DEVELOPMENT IN DIRECT PAYMENTS

Edited by Janet Leece
Joanna Bornat

FHSW

First published in Great Britain in January 2006 by

The Policy Press
University of Bristol
Fourth Floor
Beacon House
Queen's Road
Bristol BS8 1QU
UK

Tel +44 (0)117 331 4054
Fax +44 (0)117 331 4093
e-mail tpp-info@bristol.ac.uk
www.policypress.org.uk

British Library Cataloguing in Publication Data
A catalogue record for this book is available from the British Library.

Library of Congress Cataloging-in-Publication Data
A catalog record for this book has been requested.

ISBN-10 1 86134 653 0 paperback
ISBN-13 978 1 86134 653 7

A hardcover version of this book is also available.

Cover design by Qube Design Associates, Bristol.
Front cover: image kindly supplied by www.JohnBirdsall.co.uk
Printed and bound in Great Britain by Hobbs the Printers, Southampton.

Contents

List of tables and boxes

Tables

Boxes

Notes on contributors

Simone Baker is 42 years old and was born with severe shortening of her arms and legs as a consequence of the drug Thalidomide that her mother took during pregnancy to counteract the effects of severe morning sickness. Despite her physical impairment, she describes her life as "fairly normal", having never needed to rely on a huge amount of personal support until she became a parent in 1996. Simone's daughter, Lois, is now aged eight. Simone has used direct payments since 2002, primarily to assist in her parenting role.

Joanna Bornat is Professor of Oral History in the Faculty of Health and Social Care at The Open University, UK. She has a particular interest in biographical and oral history research and has researched and published in this area for some years. She has edited and co-edited collections including: *Reminiscence reviewed: Perspectives, evaluations, achievements* (1993); *Community care: A reader* (1993); *Oral history, health and welfare* (2000); *The turn to biographical methods in social science* (2000); *Understanding health and social care* (2002); *Biographical methods in professional practice* (2004).

Jane Campbell is chair of the Social Care Institute for Excellence (SCIE), a government-funded, independent organisation dedicated to improving the quality of social care across the UK. She became a Commissioner of the Disability Rights Commission at its inception in 2000. Jane has written a number of books on disability issues and speaks at a wide range of conferences and events.

Jeanne Carlin MASW, CQSW has worked as a freelance social work consultant in children's disability services for the past four years. She has written two books on direct payments and delivers training and lectures in this area across the UK. She is also a parent of a disabled young woman with multiple impairments.

Dr Heather Clark is a Reader in Social Gerontology at University College Chichester, UK. She has extensive experience of research with and involving older people and is the lead author of *Going home: Older people leaving hospital*; *'That bit of help': The high value of low level preventative services for older people*; *Piloting choice and control for older people*; and *'It pays dividends': Direct payments and older people*. She is currently a member of the secretariat team to the Older People's Inquiry into 'That Bit of Help' established by the Joseph Rowntree Foundation.

Antony Clayton is married and lives with his wife in Middlewich. He has worked as a health care professional for 14 years in the UK and America. He holds a BA degree in Social Studies and a HND in Sport and Disability.

Etienne d'Aboville is chief executive of the Glasgow Centre for Inclusive Living (GCIL), UK. GCIL is a user-controlled organisation that has been providing a range of support, training, housing and employment services since 1996. Etienne previously worked for the Spinal Injuries Association and the Living Options Partnership (based at the King's Fund). He has been an active member of the Independent Living Movement since 1985 and was closely involved in the campaign to legalise direct payments.

Christine Erskine trained as a nursery school teacher and raised three children before moving into the commercial world, where she ran a successful sign business before retiring. Christine has always had an empathy with youngsters with learning disabilities and has worked for a local charity in this field.

Margaret Fletcher has been the director of UK operations with the Princess Royal Trust for Carers since September 2003. She has a Bachelor of Social Work degree from the University of New South Wales, Australia, majoring in community development. Margaret has over 25 years' experience working in the health, social services and voluntary sectors in Australia and the UK.

Jackie Gelling is a nurse, and she met her husband, Colin, when they were both in the army, over 38 years ago. They have three grown-up children, who now have children of their own. Jackie and Colin became involved with direct payments while working as trainers for Cambridgeshire Social Services. They were the first people in the county to receive money for direct payments.

Kathryn Gilbert is a linguist who qualified as a stockbroker and worked in stock market analysis and as an IT contractor for international blue chip companies before an industrial injury put her on the corporate scrap heap. Working in the voluntary sector with support from Access to Work has proved that her working life is not over.

Kathryn is an active trade unionist and a passionate believer in equality for all, especially for disabled people with whom she identifies.

Dr Jon Glasby is a senior lecturer and head of health and social care partnerships at the Health Services Management Centre, University of Birmingham, UK. A qualified social worker by background, he is also a board member of the Social Care Institute for Excellence (SCIE) and the Centre for the Advancement of Interprofessional Education (CAIPE).

Caroline Glendinning is Professor of Social Policy and assistant director of the Social Policy Research Unit at the University of York, UK, where she directs a Department of Health research programme on choice and independence across the life course. Prior to this she was Professor of Social Policy at the National Primary Care Research and Development Centre, University of Manchester, UK, where the research reported in this book was carried out.

Frances Hasler is head of user and public involvement at the Commission for Social Care Inspection, UK. She was co-founder and chief officer of the National Centre for Independent Living. She was active in the campaign to legalise direct payments and has researched and written extensively on direct payments. Her publications include *Direct routes to independence* and *Making direct payments work*.

Andrew Holman works for Inspired Services (previously known as Community Living) and has written extensively about the use of direct payments by people with learning difficulties. Recent work includes the support of service user involvement in the development and implementation of the government's White Paper, *Valuing people* (the National Forum), as well as the production of easier-to-read information.

Peggy Hutchison is a Professor in Recreation and Leisure Studies at Brock University in St Catharines, Ontario, Canada. She has been actively involved in research and education related to inclusion, empowerment, the independent living movement, individualised funding, and community building. One of her recent publications, *A textured life: Empowerment and people with developmental disabilities*, researched individualised funding's impact on people's lives.

Helen Lee is a support worker for Stockport Sharecare, working in both specialised childcare and play scheme support. During the week she is a sixth-former at Tytherington High School studying for A levels. She hopes to go on to do a degree in architecture.

Janet Leece is a registered social worker working as a commissioning officer for Staffordshire Social Care and Health Directorate, UK. She is also an honorary research fellow at Staffordshire University. Janet has written extensively in the area of direct payments, her publications including the *Practitioner's guide to direct payments* published by Venture Press in 2003.

Christine Lenehan is director of the Council for Disabled Children, UK. She has worked with disabled children and their families for over 20 years as a social worker in residential and fieldwork settings and for voluntary and statutory agencies and has a particular interest in family support services.

Rosemary Littlechild is a lecturer in social work in the Institute of Applied Social Studies, University of Birmingham, UK. She is a qualified social worker and has worked in local authority social services departments. Her research and publication interests include community care and older people, and the health and social care divide.

Annette Lomas is a qualified social worker currently employed full time by a local authority in the north-west of England to work with older people. She completed her post-qualifying award in social work at Staffordshire University in 2003.

Dr John Lord is a researcher, consultant, and parent from Waterloo, Ontario, Canada. He is a founder and first coordinator of the Centre for Research and Education in Human Services, a non-profit, independent community-based research centre. John has published widely in areas such as deinstitutionalisation, the new paradigm, and individualised support and funding. John was recently chair of the Ontario Round Table on Individualized Funding.

Laura Luckhurst is a freelance disability researcher and consultant specialising in direct payments and independent living. Much of Laura's work has focused on the needs of people excluded from direct payments, such as people with learning disabilities and survivors/users of the mental health system. Her report *Wider options* was published by the National Centre for Independent Living in 2005.

Charlotte Pearson is a lecturer in public policy at the Department of Urban Studies, University of Glasgow, UK. She has been researching direct payments over the past eight years and is currently working with colleagues at Edinburgh and Leeds Universities on an ESRC-funded study, which is examining their impact across the UK.

Dr Julie Ridley is a freelance researcher who live and works in Scotland. While employed by Scottish Health Feedback, she was commissioned by the Scottish Executive to carry out research into direct payments for people with mental health problems. She also brings to direct payments an insight from a community care planning perspective, as well as an advocacy perspective through supporting individuals with learning disabilities to be part of their community. Over the past 20 years she has carried out research in various aspects of health and community care policy and practice. Her main research interests include supported employment, user involvement and participation, and participatory research.

Brian Salisbury is a part-time faculty member in the Community Support Worker Program at Kwantlen University College in Langley, British Columbia, Canada. He has consulted extensively in the US, Canada, Australia and the UK on various disability policy issues including individualised funding and independent planning support. Most recently he has been a senior advisor to the Ministry of Children and Family Development and interim authority for Community Living British Columbia on that province's move to a community governance model.

Louise Smyth is a direct payments user now living in Kent. She employs personal assistants.

Hilary Sparkes is 50 years old and has been working in the care sector for the last 20 years doing various different types of work. She is currently studying with The Open University, UK. Hilary has two grown-up children and has been married for 30 years.

Simon Stevens is chief executive of Enable Enterprises, a leading provider of disability and accessibility services. In 2004, he won the community category of Enterprising Young Brits. He has employed personal assistants since 1992. For more information, visit his website (www.enableenterprises.com).

Angie Stewart is 27 years old and lives in Newcastle upon Tyne with her assistance dog, who is called Lulu. Angie works as a case advocate with people who have learning disabilities and are leaving long-stay residential hospital to live in their own homes in the community. In her spare time, Angie does disability equality training and enjoys going out with friends.

Lyn Tidder is 54 years old and divorced, with three daughters, two of whom are identical twins. She ran her own curtain business for 27 years, before going into care work five years ago. Lyn is currently not working due to ill health.

Clare Ungerson is Emeritus Professor of Social Policy at the University of Southampton, UK, and is currently Honorary Professor of Social Policy at the University of Kent, UK. She has written extensively on gender and social policy in general, and gender and care in particular, and much of her more recent research has been conducted within a cross-national perspective.

Val Williams is a researcher at the Norah Fry Research Centre, University of Bristol, UK. She is particularly interested in inclusive ways of working with people with learning difficulties and other disabled people to enable them to conduct their own research and take part in projects. She previously worked with Swindon People First on their research about direct payments and is currently working with the West of England Centre for Inclusive Living on a project called 'Skills for Support'.

Rob Wilson is chief executive of the Rowan Organisation, which is one of the largest direct payments support organisations in the UK. He has previously worked for Birmingham Social Services in both older people's services and disability services, having originally started his working life as a child care officer.

ONE

Introduction

Joanna Bornat

When Vic Finkelstein, the veteran disability rights activist, was imprisoned under the apartheid regime in South Africa, he recalls that, having insisted on the right to exercise, twice each day a black prisoner was detailed to push him "... round and round the courtyard (after I had been to the toilet)". He remarks wryly that this was "[the] only time I have ever been given a free personal helper" (Finkelstein, 2002).

Forty years on, in another country, and under somewhat different conditions, direct payments legislation (the 1996 Community Care Direct Payments Act; the 2000 Carers and Disabled Children Act; the 2002 Community Care and Health (Scotland) Act) means that someone who has been assessed for community care can now be given a budget and choose how to spend the money allocated to them. If they want to pay for someone so that they can visit friends, go to a meeting, eat out at a restaurant, buy helpful equipment, spend time away from home or simply buy help with the basic tasks that use up all their energy, then the choice is theirs. As the website of the UK Department of Health (DH) explains: "Direct payments create more flexibility in the provision of social services. Giving money in place of social care services means people have greater choice and control over their lives, and are able to make their own decisions about how care is delivered". (DH, 2004a).

For Vic Finkelstein and other disabled people, direct payments came into being as the result of decades of campaigning against a society which turns disabled people into dependants without choice, control or independence in their lives. Their organisations, the Union of Physically Impaired Against Segregation, the Disability Alliance and the British Council of Disabled People (BCODP), have been at the head of an international movement that sought and still seeks to establish a citizenship-based, human rights-defined case against disabled people's exclusion from society (Campbell and Oliver, 1996). With the establishment by Act of Parliament in 2000 of the UK Disability Rights

Commission came the incorporation in policy terms of independence and participation as rights:

> 4.1 There should be a basic enforceable right to independent living for all disabled people. Policy objectives for social care services need to include guaranteed minimum outcomes, backed up by a right to independence. The provision of social care must extend beyond functional 'life and limb' support to include support to enable participation in social and economic activities.
>
> 4.1.1 All social care support services should be based on the principles of independent living. All organisations commissioning and providing services should be aware of the social model of disability and be fully committed to delivering services that enable choice, control, autonomy and participation. (Disability Rights Commission, 2002)

The chapters in this book, each in their different way, pay eloquent testimony to this determination and campaigning, as well as the political and theoretical conceptualisation of disabled people's lives and their "real needs and wishes" (Campbell and Oliver, 1996, p 1). Indeed, leading participants in that movement are contributors to this collection. They have personal and policy-based experience as well as research evidence to contribute to an understanding of the development of direct payments.

However, this is not yet a story with an ending, or even an ending that might be predicted. Our inclusion of a chapter (Chapter Four) describing developments in North America, which have a much longer history, confirms that even there the course of personalised payments is not yet clearly defined. And comparisons with other European countries, set out in another chapter (Chapter Fifteen), show how arrangements building on rather different welfare systems are identifying issues that those of us in the UK may need to pay heed to. We chose the title 'Developments in Direct Payments', because we are aware that in these different accounts and analyses we are capturing a moment when the workings of a challenge to traditional provision of care and support are being exposed to critical comment and evaluation. Despite government espousal of the principle of direct payments and despite evidence of the very real and positive difference such a new system of support can make to people's lives this is not proving a straightforward transformation. More than that, the very nature of direct payments raises questions about the future direction of health and social care provision in the 21st century. It is with such a sense of proviso that the introduction to this book has been written.

The many facets of direct payments reflected in the contributions make up a complex picture once they are assembled. In writing this introduction I am attempting not only to introduce the parts that make up this whole, but also to suggest some organising edges from which it might be viewed. From these it might be possible to scan the terrain, noting similarities and links as well as differences and discontinuities. With this to hand, the challenges that direct payments make to support systems, to providers, and to users and workers may become plain. Before going on to identify these edges, I provide a brief sketch of the antecedents and the run-up to direct payments.

The route from the out-relief of the Poor Law to direct payments is a troubled and winding course, but the tracing of continuities and discontinuitites along the way is illuminating. Glasby and Littlechild's chapter in this volume (Chapter Two) provides an outline account of the history of the late 20th-century re-emergence of cash payments in the UK welfare system. From this, it seems that the resurrection of cash payments provides an ending, one can only hope, to the stigma of a form of support that had been deliberately associated with workhouse ideology (Thane, 1982, 2000).

The story of direct payments is closely linked to the development of representative and campaigning organisations in response to negative and disabling stereotypes. Some groups of disabled people had formed their own organisations (in 1890 the British Deaf Association; the National League of the Blind in 1899; and the Disabled Drivers Association in 1947), but otherwise, until the Disablement Income Group was set up in 1965, people looking for ways to change social attitudes to disability tended to be represented by non-disabled parents, relatives and others through charities and other voluntary organisations. As Borsay argues, disabled people's rights "... were a low priority within (the) agenda of rebuilding post-war Britain" (2005, p 161). Of course, individual disabled people were drawing on experience of oppressive and segregated treatment to press for equal treatment (Humphries and Gordon, 1992) and some older people were beginning to formulate specific demands (Bornat, 1998). Campbell and Oliver's history of disability politics uses testimony to plot the changes in awareness and commitment that led to the politicising of a generation of disabled people, culminating in the movement that, following the United Nations Declaration of the Rights of Disabled Persons in 1975, "... saw a transformation in our understandings of disability" (1996, p 19).

The idea of independence as a right, which disabled people promoted in securing the steps towards the 1996 direct payments legislation, is well documented. Glasby and Littlechild's chapter (Chapter Two) provides the background to the new law and the role of the disabled people's movement in achieving this. With subsequent Labour government support, direct payments have now become a change agent in social care provision, with self-assessment being identified as a natural precursor. The implications for service providers are as dramatic as they are for service users, as a Minister for Community Care explained to a meeting of people working in the mental health services:

> What's being asked of you is not easy, I know that. It means a change in approach. It means going much further in treating people you work with as individuals and tailoring support around them. It means letting them be in charge. And it means really signing up to the principle of independent living, and helping people move away from being dependent on you for help to being dependent only on themselves. (Ladyman, 2004)

How can we understand this shift in policy and identify the direction in which direct payments may be taking social welfare? Earlier, I mentioned the idea of edges from which to oversee this new landscape. As vantage points I offer four such edges: disability's influence; direct payments as co-production; costing support; and the worker as stakeholder.

I will begin with disability's influence. Several of the chapters included here allude to an unevenness in take-up across the UK. Some, such as Charlotte Pearson (in Chapter Three), point to resistance to the mixed economy of care in Scotland. Where the ethos of public service has survived longest there seems to be the greatest reluctance to move towards a more personally oriented system. Annette Lomas (in Chapter Seventeen) looks to poor levels of awareness and support for care managers for explanation, while chapters from Heather Clark, Frances Hasler, and Rob Wilson and Kathryn Gilbert (Chapters Six, Eleven and Twelve, respectively) emphasise the significant role of support systems and their uneven spread across the UK. However, none of these has perhaps had such a broad influence as the leadership role of the disability movement in unwittingly contributing to a stereotypical image of the direct payments user. Although older disabled people shared many of the early apprehensions concerning the administration of direct payments and their own personal safety in employing personal assistants (Barnes, 1997), younger disabled people had few such concerns. This, together with their established campaigning role and organisational networks of support, meant that for many professionals the younger physically disabled person became the archetypical direct payments user.

Care managers often found it difficult to stretch the idea to fit the needs of other groups, for example, older people, who only came to be included as eligible after 2000 (Valios, 2000). People with mental health problems have perhaps seen the lowest rate of take-up, as Julie Ridley's chapter (Chapter Seven) suggests. Here, too, disability's influence may have played a part. Personal assistants have come to be synonymous with direct payments in a way which is, of course, quite inaccurate. Direct payments may be used to buy a variety of goods and services, not only physical help with daily living. People with mental health needs may well find that employing a personal assistant is helpful to them; however, there may be other activities and services which could be more appropriate. Their conditions tend not to require physical support and may often fluctuate (Sale and Leason, 2004). In the evaluation of a pilot study of direct payments in Norfolk a member of a mental health team commented: "It is written from a physical disability perspective ... the way it's written and designed is discriminatory in a way". (Dawson, 2000, p 23).

Research such as this points to a need to:

> ... introduce ... a more appropriate definition of 'disabled person' for the purpose of community care services that is consistent with the DDA [Disability Discrimination Act] definition and takes account of the implications for disability across all ages. (Cabinet Office, 2005, p 81)

The label 'disabled' may also conceal the particular barriers which people with learning difficulties have faced in securing direct payments. Val Williams' and Andrew Holman's chapter (Chapter Five) discusses their achievements as well as the particular problems they have encountered. Questions of consent and capacity tend to dog the setting up of arrangements despite the fact that two organisations of people with learning difficulties, Swindon People First and Values into Action, have collaborated with the DH in writing guidance materials (DH, 2004b, 2004c).

Identifying the part that direct payments could be playing in the production of welfare is the second of the 'edges' from which to view the scene. The shift towards a welfare policy of individual ownership and responsibility has been viewed with apprehension by some commentators seeing this as a shift towards a 'desocialising' of social divisions, undermining more integrating tendencies and risking the generation of conflicts where there might be shared interest. This individualising tendency may also prevent the setting of standards and the development of what might be best practice (Spandler, 2004, pp 194-5). Yet such a change might also lead to people becoming less compliant and dependent, and more informed and articulate partners with providers concerning their specific needs (Priestley, 2000; Clarke, 2004, pp 62-71).

This move towards a more participative role on the part of the consumer of services in this new relationship has also been identified as 'co-production':

> Consumers who first purchase and then assemble furniture bought from IKEA or a similar store must contribute their time to assemble the product in order to realize the full and final value of the items purchased. In this respect they become co-producers of their own furniture. (Pestoff, 2004)

From buying furniture to buying personal services may seem a long stretch, but, in considering the operation of direct payments, it may not be too far-fetched. Several of the chapters in this book illustrate a shift towards some form of active partnership with providers of services on the part of direct payments users. There are, for example, the centres for independent living (CILs) run by disabled people providing information and support, the people who find their own carers, those who account for their own spending and others who act in a third party capacity for people not able to manage direct payments themselves. All these could be said to be occupying territory that, under different circumstances, might be occupied by professional care workers (Spandler, 2004). This is indeed a form of empowerment that brings with it choice and control over how a life is lived. Leadbetter describes this as 'personalisation': "... by putting users at the heart of services, enabling them to become participants in the design and delivery, services will be more effective by mobilising millions of people as co-producers of the public goods they value" (2004, p 19).

In a comparative review of direct payments in the US, the UK, Sweden and Norway, Askheim adds a cautionary note to enthusiasts for co-production, suggesting that a touch of 'paternalism' may be 'protective' for those who are most vulnerable in order to "... secure their needs and to prevent user control being used as a cover for financial cuts" (Askheim, 2005, p 257). His contribution to the debate is a reminder to the disability movement of the need to "... be aware of the diversity of disabled people" when representing the most vulnerable people (Askheim, 2005, p 258).

Co-production can of course attract a range of interpretations; cost, the third 'edge' for our overview, has also played a significant role as the story of direct payments attests. The Conservative government's support for cash payments for service users in 1996 may have been borne from a commitment to independence on the part of service users, yet was helped by pressure from the disabled people's movement that made a case for cost-effectiveness (Zarb and Nadash, 1994). This, as Pearson argues, seems to have clinched the issue (2000, pp 461-2).

Several years later it is clear that the costing of support is still a concern (Spandler, 2004). For example, cost controls may be the reason for the uneven spread of direct payments, given the varied impact of spending priorities, eligibility criteria and costing policies in different localities: the 'postcode lottery', which some of the direct payments users mention in the 'Voices of experience' chapter (Chapter Nine). Costing inequalities also affect the choices available to different groups. As Clark et al point out, older people may be offered lower levels of funding when social care professionals make the ageist assumption that lifestyles in late life are more limited in contrast with those of younger disabled people (Clark et al, 2004). And if, as in other areas of public service, availability tends to be linked to immediate risk rather than the goal of full participation then the result may be traditional and conventional assessments. As Zarb explains:

> ... practically all of the existing support systems place some kind of ceiling – either in terms of cost or eligibility criteria, or often both of these – on the level of resources at which independent living is considered to be cost-effective. (Zarb, 2003)

However, even the most eloquent rights-based case for the economics of independence may have to recognise that the day-to-day operation of direct payments and other similar systems of payment for care and support introduces a cost element into relationships in such a way as to attract the label 'commodification' (Ungerson, 2002; Leece, 2004). For some people, the opportunity to pay friends and relatives for the contribution they make to their support is to be welcomed (Age Concern England, 1998); however, the introduction of financial accountability and audit may be an unwelcome intrusion into such relationships (Pearson, 2000). Cost too is an issue where, as Glendinning in Chapter Eighteen of this volume suggests, people with very intensive or specialised needs may find it difficult to recruit and retain staff on the funding they are offered if this is calculated with reference to the local authority home care staff costs. Problems also arise given that health and social care needs of individual direct payment users are differently funded and managed. People's lives are not organised in such an orderly way that what relates to health and to social care can easily be disentangled and separately costed (Glendinning et al, 2000).

The fourth and last 'edge' from which to scan the scope of direct payments is provided by the idea that care workers may also have a stake in this newly emerging form of provision. That personal assistants and support workers paid for by direct payments might also have an interest is a position which has only recently come into view (Ungerson, 1997; Shakespeare, 2000; Ungerson, 2002; Spandler, 2004; Leece, in this volume). High levels of enthusiasm for the freedom that direct payments bestow on lives otherwise restricted by narrow expectations and outright discriminatory and oppressive practice on the part of some powerful professionals have tended to overshadow their impact on those employed to carry out the support work. As the disabled activist and academic Tom Shakespeare points out, "It would deeply unfortunate if the liberation of disabled people from dependency contributed to the exploitation of another disempowered section of the population" (2000, p 68).

Testimony from personal assistants, included in this book and elsewhere, points to satisfaction with this particular form of employment. Like cash payments, there is continuity with the past, although in what exact form it would be hard to say. Are personal assistants a special kind of servant, rather like a companion, or perhaps a valet or a maid? To draw too close a comparison with the past might be invidious, even though it could be instructive. Names might change, yet employments do continue. Although domestic service has lost many of its descriptors and much of its operational language, the roles remain, embodied in such posts as butlers, chauffeurs, au pairs, 'cleaning ladies', and nannies. Labels such as these provide instant identification with the work required, although evidence of the porosity of the boundaries demarcating such jobs is widely available in the literature and is gaining recognition from studies of the internationalisation of such employment (Ehrenreich and Hochschild, 2003; Williams, 2004).

Spandler (2004, p 190) identifies the varied vocabulary used to describe those she labels 'the recipients' of direct payments. She lists a whole range of words, each with their own particular political weight and meaning: "'disabled people' ... employer, service user, PA user ... customer" (2004, p 189). And it may be here that the difference lies between domestic service and direct payments. For the very complexity of a relationship where someone is both employer as well as a user of services paid for out of public funds presents a challenge to all involved. The norms and accepted practices of such involvements are emerging through individual experience and have yet to be settled as some of the voices of personal experience in this volume attest.

The personal assistant as an identifiable stakeholder in direct payments may emerge, with a move towards co-operatives or some form of collective organisation. This might militate against the individualised relationships, often low paid and unsupported, that are at present the more typical experience of personal assistants. More solidaristic movements might help to provide training and open up debates about standards of care (Spandler, 2004). They may also lead to demands for more equitable forms of pay in what is typically a low-wage area of employment. Indeed, despite his reservations, Shakespeare goes on to suggest that exploitation may not be inevitable if the outcome is "... redistributing money from those with jobs to those on the periphery of the economy" (2000, p 69). Even so, issues of funding are persistently relevant, raising the issue of how direct payments are costed and to what extent funders acknowledge the need to raise standards in employment, including improvements in pay for what has traditionally been seen as women's work (Equal Pay Task Force, 2001; Employers Organisation for Local Government, 2004).

I have set out four 'edges' from which to view and consider the terrain of direct payments: disability's influence; direct payments as co-production; costing support; and the worker as stakeholder. These vantage points, I suggest, may help to resolve the complexity of issues from the perspective of user and worker to the level of government-led policy formation. The contributors to this book, in their different ways, engage with these issues, provoking argument, confirming stances and marking their engagement in a movement that is likely to transform the lived experience of care and support in UK society.

When we invited people to contribute we were aware that they would be starting from very different points: some are full-time researchers, others are campaigners for disabled people's rights, others combine these roles. Some are involved in using direct payments, some are researching their impact, others in managing their distribution, and others again are the very embodiments of the direct payment, the personal assistant and the recipient. All are in the thick of understanding and implementing this new way of working and supporting people.

Our contributors present their cases in very different ways, their writing styles follow no one pattern; indeed, a reviewer of the original typescript suggested that these contrasts are "one of the book's strengths". We had no hesitation in juxtaposing writing by people who keep to the conventions of academic presentation side by side with contributions from people who write directly from experience and with passion and conviction about what is their daily life and work. Some chapters are steeped in references and evidence, while others move straight to the point with statements which draw on what they personally know and have observed. Our authors complement each other, responding to the wide variety of contexts, in the UK and beyond, where debates about direct payments are being held.

Earlier, mention was made of a government document (Cabinet Office, 2005), which raises the issue of terminology with respect to disability and impairment across all age groups. In this collection we have sought consistency among the many terms used. So, for example, we find our authors distinguishing 'disability' from 'impairment', as in the chapters by Frances Hasler, Caroline Glendinning, and Jon Glasby and Rosemary Littlechild. There, 'impairment' is used to refer to particular conditions, physical, cognitive, or health-linked, while 'disability', following the distinction drawn up by members of the disabled people's movement, refers to the way those conditions are defined and acted upon by society (French, 2001, pp 10-11). You will therefore read about 'someone who has a physical impairment' (p 23) as well as 'disabled people' (p 199) in relevant contexts. However, sometimes these words are not specific enough, and so terms such as 'people with mental health problems' (p 101) and 'people with learning difficulties' (p 68), even 'people with substantial, ongoing nursing needs' (p 255) are more fairly explicative. Given the personal and political significance of these wordings, it seems debateable that a single inclusive term, as the Cabinet Office document cited above calls for, will ever be identified.

We have sought to standardise use of language across the chapters, but this has not always been possible. In the case of Peggy Hutchison, John Lord and Brian Salisbury's chapter (Chapter Four), we did not think such a move was appropriate. On a different continent, words have a different history, even when we are speaking the same language. We therefore decided to leave our North American contributors' chapter as it is. There, readers will encounter terms such as 'people with developmental disabilities', 'labeled people' and 'people with a physical disability'.

The five sections of this book illustrate these differences of style and language. It is our intention that the contents will have relevance for the disabled people's movement, however defined and delineated, thereby encompassing as many perspectives and understanding as we are able.

In Section One, 'Setting the scene', three chapters go into some detail in identifying the main characteristics of direct or personalised payments in three different welfare systems. Jon Glasby and Rosemary Littlechild provide an overview of the origins, implementation and development of direct payments in England and Wales (Chapter Two). Charlotte Pearson (in Chapter Three) explores some of the key problems which have prevented successful implementation of direct payments in Scotland and examines some of the challenges that will be raised with the widening of users groups to include, for example, people fleeing domestic violence, as set out in the 2002 Community Care and Health (Scotland) Act. Finally, Peggy Hutchison, John Lord and Brian Salisbury (in Chapter Four) explore the relationships between the concepts of 'individualized planning' and 'individualized funding' in Canada and the US. They provide an opportunity to draw comparisons where systems have undergone an earlier experience of development.

Section Two, 'Policy into practice', presents an opportunity to compare the experience of the take-up of direct payments among different groups of users. Val Williams and Andrew Holman (in Chapter Five) consider the position of people with learning difficulties in relation to direct payments, raising issues of implementation and exclusion. Heather Clark considers how older people, including those from a minority ethnic community, value direct payments (Chapter Six). Julie Ridley looks at research which reviews the experiences of Scottish mental health service users, including people with dementia, and their views of direct payments (Chapter Seven). The section concludes with a study by Jeanne Carlin and Christine Lenehan (in Chapter Eight) of the key issues and challenges in implementing and expanding direct payments to users of children's services.

Section Three, 'Voices of experience' is an anthology of writings commissioned especially from users of direct payments and by people working as personal assistants. These are accounts that speak with authenticity about having control, exercising choice and opportunities for independence. They are also the voices of people who are working, sometimes for the first time with commitment and enjoyment. However, these are also stories that ask challenging questions and that call for attention.

Section Four, 'Reporting from the field', includes a number of brief contributions from people who are engaged directly in the implementation and take-up of direct payments. Etienne d'Aboville recounts (in Chapter Ten) the experience of Glasgow's Centre for Inclusive Living, an organisation of disabled people, and its engagement with direct payments. Frances Hasler (in Chapter Eleven) recounts the National Centre for Independent Living's involvement as the evaluator of projects funded by a major government initiative, the DH's Development Fund for Direct Payments. Rob Wilson and Kathryn Gilbert describe the opportunity that this funding gave their organisation to promote the adoption of direct payments by under-represented groups (in Chapter Twelve). Finally (in Chapter Thirteen), Margaret Fletcher provides an account of working with carers who are now also eligible for direct payments.

In Section Five, a group of chapters with the title 'Working with direct payments' looks at the roles and understanding of different groups of practitioners involved in direct payments provision. Jan Leece, drawing on UK data (in Chapter Fourteen), compares the relationship between direct payments users and their personal assistants with that of users of traditional home care services and home care workers. Clare Ungerson (in Chapter Fifteen) draws on cross-national research to seek out an understanding of a new employment: the personal assistant. With awareness of low take-up among certain groups of potential direct payments users, Laura Luckhurst reports (in Chapter Sixteen) on research into some intensive support schemes, while Annette Lomas (in Chapter Seventeen) reports on a study of care managers in order to identify their knowledge and views of direct payments and how this affects their take-up by older people.

The final section of the book, 'Developments in direct payments' comprises three chapters, each of which raises issues for the future settlement of direct payments as a form of support in the UK. Caroline Glendinning (in Chapter Eighteen) describes the continuing complexity and ambiguities surrounding the provision of direct payments for people whose needs cross the health and social care boundaries and the challenges involved in overcoming this divide. In the penultimate chapter, she, Jon Glasby and Rosemary Littlechild draw some conclusions about the way direct payments are developing and raise issues about future developments and trends. Finally, in Chapter Twenty, 'Holding the dream', Frances Hasler weighs up the issues as she sees them, after 20 years of campaigning with a discussion of the questions that direct payments implementation raise for all the stakeholders in the quest towards independent living.

We believe that in this collection we have assembled some of the very best writing available on the subject of direct payments. In the chapters that follow you should find yourself rewarded and perhaps provoked. This is in the nature of debate and we make no apologies. Our only intention is to provide more opportunities to link theory, policy and practice in ways that will ensure a richly informed discussion.

References

Age Concern England (1998) *Direct payments review: Age Concern's response*, London, Age Concern England.

Askheim, O.P. (2005) 'Personal assistance – direct payments or alternative public service: does it matter for the promotion of user control?', *Disability & Society*, vol 20, no 3, pp 247-60.

Barnes, C. (1997) *Older people's perspectives of direct payments and self operated support schemes*, Leeds: BCODP Research Unit.

Bornat, J (1998) 'Pensioners organise: hearing the voice of older people', in M. Bernard and J. Phillips (eds) *The social policy of old age*, London: Centre for Policy on Ageing, pp 183-99.

Borsay, A. (2005) *Disability and social policy in Britain since 1750*, Basingstoke: Palgrave Macmillan.

Cabinet Office (2005) *Improving the life chances of disabled people*, London: The Stationery Office.

Campbell, J. and Oliver, M. (1996) *Disability politics: Understanding our past, changing our future*, London: Routledge.

Clark, H., Gough, H. and Macfarlane, A. (2004) *'It pays dividends': Direct payments and older people*, Bristol: The Policy Press.

Clarke, J. (2004) *Changing welfare, changing states: New directions in social policy*, London: Sage Publications.

Dawson, C. (2000) *Independent success: Implementing direct payments*, York: Joseph Rowntree Foundation.

DH (Department of Health) (2004a) *Policy and guidance: Direct payments*, (www.dh.gov.uk/PolicyAndGuidance/PolicyAZ/fs/en?CONTENT_ID=4055548&chk=XlLN/p), accessed 15 February 2005.

DH (2004b) *An easy guide to direct payments: Giving you choice and control*, London: The Stationery Office/DH.

DH (2004c) *Direct choices – what councils need to make direct payments happen for people with learning disabilities*, London: The Stationery Office/DH.

Disability Rights Commission (2002) *DRC policy statement on social care and independent living*, (www.drc-gb.org/publicationsandreports/), accessed 17 September 2005.

Ehrenreich, B. and Hochschild, A.R. (2003) *Global woman: Nannies, maids and sex workers in the new economy*, London: Granta.

Employers Organisation for Local Government (2004) *Social services workforce survey, 2003, Report no 33* (www.lg-employers.gov.uk/documents/recruitment_careers/workforce_surveys/ssws_report_2003.pdf), accessed 30 September 2004.

Equal Pay Task Force (2001) *Just pay, reports to the Equal Opportunities Commission*, Manchester: Equal Opportunities Commission.

Finkelstein, V. (2002) 'Whose history???,' Keynote address at the Disability History Week, Birmingham, 10 June, (www.leeds.ac.uk/disability-studies/archiveuk/archframe.htm), accessed 15 February 2005.

French, S. (2001) *Disabled people and employment: A study of the working lives of visually impaired physiotherapists*, Aldershot: Ashgate.

Glendinning, C., Halliwell, S., Jacobs, S., Rummery, K. and Tyrer, J. (2000) *Buying independence: Using direct payments to integrate health and social services*, Bristol, The Policy Press

Humphries, S. and Gordon, P. (1992) *Out of sight: The experience of disability 1900-1950*, Plymouth: Northcote House.

Ladyman, S. (2004) 'New directions for direct payments for people who use mental health services', Speech at the Health and Social Care Advisory Service conference, 18 May.

Leadbetter, C. (2004) *Personalisation through participation: A new script for public services*, London: Demos.

Leece, J. (2004) 'Money talks, but what does it say? Direct payments and the commodification of care', *Practice: the Journal of the British Association of Social Workers*, vol 16, no 3, pp 211-21.

Pearson, C. (2000) 'Money talks? Competing discourses in the implementation of direct payments', *Critical Social Policy*, vol 20, no 4, pp 459-77.

Pestoff, V. (2004) 'Co-production and personal social services: childcare in eight European countries', Paper given at the European Group for Public Administration Annual Conference, Ljubljana, Slovenia, 1-4 September.

Priestley, M. (2000) 'Adults only: disability, social policy and the life course', *Journal of Social Policy*, vol 29, no 3, pp 421–39.

Sale, A.U. and Leason, K. (2004) 'Is help easily at hand?', *Community Care*, 6-12 May.

Shakespeare, T. (2000) *Help: Imagining welfare*, Birmingham: British Association of Social Workers/Venture Press.

Spandler, H. (2004) 'Friend or foe? Towards a critical assessment of direct payments', *Critical Social Policy*, vol 24, no 2, pp 187-209.

Thane, P. (1982) *The foundations of the welfare state*, London: Longman.

Thane, P. (2000) *Old age in English society, past experiences, present issues*, Oxford: Oxford University Press.

Ungerson, C. (1997) 'Give them the money: is cash a route to empowerment?', *Social Policy and Administration*, vol 31, no 1, pp 45-53.

Ungerson, C. (2002) 'Care as a commodity', in B. Bytheway, V. Bacigalupo, J. Bornat, J. Johnson and S. Spurr (eds) *Understanding care, welfare and community: A reader*, London: Routledge.

Valios, N. (2000) 'Cash in hand', *Community Care*, 14-20 December.

Williams, F. (2004) 'Trends in women's employment, domestic service and female migration: changing and competing patterns of solidarity', in T. Knijn and A. Komter (eds) *Solidarity between the sexes and the generations*, Cheltenham: Edward Elgar.

Zarb, G. (2003) 'The economics of independent living', internet publication (www.independentliving.org/docs6/zarb2003.html).

Zarb, G. and Nadash, P. (1994) *Cashing in on independence: Comparing the costs and benefits of cash and services*, Derby: BCODP/PSI.

Section 1
Setting the scene

TWO

An overview of the implementation and development of direct payments

Jon Glasby and Rosemary Littlechild

As is often the case with any new and fundamentally different policy initiative, the passage of the 1996 Community Care (Direct Payments) Act was greeted with a range of different responses from a range of different stakeholders. For some disabled academics and activists, direct payments held out "the potential for the most fundamental reorganisation of welfare for half a century" (Oliver and Sapey, 1999, p 175). However, for some local authorities, direct payments were little more than a form of "privatisation by the back door" (Hasler, 1999, p 7), introduced by a Conservative government as part of a series of measures to erode traditional public services. For some social workers, direct payments are an exciting new way of working that has the potential to deliver traditional commitments to empower service users and work *with* them rather than *for* them. For others, direct payments are a step too far too soon, and doubts remain as to whether so-called 'vulnerable people' are truly able to manage their own services (Fruin, 2000, p 17):

> "I am very worried about direct payments – vulnerable people managing their own services." (Social worker in a multi-disciplinary team)

> "Can I risk [direct payments] ... on behalf of clients?" (Adults team social worker)

For policy makers too, direct payments have attracted very different responses. As we shall see below, the former Conservative government was, for a long time, resistant to the concept of direct payments. However, over time the efficacy of direct payments has found favour with politicians of all persuasions. As we shall argue in this overview of the implementation of direct payments, these contradictory responses are the result of two main factors. First, direct payments are a considerable challenge to previous ways of working, and this tends to evoke polarised responses (either clear and vocal commitment or considerable hostility). Second, the policy of direct payments, as initially conceived, had a number of discrepancies and inconsistencies. While these could be overlooked while the policy was in its infancy, direct payments are now sufficiently mainstream that these issues need to be explicitly addressed if the number of recipients is to expand significantly.

Despite this, our own view is that these issues are all limitations in the way in which direct payments have been operationalised and implemented, not a product of the concept of direct payments itself. Direct payments are extremely simple: what has proved difficult so far to do is to turn these basic principles and philosophy into a practical policy that commands widespread support from all key stakeholders. As a result, we believe that it is important to resolve any underlying tensions and inconsistencies in direct payments policy and practice in order to focus attention back onto more important issues such as the centrality of direct payments and other individualised funding mechanisms to achieving independent living.

Against this background, the first section of this chapter summarises the build-up to the 1996 Act, placing the advent of direct payments in its historical and social policy context. This draws on previously published material (Glasby and Littlechild, 2002), but is necessary in order to illustrate the origins of current problems and tensions. Next, a second section considers the legacy of this history for current policy and practice, linking to other chapters in this book that explore these issues in more detail.

The introduction of direct payments

The introduction of direct payments paid to individuals to enable them to purchase and arrange their own care involved a fundamental shift in the thinking of British social workers. In order to understand the extent of this shift, it is necessary to have an understanding of the historical legacy of social work and its relationship to financial issues which predated direct payments.

Overturning 50 years of established practice

British social work had its roots in 19th-century philanthropy and the establishment of charitable organisations that would dispense money to those people in need who were deemed deserving of assistance (Thane, 1996). For those who did not fall into that category, the Poor Law provided support via the workhouse and via outdoor relief (Englander, 1998). However, the abolition of the Poor Law in 1948 and the introduction of a national system of social security benefits saw the end of social workers making cash payments to those in need. The domain of social workers then became the assessment for and provision of welfare services for older people, disabled people and families. This separation of financial and non-financial assistance did not occur in most European countries and the US (Davis and Stephenson, 1999), and has been a major cause of British social work not developing a significant anti-poverty perspective (Becker, 1997).

This position was confirmed in the early 1990s by the then Health Secretary, Virginia Bottomley, who, in response to a Private Member's Bill attempting to legalise direct payments, wrote: "Social services legislation is concerned with the arrangements of services and not with direct payments, which is the province of the social security system" (quoted in Hatchett, 1991, pp 14-15).

The campaign for direct payments

Although the introduction of post-war social policy legislation saw the start of the move from residential to community-based services (Means and Smith, 1998), there was a growing dissatisfaction among disabled people themselves about the nature and provision of such services (Zarb and Nadash, 1994). In part, their dissatisfaction was due to the inflexibility and unreliability of directly provided services and the increasing tendency following the 1990 NHS and Community Care Act for services to be restricted and subject to ever-tightening eligibility criteria (Department of Health (DH), 1990). Also developing during the 1980s was the independent living movement, whose philosophy is based upon disabled people having the right to choice and control over their own lives (Evans, 1993). Alongside this, there was emerging a number of national and international forums, set up and run by disabled people themselves, whose prime focus was the promotion of independent living (Morris, 1993).

The 1986 Social Security Act made changes to payments for disabled people, introducing much stricter eligibility criteria and financially disadvantaging many disabled people (Hudson, 1988). The disabled people's movement successfully pressurised the government to introduce a new Independent Living Fund (ILF) for people on low incomes who had to pay for personal care. However, with an initial budget of £5 million over five years, the demands on the ILF far exceeded the government's expectations as people who accessed it found they had greater autonomy and control over purchasing their own care (Kestenbaum, 1993). Concerned about the financial implications of such demand, in 1993 the government introduced a new ILF which was restricted to people under 66 years of age and was essentially a 'top-up' for those people already receiving extensive care packages from their local authority.

Meanwhile, although the 1948 National Assistance Act had prohibited the making of cash payments to individuals in England (in Scotland they were permissible in some circumstances but rarely used), a number of local authorities began experimenting with different forms of payments schemes. Some had successfully introduced the concept of indirect payments, either via a voluntary organisation or via a trust fund. The British Council for Disabled People (BCODP) was a key player in the campaign for direct payments and actively lobbied MPs for their support in changing legislation. It found a committed supporter in Andrew Rowe, a Conservative MP, who proposed an amendment to the NHS and Community Care Bill going through Parliament in 1990. This was unsuccessful and resulted in the government explicitly stating in the guidance on the 1990 NHS and Community Care Act that current legislation "prohibit(ed) the making of cash payments in place of arranging services" (DH, 1990, p 26). Research shows that, as a result, some local authorities ceased making payments to individuals, despite the majority being committed in principle to the idea of direct payments (Zarb and Nadash, 1994).

As pressure mounted to change the law on direct payments, the government was faced with considerable dilemmas. On the one hand their experience of the ILF raised major concerns about an escalation of public expenditure, but on the other the concept of direct payments accorded with the principles of consumer involvement and choice that were at the heart of the community care reforms. Its commitment to New Right or neo-liberal social and economic policies, discussed later in this chapter, may have had a greater influence on its decision in November 1994 to change the legislation on direct payments than its commitment to user empowerment and involvement. There is speculation too that its apparent change of heart was influenced by the imminent publication of some research commissioned by BCODP on the cost implications and effectiveness of direct payments schemes. The study, *Cashing in on independence*, showed that direct payments were not only cheaper than directly provided services but that they resulted in higher quality services (Zarb and Nadash, 1994; see Glasby and Littlechild, 2002, for further evidence on cost-effectiveness).

The government's decision in 1994 to change the legislation and make cash payments available to disabled people was greeted ecstatically by key disability rights campaigners – the pressure they had brought to bear over many years had at last come to fruition.

The 1996 Community Care (Direct Payments) Act

The government set about a consultation exercise on the implementation of direct payments having stated that it intended initially to restrict those people who would be eligible in order to allow local authorities to test payments out on a limited scale. Another key issue was the intention to restrict the employment of partners or close family members by direct payments recipients, justified by a wish not to formalise informal caring arrangements, but also undoubtedly influenced by an unwillingness to pay for existing unpaid caring activities (Glasby and Littlechild, 2002).

In 1996 the Community Care (Direct Payments) Act was passed, simply giving local authorities the *power* (not the *duty*) to make payments to disabled people. The accompanying Regulations, and policy and practice guidance (DH, 1997) stated that from 1 April 1997 direct payments could be made to disabled people aged 18 to 65 (or to those above the age of 65 where payments had started before their 65th birthday); could not be used for more than four weeks' residential care in any 12-month period; and could not be used to employ close family members.

As a result of further campaigning by organisations of disabled people, the government changed its intention to exclude people with learning difficulties from direct payments. Direct payments were therefore initially available to disabled people under 65, including people with physical impairments, learning difficulties, mental health problems and HIV/AIDS, but excluding certain people in the mental health or criminal justice system (see Glasby and Littlechild, 2002, p 34). The local authority had to satisfy itself that recipients consented to receiving the services and understood the financial and legal implications they were undertaking, an element that has been termed subsequently as being 'willing and able'.

From the beginning, local authorities therefore had considerable discretion over whether or not they offered direct payments to people assessed as needing community care services. The payment could not be used to make payments for any other services, including health services, an issue which has become increasingly contentious as the latter part of this chapter illustrates.

The extension of direct payments

Since the original 1996 Act and 1997 policy and practice guidance, four main developments have taken place. On 1 February 2000, new regulations extended the age limit for recipients of direct payments to include people aged 65 and over in England. Similar changes have taken place subsequently in the rest of the UK. In July 2000, the Carers and Disabled Children Act extended the range of people to whom direct payments could be paid, to include carers (including 16- and 17-year-old carers) for services that meet assessed needs, people with parental responsibility for disabled children for services to the family, and 16- and 17-year-old disabled children for services that meet their own assessed needs.

In an attempt to encourage people from these new groups to access direct payments and to increase the number of people generally receiving direct payments, the government launched a £9 million Direct Payments Development Fund in 2003. The purpose of the Fund is to encourage voluntary organisations to provide information and support services for people wanting to access direct payments, as this has been a key issue identified from the inception of direct payments.

Finally, an important change has been that direct payments have now become mandatory, not discretionary. Under section 57 of the 2001 Health and Social Care Act, local authorities are *required* to offer direct payments to all eligible individuals (that is, those eligible for community care services, who consent to and are able to manage payments).

From the start, the take-up of direct payments has been slow and patchy, with different local authorities adopting different approaches. Figures show a very varied pattern of take-up across the country and across different potential user groups (see Table 2.1). The benefits of direct payments over conventional services to service users have been well documented (see Glasby and Littlechild, 2002, for a review of the literature), but the barriers to effective take-up are considerable and are addressed in detail in later chapters of this book.

Table 2.1: Take-up of direct payments by different user groups

Receiving direct payments, England	30/9/2001	30/9/2002	30/9/2003
Total number of recipients	5,423	7,882	12,585
Older people (aged 65+)	537	1,032	1,899
People with learning disabilities	353	736	1,377
People with physical disabilities	4,274	5,459	6,944
People with sensory impairment	100	159	207
Young carers	3	3	12
People with mental health problems	61	132	229
Carers of disabled children	66	228	875
Disabled children (aged 16-17)	8	38	125
Carers (for carers' services)	21	95	957

Source: CSCI (2004, p 8)

The implications for current policy and practice

As this overview of the introduction of direct payments suggests, the campaign for direct payments was initiated, led and brought to successful fruition by disabled people. Despite support from a number of non-disabled allies, it was disabled people who pioneered, researched and campaigned for direct payments, and disabled people who continued to circulate information, raise awareness and provide practical support. More than almost any other policy, this is something that was developed *by* disabled people *for* disabled people. As a result, promoting direct payments offers a unique opportunity for social care staff to respond to the needs, wishes and aspirations of service users and to help existing services to change in order to promote greater independent living. Despite this, the way in which direct payments were introduced has generated a number of tensions and complexities that have implications for current policy and practice and which we go on to look at now.

The challenge of direct payments to traditional social care practices

Direct payments are fundamentally different from previous ways of working in social care. As a result, winning workers and other key stakeholders over to the concept of direct payments was always going to be an uphill struggle, and this has indeed proved to be the case. In many studies, the attitudes of front-line workers have been particularly important in determining whether or not potential direct payments recipients receive accessible information and appropriate support. While some may be resistant to change, others can be excited by the potential of direct payments. These two extremes are summarised by Bewley

(2000, pp 14-15) in relation to direct payments and people with learning difficulties:

> The care management system is under many pressures and the truth is that direct payments are not a daily priority for many care managers.... This is a shame because the ethos of direct payments is extremely exciting. Care managers now have the chance to actually give service users the money to buy their own services. This sharing of power, this chance to see individual lives flourish whilst practical support needs are met, is a fantastic opportunity for care managers to be inspired by their job.

Despite the key role that front-line workers play in supporting or hindering access to direct payments, there are also other important players, including social care managers and elected members. However, research consistently suggests that many key stakeholders do not know about or really understand direct payments (see, for example, Dawson, 2000; Leece, 2000; Maglajlic et al, 2000; Glasby and Littlechild, 2002). As a further example, participants in a regional learning network seeking to increase the uptake of direct payments for people with learning difficulties suggested that there was little mandatory training on direct payments and that it can be difficult to compete with other priorities to get this taken up by hard-pressed training departments. While awareness training is available in many areas for front-line workers, and direct payments are mentioned in inductions and team meetings, there tended to be little mandatory provision, no provision for managers and elected members, and few examples of user involvement in training (Glasby, 2004). With direct payments such a departure from pre-1996 ways of working, a much greater emphasis on training opportunities and organisational development interventions will be required to promote direct payments to a greater number of people.

Difficulties extending direct payments to a range of user groups

Many of the key individuals and organisations involved in the campaign for direct payments were younger people with a physical impairment. This is very much a generalisation and is probably not true of a number of early champions of direct payments. However, the fact remains that much of current direct payments policy focuses primarily on the needs of people with physical impairments and that the vast majority of direct payments recipients continue to be people with physical impairments. In many ways, this should not be surprising, since people with physical and sensory impairments have traditionally formed user groups that have been more powerful and politically active than those of other service users (Barnes, 1997). At the same time, the imperative to ensure that recipients of direct payments are 'willing and able' to manage them (alone or with assistance) is likely to have been interpreted by some local authorities as ruling out most user groups other than people with physical impairments. In some locations, staff specialising in work with people with physical impairments may also be much more familiar with the concepts of independent living and direct payments than their colleagues in mental health, learning difficulty or other teams.

Certainly this seems to have been the case in one evaluation of a direct payments scheme, which found that take-up was higher among people with physical impairments than among other user groups (Dawson, 2000). Within this local authority, staff involved in the direct payments project came from physical impairment teams and were more likely to be aware of a previous indirect payments project and familiar with the concept of users employing their own personal assistants. In contrast, managers of mental health or learning difficulty teams were not conversant with the direct payments scheme and there was a widespread assumption that people with learning difficulties and mental health problems would not be able to manage direct payments. In addition, a local coalition of disabled people represented a range of user groups, but was dominated by people with physical impairments, while the direct payments coordinator employed by the coalition moved from working at home to an office in a day centre which traditionally served people with physical impairments.

Against this background there remain a number of unresolved questions as to whether a single policy can be made to work for all user groups, or whether more creative and imaginative approaches to direct payments are needed for groups such as people with learning difficulties, older people, people with mental health problems, younger people and others.

The tension between civil rights and neo-liberal social policy

While direct payments were a victory for disabled campaigners, they were also championed by a Conservative government committed to neo-liberal social policies aimed at rolling back the frontiers of the welfare state and promoting greater consumer choice through the creation of markets in social care. As a result, the government's initial concerns that direct payments would increase public expenditure were eventually overcome once research suggested that direct payments would be more cost-effective than directly provided services. Following the introduction of direct payments in 1997, official guidance has continued to emphasise that "a local authority should not make direct payments unless they are at least as cost-effective as the services which it would otherwise arrange" (DH, 1997, p 16). As direct payments schemes have begun to develop in different areas of the country, moreover, there has clearly been a political and economic dimension to local authorities' approach. Thus, in Scotland and in Northern England, some authorities have been reluctant to promote direct payments due to a perceived threat to the funding and future of local authority services (see, for example, McCurry, 1999; Witcher et al, 2000). For one commentator, such ideological concerns may be creating something of a 'north–south divide' (Pearson, 2000, p 463), with northern and Scottish authorities perceiving direct payments as a means of eroding public sector service provision, and Conservative-led authorities in the south promoting direct payments as a means of encouraging individual choice and cost-efficiency. That this remains the case can be seen from DH (2002a) data on the number of direct payments recipients per local authority. This suggests that direct payments are most prominent in Conservative authorities such as Hampshire, Essex and Norfolk, and least prevalent in Labour councils such as Sunderland, Slough, and North and South Tyneside.

As a result, when we talk about the introduction and expansion of direct payments, we are really talking about two different processes – on the one hand, a victory for disabled campaigners who advocated greater choice and control for disabled people (a civil rights or social justice approach); on the other, an attempt by a Conservative government to introduce the values of the market into social care and reduce welfare expenditure (a neo-liberal or market approach).

Perhaps one of the reasons why direct payments were implemented in the first place was because these two very different approaches went hand in hand for so long and, albeit for very different reasons, both seemed to be pointing in the same direction. In the UK, this has happened before – during the build-up to the community care reforms there was a moral argument (that quality of life is impeded in institutions) and a political and an economic one (institutions are very expensive and individuals/families should make their own provision), which for many years both pointed in the same direction and culminated in the passage of the 1990 NHS and Community Care

Act (see, for example, Victor, 1997; Means and Smith, 1998). However, these two moral and political/economic approaches were both very different and, arguably, have begun to diverge since community care was introduced, leading to ongoing debate about quality of care, the role of the state and the extent to which individuals should make their own provision for care (see, for example, Royal Commission on Long Term Care, 1999).

Against this background, could the same thing happen to direct payments? Now that payments have been introduced, will the civil rights approach of the disability movement and the neo-liberal approach of the previous government begin to diverge? If so, what will happen when this divergence takes place and will direct payments be sufficiently established to be able to survive this process? What is certain is that policy makers and front-line workers need to be clear about their value base when implementing direct payments, and about whether they wish to promote direct payments as a means of achieving civil rights or of rolling back the frontiers of the welfare state. To continue to try to do both may not ultimately be tenable.

The contribution of direct payments to health care

Direct payments are currently a social care policy made in lieu of directly provided social services. In many ways, social care was a natural forum for direct payments due to a traditional commitment to principles of empowerment and equality and since there was already considerable experience of commissioning services from a range of different potential providers in a mixed economy of care. However, social care is increasingly being asked to work in partnership with the National Health Service (NHS), recognising that that people's needs rarely divide neatly into separate 'health' and 'social care' categories:

> Although progress has been made towards breaching the 'Berlin Wall' between health and social care there are still too many parts of the country where a failure to co-operate means that older people fail to get the holistic services they need…. We will keep the relationship between health and social services under review. Older people and other service users have the right to expect that local services are working as one care system not two. We will monitor how far the NHS Plan and these further reforms we are proposing take us towards that goal. If more radical change is needed we will introduce it. (DH, 2002b, pp 32-3)

This raises key questions about how direct payments fit into this 'joined-up' agenda. What happens when health and social care are working in integrated settings and where do direct payments fit with the current partnership agenda? In the future, could direct payments be used to promote greater choice in the NHS? How might direct payments support people with long-term conditions (a current NHS priority)? To date, the two key contributions to this debate have been a 2000 study into direct payments and the health–social care divide (Glendinning et al, 2000), and a national seminar to explore the implications of direct payments for health care (Glasby and Hasler, 2004), although other studies have also drawn attention to this issue.

Conclusion

This chapter has provided an overview of both the campaign for the introduction of direct payments and the policy shift associated with it, drawing out some of the initial tensions, gaps and inconsistencies in policy and practice. While many of these were managed (or at least overlooked) in the early years of direct payments, the policy is now sufficiently mainstream for many of these issues to form increasingly significant barriers to further progress. With several of the unresolved areas highlighted above there is a danger that local authorities sympathetic to direct payments will be held back as they each 'reinvent the wheel' trying to resolve these dilemmas, while authorities hostile to direct payments will have an excuse to avoid further action.

As a result, the implementation and expansion of direct payments to date raise a number of questions that will need further thought and a policy response if direct payments really are to transform social care. Thus, there is still some way to go in winning over certain key stakeholders who may currently be sceptical about this way of working, while further work is also required to extend the choice and control inherent in direct payments to different user groups. At the same time, the civil rights approach of the independent living movement which underpinned the campaign for direct payments is at odds with the neo-liberal approaches to social policy, and this tension needs to be acknowledged and managed. Finally, it is unclear where direct payments fit in the current partnership agenda and whether they can be extended into other areas such as health care. It is these and other key issues on direct payments that the following chapters in this book begin to address.

References

Barnes, M. (1997) *Care, communities and citizens*, London: Longman.

Becker, S. (1997) *Responding to poverty: The politics of cash and care*, Basingstoke: Macmillan.

Bewley, C. (2000) 'Care managers can be champions for direct payments', *Care Plan*, vol 6, no 4, pp 13-16.

CSCI (Commission for Social Care Inspection) (2004) *Direct payments: What are the barriers?*, London: CSCI.

Davis, A. and Stephenson, D. (1999) 'Working with poor communities: social and community work in the UK – one hundred years of change and continuity', Unpublished paper presented at Association House, Chicago, IL, 20 October.

Dawson, C. (2000) *Independent successes: Implementing direct payments*, York: Joseph Rowntree Foundation.

DH (Department of Health) (1990) *Community care in the next decade and beyond: Policy guidance*, London: DH.

DH (1997) *Community Care (Direct Payments) Act 1996: Policy and practice guidance*, London: DH.

DH (1999) 'Direct payments: cash for services', information video, London: DH.

DH (2000) *Community Care (Direct Payments) Act 1996: Policy and practice guidance* (2nd edn), London: DH.

DH (2002a) *Direct payments*, DH statistical information, accessed 25 April 2003 (www.doh.gov.uk/directpayments).

DH (2002b) *Delivering the NHS plan: Next steps on investment, next steps on reform*, London: DH.

Englander, D. (1998) *Poverty and Poor Law reform in 19th century Britain, 1834–1914: From Chadwick to Booth*, London: Longman.

Evans, J. (1993) 'The role of centres of independent/integrated living and networks of disabled people', in C. Barnes (ed) *Making our own choices: Independent living, personal assistance and disabled people*, Belper: BCODP.

Fruin, D. (2000) *New directions for independent living*, London: DH.

Glasby, J. (2004) *Direct payments and people with learning difficulties: West Midlands Regional Support Network (internet summary): Meeting 2-17 September 2003*, Notes from a regional network commissioned by the Valuing People Support Team.

Glasby, J. and Hasler, F. (2004) *A healthy option? Direct payments and the implications for health care*, Birmingham/London: Health Services Management Centre/National Centre for Independent Living.

Glasby, J. and Littlechild, R. (2002) *Social work and direct payments*, Bristol: The Policy Press.

Glendinning, C., Haliwell, S., Jacobs, S., Rummery, K. and Tyrer, J. (2000) *Buying independence: Using direct payments to integrate health and social services*, Bristol: The Policy Press.

Hasler, F. (1999) 'Exercising the right to freedom of choice', *Professional Social Work*, June, pp 6–7.

Hatchett, W. (1991) 'Cash on delivery?', *Community Care*, 30 May, pp 14–15.

Hudson, B. (1988) 'Doomed from the start?', *Health Service Journal*, 23 June, pp 708–9.

Kestenbaum, A. (1993) *Making community care a reality: The Independent Living Fund, 1988-1993*, London: RADAR.

Leece, J. (2000) 'It's a matter of choice: making direct payments work in Staffordshire', *Practice*, vol 12, no 4, pp 37-48.

McCurry, P. (1999) 'The direct route', *Community Care*, 9-15 September, pp 20–1.

Maglajlic, R., Brandon, D. and Given, D. (2000) 'Making direct payments a choice: a report on the research findings', *Disability & Society*, vol 15, no 1, pp 99-113.

Means, R. and Smith, R. (1998) *Community care: Policy and practice* (2nd edn), Basingstoke: Macmillan.

Morris, J. (1993) *Independent lives: Community care and disabled people*, Basingstoke: Macmillan.

Oliver, M. and Sapey, B. (1999) *Social work with disabled people* (2nd edn), Basingstoke: Macmillan.

Pearson, C. (2000) 'Money talks? Competing discourses in the role of direct payments', *Critical Social Policy*, vol 20, no 4, pp 459-77.

Royal Commission on Long Term Care (1999) *With respect to old age: Long term care – rights and responsibilities*, London: The Stationery Office.

Thane, P. (1996) *Foundations of the welfare state* (2nd edn), London: Longman.

Victor, C. (1997) *Community care and older people*, Cheltenham: Stanley Thomas.

Witcher, S., Stalker, K., Roadburg, M. and Jones, C. (2000) *Direct payments: The impact on choice and control for disabled people*, Edinburgh: Scottish Executive Central Research Unit.

Zarb, G. and Nadash, P. (1994) *Cashing in on independence: Comparing the costs and benefits of cash and services*, London: BCODP.

THREE

Direct payments in Scotland

Charlotte Pearson

The initial implementation of the 1996 Community Care (Direct Payments) Act in April 1997 as enabling legislation gave local authorities in England, Wales and Scotland and health and social service trusts (HSS) in Northern Ireland the option whether to offer direct payments or maintain existing modes of service provision (see Pearson, 2004a for a discussion of this). In exploring some of the key problems underpinning this trend, this chapter focuses specifically on the impact and future directions of policy in Scotland.

The impact of the early years of direct payments across the UK may be described as limited. Indeed, although many areas largely in the south-east of England have consistently increased their user take-up (see Riddell et al, 2005), access has remained fairly marginal elsewhere.

This chapter begins by mapping the early impact of indirect payment and third party schemes in Scotland through the actions of local alliances of disabled people. Discussion then follows the initial take-up of policy in the period from April 1997 to 2000. Policy development at this time is shown to be especially poor, with only a small number of local authorities enabling access to direct payments. Indeed, changes since 2003 have seen a heightened drive from both the Scottish Executive and local authorities in promoting policy and encouraging a more diverse user population. However, drawing on preliminary analysis from the Economic and Social Research Council (ESRC) funded study, 'Disabled People and Direct Payments: A UK Comparative Study', being carried out by researchers at Glasgow, Edinburgh and Leeds Universities, the discussion outlines some of the key trends and policy issues that have emerged in relation to direct payments in Scotland over the past eight years.

This includes a focus on practitioner roles, which, in many areas, have been responsible for resistance to direct payments, thereby creating attitudinal and structural barriers to change. Such problems have often been linked to concerns from trades unions over the promotion of policy as a means to privatise social care services. Commentary at this stage examines some of these issues more closely and questions the emergence of these debates over the past few years. This is then extended to examining the development of support services for direct payment users. Despite the promotion of a 'user-led' model for this type of support, there has been a shift towards alternative providers as user groups diversify and a 'support market' emerges in Scotland. The chapter concludes by discussing these broader trends and questioning their impact on the future development of policy.

Early routes to payments: the impact of local alliances in Scotland

Prior to implementation of the 1996 Act, confusion surrounded the legality of direct payments across the UK. Whereas, in England and Wales, the 1948 Social Security Act stipulated that only services and *not* payments could be made by local authorities, the position differed slightly in Scotland. Indeed, through the 1968 Social Work (Scotland) Act, cash payments could be made in exceptional circumstances and emergencies. However, the impact of this ruling was limited, as local authority planners had minimal knowledge of this provision (Pearson, 2000) and only one local authority justified making payments through this route (Witcher et al, 2000).

The administration of indirect payments during the 1980s and 1990s through third parties, such as voluntary sector organisations or independent local trusts, sought to overcome these restrictions. These emerged as a result of the actions of small groups of disabled people demanding cash rather than services to employ personal assistants, and formed the locus of local and national campaigns for legislation. While most of these payments were found in English areas such as Derbyshire, Essex, Hampshire and Norfolk, in Scotland activists in the former Lothian region also successfully pioneered change.

A few other examples of indirect payments during the early 1990s were found in Scotland. Notably, in the former Strathclyde region, monies paid from Independent Living Funds (ILFs) helped establish an alternative approach to indirect payments (see Kestenbaum, 1995). While this proved very popular with local disabled people, its position as a separate service option, rather than as part of mainstream disability services, made it susceptible to cuts, and new users were denied access.

Therefore, akin to early payment coverage in Wales and Northern Ireland, the starting point for direct payments when they were initially implemented in April 1997, was considerably weaker than in many parts of southern England. The next section details the early impact of policy change.

Initial take-up: 1997-2000

The first major study of direct payments in Scotland was carried out by Witcher et al (2000). This research, commissioned by the Scottish Executive, confirmed the limited availability of direct payments, with only 13 out of the 32 local authorities having fully operational or pilot schemes, and a total of 143 users. Although figures have since risen (this will be returned to shortly), take-up is still proportionately lower than in England. Findings from the research also highlighted an imbalance between impairment groups with nearly 90% uptake for persons with physical and sensory impairments, and only marginal use for persons with perceived learning difficulties. At this time, there were no users with reported mental health problems, and persons from black and minority ethnic communities were also disproportionately poorly represented.

Policy developments since 2000

As discussion so far has indicated, the success of direct payments in Scotland in the early years of the scheme's implementation (from April 1997) was marginal and proved to be something of a 'false dawn'. Since then, in line with developments elsewhere in the UK, the Scottish Executive has underlined its commitment to direct payments through a series of legislative changes. Primarily, it is clear from these initiatives that there is a strong commitment to extending policy to a more diverse user population, and changes have been presented as an integral part of the modernising agenda for social care and social inclusion programmes (see, for example, Scottish Executive, 2003). Therefore, following on from expansion of the scheme to persons over the age of 65 in 2000, the main focus of change in Scotland was set out in the 2002 Community Care and Health (Scotland) Act. At the forefront of this was the enforcement of a mandatory duty placed on all local authorities to offer direct payments to all community care users requesting them from June 2003. Although the same shift was made across the UK, the implications of this shift outside England look to be more strongly felt and there has been a much more concerted push to develop policy than at the time of initial implementation in 1997. This will be returned to shortly. Other changes made in the 2002 Act allowed parents of disabled children to receive payments. It is clear that the immediate impact of this change has remained limited, as many local authorities have struggled to reorganise their services (Pearson, 2004b). This level of concern is also reflected in the decision to exclude 'carers' from direct payments in Scotland – a move that differs from the changes made in all other parts of the UK.

Despite the rationale for excluding 'carers', the Act stipulated that *all* persons assessed as having 'community care needs' would be eligible for direct payments. This covers persons who are frail, receiving rehabilitation after an accident or operation, fleeing domestic violence, refugees, homeless or recovering from drug or alcohol dependency. The change was initially planned for April 2004; however, amid concerns that local authorities and support organisations would be unable to cope with new user groups, the shift was deferred for gradual implementation from April 2005. At the time of writing it was still unclear whether the Executive was going to proceed with these changes from the revised date.

Given the Scottish Executive's aim to widen user access, it is likely that a different payment pattern will emerge over the next few years. As such, the shift has important implications for a number of reasons: first, in terms of the discourses underpinning policy, and second, in terms of user support, which has tended to be provided by user-controlled disability organisations. From this standpoint, the move to make payments available to all community care users raises broader questions over the policy direction and the values promoted by the disability movement. These debates will be returned to shortly.

Other important differences in the structure of direct payments within the UK relate to the provision of monies for support service roles from the related government departments. In October 2002, the Department of Health (DH) announced the introduction of the Direct Payments Development Fund in England. This centred on a package of £9 million, made available over three years, which was targeted at developing direct payment support structures through partnerships between local authorities and voluntary agencies in England where user uptake was poor (DH, 2003). In July 2003, the first round of successful bids was announced and 45 organisations were allocated £4.5 million to develop projects. The second round of funding was released in June 2004; at both stages projects were funded for 18 months. See Hasler in Chapter 11, 'The Direct Payments Development Fund', for more details.

Elsewhere in the UK, in Northern Ireland support has been centred around the work of the Centre for Independent Living (CIL), which to date has received funds from the Eastern and Southern Boards to undertake these roles in HSS. In Wales, limited funds for support have been targeted at local authorities rather than organisations themselves.

In Scotland, the approach also differs. Unlike the Development Fund model and/or targeting funds at local authorities or the HSS or other organisational groups, the focus on increasing information access and service support has been made through the establishment of Direct Payments Scotland (DPS) in 2001. This project was set up with an initial allocation of £530,000 from the Scottish Executive and renewed funding to support work until 2006. Like the Direct Payments Development Fund, DPS has a clear remit to help establish support organisations. However, its focus is centred more on promoting awareness of policy among users, local authority staff and service providers, alongside conducting widespread training for personnel in these areas. While the Executive has emphasised the importance of developing support roles for direct payments users (see, for example, Scottish Executive, 2003), unlike the Development Fund, funding has been restricted to DPS with no additional monies being made available to promote local initiatives.

Mapping the UK payment pattern

As Table 3.1 shows, preliminary analysis of the ESRC study undertaken in February 2004 indicated that there were 534 direct payments users in Scotland in 2003. Although this is a higher rate than in both Northern Ireland and Wales, it remained proportionately lower than take-up in England, which at the time stood at 12,585 and represented 95% of the overall total of payments made.

Furthermore, when looking at direct payments figures alongside those recorded for 'long-term illness or disability' (LTID) in the UK, a clear mismatch is highlighted. Although England covers a significantly larger population, it has the lowest rate of LTID at 18%, but has over 90% of all direct payments users in the UK. While Scotland scores second in terms of the number of payment users, this only amounts to 4% of the total. This figure is perhaps more striking when placed alongside the LTID rate, which is 2% higher than in England at 20%. While it is acknowledged that eligibility to direct payments would be restricted to a limited number in this population through the community care assessment system, the figures are useful in that they highlight the geographical inequity in policy take-up. Hence it is clear that policy is not being used to its full potential as a mainstream service option.

More recent figures released in October 2004 by the Scottish

Executive (2004) revealed a further increase to 912 users in Scotland. While this clearly represents a considerable rise over the past three years from the 143 payments identified in Witcher et al's (2000) research, some of the key patterns remain the same. Indeed, when looking at take-up among impairment groups, although some shifts have occurred, the overall imbalance is still prominent. Notably, 72% of payments (606) were made to persons with physical impairments, and take-up for persons with learning difficulties and mental health problems remains fairly marginal. However, the main area of increase is for older people, since a third of all claimants are now aged 65 or over, compared to only 7% in 2001.

Political control, local support: emerging issues in Scotland

As the figures in Table 3.1 show, there is a concentration of direct payments in England, with a far more restricted spread elsewhere. In looking at these figures in more detail, preliminary analysis for the ESRC study identified two key factors which appeared to impact on this pattern: political control and the type of direct payment support scheme in place (Riddell et al, 2005).

Table 3.1: Number of direct payment users in each part of the UK between 2000/01 and 2003

Country/province	% LTID	2000/01	2002/03	2003	% of direct payments in the UK
* England	18	5,423	7,882	12,585	95
** Scotland	20	207	292	534	4
†Wales	23.5	*	185	*	2
‡ Northern Ireland	22.5	33	49	128	1

Notes: (1) LTID refers to the percentage of people reporting a long-term limiting illness or disability in the 2001 Census. (2) Figures for Wales not available for 2000/01 and 2003 due to recording methods of the Welsh Assembly. (3) Percentages in the column '% of direct payments in the UK' do not add to 100 due to rounding. All direct payment figures cited in this paper are based on publicly available statistics and statistical breakdowns available on 18 February 2004. All figures include all direct and indirect payments recorded by relevant authorities. The term 'direct payments' has therefore been used generically to cover all cash payments made to individuals to purchase services, whether or not made through a third party.

Sources: *DH (2003); **Scottish Executive (2003); † the Local Government Data Unit in Wales (LGDUW). This has responsibility for producing community care output figures but was not established until April 2001. The Welsh Executive, which had prior responsibility, did not produce direct payment statistics by users, but by expenditure. Therefore, figures shown here are adapted from LGDUW figures at 10/10/03 and those held by the National Centre for Independent Living. ‡ Figures supplied by the information branch at the Department for Health, Social Services and Public Safety for 31/3/03.

Taking the UK as a whole, it appears that the political control of an authority may indeed be a significant factor in accessing direct payments, with many Conservative areas more likely to embrace policy than those in traditional Labour heartlands. Indeed, out of the 10 local authorities with the highest numbers of direct payments users (all of which are located in England), seven are Conservative controlled. Therefore, as already documented in the literature (Pearson, 2000; Spandler, 2004), it is likely that it is the promotion of consumer markets, individual 'choice' and 'cost efficiency', enabled through cash rather than service provision, that appeals to certain Conservative-led authorities. Given the political exclusion of the Conservative Party in Scotland and the broader resistance to the marketisation of social services, it is perhaps unsurprising to see a rejection of policy. However, in order to understand the wider use of policy more fully, it is necessary to explore support and practitioner roles and their position in promoting take-up.

Practitioner roles

Across the UK, social work roles in relation to direct payments have been largely mixed. Examples of good practice have been highlighted (Stainton, 2002; Clark et al, 2004), but there has also been a substantive critique on the values and approaches informing some practice. This has centred on the position of social workers as 'gatekeepers' to cash-limited 'care' budgets and a perceived lack of awareness of the principles of independent living and social justice promoted by the disability movement in their campaign for policy change (see Dawson, 2000; Pearson, 2000). In Scotland, these issues were initially highlighted by Witcher et al (2000) and have remained a key concern among policy advocates (Pearson, 2004a). Since then, a number of training initiatives have been developed to tackle some of the structural and attitudinal barriers apparent in social work departments. Notably, the work of DPS has played an important role in promoting good practice by offering a range of training sessions and related materials (see, for example, DPS, 2002).

Direct payments and the marketisation of social care

However, as suggested, there remains broader ideological resistance over the use of direct payments in Scotland as a mode of service provision (see also Pearson, 2004a, 2004b). This has linked in both with concerns over the marketisation of social care, and broader anti-privatisation campaigns across the public services (Mooney and Poole, 2004). Indeed, the public sector union UNISON has expressed particular concern over the impact of direct payments for employees in the social care sector. In a recent briefing to members (UNISON Scotland, 2004), the concerns listed focused on two main issues: the role of users as employers, and how the payments are used. In looking at the employer role, UNISON has stated:

> Direct Payments do not allow recipients to offer decent rates of pay to personal assistants. (UNISON Scotland, 2004, p 3)

This is clearly a contentious area, as rates of pay between local authorities do differ considerably. Witcher et al (2000), for example, found that hourly rates varied from £3.60 to £11.64 and, while some included contingency monies and other costs, others did not. Similarly in England, McMullen (2003) found that hourly rates varied from £4.20 to £12.30.

Furthermore, the UNISON line reiterates some of the earlier critiques of personal assistance developed in the academic literature raised by commentators such as Ungerson (1997). These have centred on the potential exploitation of personal assistants in an increasingly deregulated social care market. As Spandler (2004) observed, these concerns reflect a more general trend of devaluing social and home care work. This has seen greater job insecurity, reduced pay levels and an increase in stress, overwork and other health problems for workers (UNISON, 2001). In turn, these changes are more likely to impact disproportionately on women and people from black and minority ethnic communities (Begum, 1992).

Clearly, issues around the provision of secure and comparable employment packages through direct payments are vital in promoting policy as a viable service option. Indeed, the pool of labour for personal assistance is currently limited both in Scotland and across the UK. As Morris (2004) has observed, poor rates of pay inevitably create situations where disabled people are forced to take on personal assistants who cannot provide them with a good service. This is therefore an area that must be addressed by local authorities and central government so that it can be developed as a service and career option. Hence, it is important that resistance to direct payments does not become further ingrained in a broader anti-market discourse that is positioned separately from the rights and choices of disabled people and/or the promotion of employment rights of personal assistants.

The shift towards direct payments has also raised questions for UNISON over the role of disabled people as employers. As the briefing states:

> There are also a number of employment rights issues about the impact of recipients as 'employers' of personal assistants providing care to them. (UNISON Scotland, 2004, p 3)

Indeed, during the early phase of policy implementation, what is now referred to as the 'South Lanarkshire case' caused alarm among local authorities. In this instance, it was ruled that, in a case of sexual harassment against a direct payment user, the local authority rather than the user was to be regarded as the employer (Hunter, 1999). It is clear from subsequent commentary on this case (see, for example, Glasby and Littlechild, 2002) that the situation could have been avoided if there had been more clarity over roles and responsibilities. Moreover, union concern over the shift from user to employer once again questions the need to promote the independent living principles of policy and, in turn, to encourage a more diverse understanding of disabled people's identities.

Issues relating to how direct payments are used also raised by UNISON clearly centre on the impact of payments as a means of challenging existing service provision. This revisits arguments as to accountability, which have been raised by a number of local authorities through their policy transition (see Pearson, 2000). As such, UNISON questions whether "recipients [will] opt to keep some or all of the cash instead of purchasing services?" (UNISON Scotland, 2004, p 3).

Given the rigidity of community care assessments and complaints of restrictive hours raised by many users (Morris, 2004; Zarb, 2004), it is difficult to see how this type of argument can hold up. To some extent, it is reminiscent of the attack on 'benefit dependency' (see, for example, Cook, 1993) promoted by the New Right from the late 1980s and sustained by New Labour. Likewise, this type of attack on direct payments reiterates a failure to acknowledge the independent living discourses underpinning policy.

While efforts by DPS, the Scottish Personal Assistance Employers Network (SPAEN) and the centres for independent/integrated living (CILs) in Edinburgh and Glasgow continue to promote policy more positively, the link between direct payments and service privatisation clearly remains prominent.

User-led or in-house? The development of 'support markets'

Alongside the need to promote direct payments positively as part of a network of independent living services for disabled people, the role of support organisations in facilitating this has become a prominent area of discussion. The importance of this role has been emphasised from within the disability movement (Evans and Hasler, 1996; Hasler et al, 1999), by users themselves (Carmichael and Brown, 2002; Clark et al, 2004) and by policy planners (Scottish Executive, 2003).

Preliminary analysis for the ESRC study showed that support schemes undoubtedly have a positive impact on direct payments use, encouraging take-up by up to 80% when tested at UK level (Riddell et al, 2005). Yet despite this recognition, local authorities are not obliged to meet these costs as part of community care assessments. As detailed earlier in this chapter, the establishment of the Direct Payments Development Fund in England was targeted specifically at developing support structures through partnerships between local authorities and voluntary agencies in areas where take-up has been particularly low (see Hasler, in Chaper Eleven of this book). While DPS has worked rigorously to develop user-led support organisations (DPS, 2002), to date no direct funding from the Scottish Executive has been made available to develop individual groups. In some instances, this has meant that CILs – traditionally the main providers of user-led support – have been required to negotiate separate contracts with local authorities. While this has worked effectively when councils have bought in block service contracts, it has been far more difficult to sustain a level of service provision when only spot contracting has been offered. Consequently, CILs have often found themselves in a precarious position where it is assumed that they are willing and able to support an expanding and increasingly diverse user population, but often without additional funding. Indeed, as reported in an earlier study (Pearson, 2004b), the two Scottish CILs and the related SPAEN reported considerable variation in local authority willingness to cover support payments. These ranged from councils who make core funding for support services to those who make no or limited contributions.

The study also found that, as Scottish legislation moves to permit access to direct payments for all community care users, the idea of offering support to more diverse groups of direct payment users raised concerns for the CILs (Pearson, 2004b). Questions were raised over the feasibility of providing support to other groups based on the experiences of disabled people. The option of employing specialist workers for the new user groups within CILs was also discussed. In taking this approach, direct payment support would be specifically framed around different user needs and would provide a 'one-stop shop' for all groups. However, as the study details, although this would perhaps provide a more specialist level of knowledge for more diverse user needs as part of CIL structures, concerns were raised over the implications of this type of shift for the management and constitution of CILs.

Indeed, despite the prominence of CILs and other user-led organisations as support providers for direct payments, in recent years there has been a considerable growth in other groups taking on this role. Across the UK, these have assumed a number of different guises and have been set up by private or voluntary sector companies or established 'in-house' within social work departments. In Scotland, despite a concerted push to promote a user-led framework by key proponents like DPS (see DPS, 2002), a number of other providers have emerged. For the disability movement, this shift towards a 'support market' where the favoured user-led framework has been marginalised in some areas by other providers, has raised a number of concerns. Conversely, for local authority planners seeking to develop policy, concerns have appeared to focus primarily on offering users choice and the need for these organisations to be able to adapt and include any new user group (Pearson, 2004b).

Discussion

As commentary in this chapter has shown, the emergence of direct payments in Scotland over the past eight years has been slow and fraught with difficulties and contradictions among different interest groups. While many of the issues and patterns are replicated at UK level, there remain a number of competing discourses which have acted as significant barriers to mainstream implementation.

On the one hand, in line with calls to promote cash payments for personal assistance throughout the UK (see Campbell, 1996) and internationally (Roeher Institute, 1993; Lord and Hutchison, 2003), disability activism has been an important impetus to securing change. In Scotland, at an organisational level this has seen the two CILs in Edinburgh and Glasgow, together with SPAEN, take a leading role in developing support and training for disabled people who have chosen to take on the role of personal assistance employer. However, despite the renewed emphasis on local authorities to develop schemes, the increase in the number of support organisations outside the user-led model has been raised as a worrying trend for the movement as a whole. Indeed, given the likely shift to allow all community care users access to direct payments, policy direction in Scotland has the potential to look quite different from the rest of the UK over the next few years. For user-led organisations with constitutions framed around the needs of disabled people, this is clearly an important time in considering their future roles as support providers and/or competitors as user needs diversify.

Concerns raised by union workers and some practitioners have, however, been more prominent in Scotland than in the rest of the UK. As Mooney and Poole (2004) have outlined in their overview of social policy in post-devolution Scotland, historical alliances between local authorities, trades unions and the Scottish Labour Party, which were cemented in the 1980s and 1990s, have been significant in resisting Conservative agendas. From this standpoint, the perception of direct payments as part of a wider privatisation of social care has clearly been damaging and once again erodes its independent living foundations. Clearly, the positioning of direct payments as an appendage to community care legislation and wider network of local authority services for disabled people has made these links inevitable. It is therefore important for both policy planners and public sector unions to focus on developing sustainable employment packages for personal assistants, thereby separating the ethos of direct payments from the privatisation of social care. Inevitably, for this to occur successfully, the policy framework for direct payments needs to be re-examined in the wider context of how both local and central government provide services for disabled people. In the meantime, it is important that the views of disabled people and other new user groups are represented in planning and support structures to secure wider access.

It is of course important not to negate the significant increase in the numbers of direct payments users in Scotland over the past three years. Indeed, the shift to mandatory implementation in 2003 has clearly acted as a major stimulus to change and encouraged a much-needed relaunch of the 1996 Act. As local authorities now seek to develop schemes, the new era for policy in Scotland does perhaps indicate a shift by many practitioners in taking change on board and challenging more rigid service structures.

References

Begum, N. (1992) 'Independent living, personal assistance and black disabled people', in C. Barnes (ed) *Making our own choice: Independent living, personal assistance and disabled people,* London: British Council of Disabled People and Ryburn Press.

Campbell, J. (1996) 'Implementing direct payments: towards the next millennium', National Institute of Social Work Conference, 12 November.

Carmichael, A. and Brown, L. (2002) 'The future challenge for direct payments', *Disability and Society*, vol 17, no 7, pp 797-808.

Clark, H., Gough, H. and Macfarlane, A. (2004) *'It pays dividends': Direct payments and older people*, Bristol/York: The Policy Press/Joseph Rowntree Foundation.

Cook, D. (1993) 'Defrauding the state: who benefits? Social inequality and the responses to tax and social security fraud', in A. Sinfield (ed) *Poverty, inequality and justice*, New Waverley Papers, Social Policy Series No 6, Edinburgh: Department of Social Policy, University of Edinburgh.

Dawson, C. (2000) *Independent successes: Implementing direct payments*, York: York Publishing Services.

DH (Department of Health) (2003) *Direct payments guidance: Community care, services for carers and children's services (direct payments) guidance, England 2003*, London: DH.

DPS (Direct Payments Scotland) (2002) *Five steps: A guide for local authorities, implementing direct payments*, Edinburgh: DPS.

Evans J. and Hasler, F. (1996) 'Direct payments campaign in the UK', Presentation for the European Network on Independent Living Seminar, Stockholm, 9-11 June.

Glasby, J. and Littlechild, R. (2002) *Social work and direct payments*, Bristol: The Policy Press.

Hasler, F., Campbell, J. and Zarb, G. (1999) *Direct routes to independence: A guide to local authority implementation of direct payments*, London: Policy Studies Institute/National Centre for Independent Living.

Hunter, M. (1999) 'Case threatens direct payments', *Community Care*, 12-18 August, pp 10-11.

Kestenbaum, A. (1995) *An opportunity lost? Social services use of the Independent Living Transfer*, London: Disability Income Group.

Lord, J. and Hutchison, P. (2003) 'Individualised support and funding: building blocks for capacity building and inclusion', *Disability and Society*, vol 18, no 1, pp 71-86.

McMullen, K. (2003) *The direct approach: Disabled people's experience of direct payments*, London: Scope.

Mooney, G. and Poole, L. (2004) 'A land of milk and honey? Social policy in Scotland after devolution', *Critical Social Policy*, vol 24, no 4, pp 458–83.

Morris, J. (2004) 'Independent living and community care: a disempowering framework', *Disability and Society*, vol 19, no 5, pp 427-42.

Pearson, C. (2000) 'Money talks? Competing discourses in the implementation of direct payments', *Critical Social Policy*, vol 20, no 4, pp 459-77.

Pearson, C. (2003) *Exploring the role of support organisations for direct payments*, Report prepared for Direct Payments Scotland, August 2003 (www.dpscotland.org.uk/).

Pearson, C. (2004a) 'Keeping the cash under control: what's the problem with direct payments in Scotland?', *Disability and Society*, vol 19, no 1, pp 3-14.

Pearson, C. (2004b) 'The implementation of direct payments: issues for user-led organisations in Scotland', in C. Barnes, and G. Mercer (eds) *Implementing the social model of disability: Theory and research*, Leeds: Disability Press.

Riddell, S., Pearson, C., Jolly, D., Barnes, C., Priestley, M. and Mercer, G. (2005) 'The development of direct payments in the UK: implications for social justice', *Social Policy and Society*, vol 4, no 1, pp 77-85.

Roeher Institute (1993) *Direct dollars: A study of individualised funding in Canada*, Ontario: Roeher Institute.

Scottish Executive (2003) *Direct Payments Social Work (Scotland) Act 1968: Sections 12B and C: Policy and practice guidance*, Edinburgh: Scottish Executive Health Department, Community Care Division.

Scottish Executive (2004) *Statistics release: Direct payments Scotland 2004*, (www.scotland.gov.uk/stats/bulletins/00370-00.asp), accessed 6 October 2004.

Spandler, H. (2004) 'Friend or foe? Towards a critical assessment of direct payments?', *Critical Social Policy*, vol 24, no 2, pp 187-209.

Stainton, T. (2002) 'Taking rights structurally: disability rights and social worker responses to direct payments', *British Journal of Social Work*, vol 32, pp 751-63.

Ungerson, C. (1997) 'Give them the money: is cash a route to empowerment?', *Social Policy and Administration*, vol 31, no 1, pp 45-53.

UNISON (2001) *Home care: The forgotten service*, London: UNISON.

UNISON Scotland (2004) *Direct payment briefing* (www.unison-scotland.org.uk/briefings/directpay.html).

Witcher, S., Stalker, K., Roadburg, M. and Jones, C. (2000) *Direct payments: The impact on choice and control for disabled people*, Edinburgh: Scottish Executive Central Research Unit.

Zarb, G. (2004) 'Independent living and the road to inclusion', in C. Barnes and G. Mercer (eds) *Implementing the social model of disability: Theory and research*, Leeds: Disability Press.

FOUR

North American approaches to individualised planning and direct funding

Peggy Hutchison, John Lord and Brian Salisbury

North America, unlike many Western countries, has a long history of service reform for people with different disabilities. Since the 1960s, complex community service systems have evolved, and many large institutions have closed. In Canada and the US, this extensive array of community-based programmes and rehabilitation services was originally based on what is known as the continuum model. In this approach, a range of services are offered from the most restrictive, such as a large residential care home, to the least restrictive, such as a supported independent living apartment. The assumption was that people would be able to progress through the continuum relatively quickly and that no one would get 'stuck' at the more restrictive end (Wieck and Strully, 1991).

In the early 1980s, there was growing awareness of the limitations of the continuum model and the rehabilitation approach as a foundation for the provision of disability supports. Users and families found that community services that placed people into programmes promised far more than they delivered. The reality was that many people were isolated, congregated in large groups with other labelled people, stuck at the restrictive end of the continuum, and experiencing very little genuine community (Pedlar et al, 2000). The desire for a better quality of life grew as a response to these limitations and as a way to further community inclusion (Renwick et al, 1996).

Individualised planning and direct funding have evolved as cornerstones of a new paradigm of disability supports for citizenship and inclusion. For more than 25 years, this new stage of service reform has been underway in Canada and the US. This chapter explores the relationship between the concepts of individualised planning and direct funding within North America by drawing on recent innovations across North America, the authors' extensive experience with direct funding projects, and research from a cross-site study conducted by two of the authors.

Evolution of supports for citizens with disabilities

The traditional community service delivery system that evolved in the 1960s and 1970s for people with disabilities in Canada and the US has many features:

- funding for disability supports is available only to agencies and not directly to individuals;
- services are provided in congregate settings, rather than being individualised;
- the development of supports is typically professionally driven;
- many community services are rehabilitation-oriented and play a major role in people's lives;
- services are usually poorly coordinated, and duplication, misutilisation, or gaps in services are common.

A new paradigm of disability supports has been responding to each of these major concerns (Roeher Institute, 1993; O'Brien, 2001; Hulgin, 2004) and is probably best understood as a move from service and placement towards capacity building and participation.

Social change toward this new paradigm has been driven by consumer/user movements of people with disabilities, the disability family movement, and the rights movement. All have been significant in the evolution away from traditional community services that reinforce compliance and clienthood toward individualised planning and direct funding. For example, the independent living movement, through its cross-disability Independent Living Resource Centres, has promoted consumer control, peer support, community integration, and empowerment skills (de Jong, 1979; Hutchison et al, 2000). The community living movement, driven primarily by parents, has built broad awareness of the value of inclusion and participation in community life for individuals with developmental and learning disabilities (Roeher Institute, 1996). Finally, human rights and the courts have helped shape the evolution of disability supports. The Americans with Disabilities Act (ADA), passed in 1990, mandates the elimination of discrimination, and in turn, promotes integration in all aspects of community life (Americans with Disabilities Act, PL 101-336, 1990). The Canadian Charter of Rights and Freedoms (the 1982 Canadian Constitution Act) identifies persons with disabilities as a core group entitled to fundamental rights and freedoms (Lepofsky, 1997).

Individualised planning and direct funding mean different things to different people

Earlier, any efforts at individual planning usually resulted in service planning, with very little attention paid to individualised needs. This is understandable given the strong influence of traditional approaches. The residue of such limited reform remains today, as many organisations continue to use person-centered language to carry out regular services and programmes. As well, individualised or direct funding initiatives have also been compromised. In many instances, direct funding has meant 'give me the money'. The metaphor of 'cash', while appealing to users, has turned out to be an illusion of change when direct funding was not accompanied by new ways of thinking, planning, and acting.

If 'services' and 'cash' were not the right metaphors for the change people need, how has the dialogue about the new paradigm been proceeding? More and more in North America, the discourse is focusing on citizenship, individualised disability supports, and quality of life. The First International Conference on Self-Determination and Individualized Funding (see http://members.shaw.ca/individualizedfunding/), which took place in Seattle in 2000, produced a declaration on key principles that can guide individualised funding implementation. Over 1,250 people from around the world attended, including self-advocates, family members, professionals, providers, and policy makers. There was a significant degree of consensus on key issues.

We know that when direct funding is accompanied by infrastructure supports for person-centred planning and facilitation, quality of life is significantly enhanced. Person-centred planning is a process that enables an individual and his/her network to develop dreams, goals, and possibilities with community as a first resort (Lord and Hutchison, 2003). It has been challenging for change agents to convince the field that direct funding is only part of the picture.

Local and state/provincial initiatives must drive the North American paradigm shift

Unlike in Britain, there has been no national policy direction or legislation in North America that enables people to access direct payments. Local initiatives and state/provincial projects drive paradigm and policy change in North America, although there have been some advantages to this approach. For one thing, there has been plenty of local innovation and experiments with individualised approaches. This has created a strong sense that each project is unique to that area, as well as contributed to citizen engagement and ownership of initiatives. Over time, this has led to a deeper understanding about what really works in local communities.

The dilemma, however, is that few states or provinces have developed direct funding policies or systems, so innovation at the local level is often piecemeal, at best. During the 1990s, self-determination projects were funded in 19 US states. These pilot projects attracted wide attention because they attempted to build direct funding mechanisms and person-centered planning approaches for people with developmental disabilities into local, and in some cases, even state systems. Despite some success, few states have evolved more comprehensive approaches to direct funding based on these experiments. In 1995, the Canadian province of Alberta legislated individualised funding for individuals with developmental disabilities or physical disabilities. Despite some positive features, the Alberta experience has had limited results, mainly because there was no infrastructure support for person-centered planning and facilitation (Uditsky, 1999). As both of these examples show, when state/province or local initiatives are not accompanied by thoughtful principles and strategies that are consistent with new policy directions, the impact on people's quality of life is minimal. To more fully understand direct funding in North America, we need to consider the dilemmas and impact of local and state/provincial change.

Three examples of projects

These three examples of local and state/provincial change have been chosen for several reasons. First, each project highlights a unique approach to direct funding and paradigm change. Second, they clearly demonstrate innovations or changes that are needed for direct funding to work effectively. Third, the projects illustrate some of the dilemmas that are experienced by all direct funding projects in North America. Finally, the projects represent a range from local to province- or state-wide initiatives.

'My Life ... My Way' project: San Diego Regional Center, San Diego, California

The 'My Life ... My Way' project (see www.selfdeterminations andiego.org/) is sponsored by the San Diego Regional Center (SDRC) and Area Board XIII and has been designed to support people with developmental disabilities who wish to use individualised funding to purchase their own supports and services. Participants can also access planning support through independent services brokers. The project seeks to empower participants "... to determine how they want to live and participate in their local communities".

Participants can apply for individualised funding by indicating in their support plan how funds will be used to support their lifestyle. To assist individuals and families to develop and implement their personal support plans, including an individual budget, the project makes independent service brokers (or facilitators) available. Where requested by participants, organisations known as 'fiscal intermediaries' are used to pay for needed supports and services and act as an 'employer of record'. Project participation is voluntary.

Participants who choose the option of hiring a broker to assist them with planning can select someone from a list of six trained service brokers. The broker meets with the participant/family, and gets to know them and their dreams and needs. This involves the broker researching options and identifying appropriate formal (paid) services and informal community resources and supports to meet the person's goals. Once a support plan and budget is completed, it is submitted to SDRC for review and approval. Once funding approval is given, SDRC distributes the funding, usually through a fiscal intermediary, to enable participants to purchase supports or equipment identified in the plan. A request to amend an allocated budget can be made by a participant as needs change.

California is currently revising implementation plans for its Medicaid Waiver (Medicaid provides federal funding for disability supports) and both individualised funding and service brokerage are key elements in what will be a broader system change initiative in the future.

Ontario Direct Funding Project: Centre for Independent Living Toronto, Toronto, Ontario

Throughout the 1980s, the Attendant Care Action Coalition in Ontario, Canada's largest province, advocated direct individualised funding as an essential option for people with a physical disability who wished to manage their own attendant services (or 'self-manage'). A review of support services in Ontario (Lord et al, 1988) presented a framework for individualised funding and identified consumer interest around the province. In 1993, the Ontario government amended the Long Term Care Act of 1990 and included legislation for direct grants to individuals. The main goals of the Ontario Direct Funding Project are:

- to create an alternative attendant care programme based on principles from the independent living movement;
- to provide a cost-effective alternative to conventional service delivery of attendant care;
- to strengthen the capacity of individual consumers to self-manage;
- to provide an attendant care mechanism which provides greater control, flexibility, and empowerment for individuals with disabilities.

People with a physical disability who want to manage their own attendant services are the project participants. Participants must be 16 years of age or above, have a condition that has been stable for one year or more, require attendant services, and be aware of the type of service required; they must, in addition, be capable of scheduling their own services, making alternate arrangements if the attendant cannot come, and hiring and firing an attendant, just to name a few eligibility criteria (Roeher Institute, 1997). Consumers can receive a maximum number of 180 hours per month.

Once accepted into the project, the consumer must sign an agreement with Centre for Independent Living Toronto (CILT), which includes a monthly budget, payroll schedule, and sample employment agreements with employees to be hired. Self-managers are responsible for everything related to employees – from hiring to remuneration, performance reviews, supervision, discipline and termination (Parker, 1995). Self-managers are required to keep a personal file for each employee and copies of all time sheets, payroll information, and termination and other notices. They must also keep a separate bank account for their direct funds, and all cheques and withdrawals must be recorded. CILT provides an attendant job description that self-managers can utilise or adapt. The *Self-manager's handbook* (Parker, 1995) provides resource material on workplace law in Ontario, which offers important guidelines regarding the employee–employer relationship.

The Ontario government is now examining ways of extending independent planning and direct funding to other people with disabilities. Much of the impetus for this change comes from the

Individualized Funding Coalition for Ontario (see www.individualizedfunding.ca).

System change in British Columbia: the role of individualised funding and independent planning support

For many years, the province of British Columbia (BC) has explored different funding initiatives. These attempts at change provided consumers with more control than previously, but more importantly, stimulated interest in broader reform. However, by the year 2000, there was wide agreement that the current system still lacked flexibility, responsiveness, and accountability.

In 2001, a stakeholder coalition began working with government to establish a community governance body known as Community Living British Columbia (CLBC). This concept is based on the belief that individuals, families, and communities know best how to meet the needs of people with disabilities. CLBC, created by the 2004 Community Living Authority Act, assumed responsibility from the Ministry for Children and Family Development for all services and supports for adults with developmental disabilities, as well as some children and their families, when the Act was proclaimed in 2005. CLBC are responsible for providing assistance to those needing community living support, managing the budget allocated by government, and stimulating communities to change how they respond to people with disabilities.

CLBC has an 11-member governance board which includes two people with disabilities. There will be two main, yet separate, divisions within CLBC. Quality Services, located centrally, is responsible for system functions such as eligibility, financial allocations, contract management, and outcome reporting. Community Planning and Development has staff located throughout the province. Known as 'facilitators', these staff provide independent planning support. Creating an organisational structure that separates independent planning support from operational decisions involving eligibility and funding is critical. This ensures that person–centered planning remains free from the constraints of service systems and the self-interest that generally ties planning with placement. Facilitators who work with individuals and families have a 'community first', not a service focus. Facilitators focus primarily on planning and network development, and use modern technology like email and cell phones to stay connected.

Individualised funding is seen as a necessary option to help transform the system. A draft policy specifies that funding allocations will be based on a support plan that identifies and justifies disability-related support needs. Allocated funding will be portable throughout the province. The policy will also specify 'eligible' supports or services, and applicants will have access to a review process. Importantly, people will not be forced to use CLBC facilitators – they will be able to access planning support from anyone with whom they have a trusted relationship.

With the implementation of the 2004 Community Living Authority Act, BC is poised to develop a new system that has independent planning and individualised guidance as its cornerstones.

Transforming services in North America: lessons and dilemmas

The three case studies, as well as the results of a multi-site review conducted by Lord and Hutchison (2003), enable us to identify several lessons and dilemmas in the transformation of services that is underway in North America.

The importance of values and principles

Whether a local or provincial/state initiative, we have found that values and principles need to guide the development of any consumer-driven, individualised disability support system and direct funding. Many of the explicit values reflect a commitment to self-determination and community participation. People receiving disability supports are viewed as citizens with the same rights as others. Often these rights promote the idea that disability supports should be an entitlement, helping ensure that people with disabilities have an equal opportunity to participate in society (Lord and Hutchison, 2003). In BC, for example, the focus on citizenship and 'community as a first resort' reflect new values and the new paradigm. Similarly, the legislated principles for the Ontario Direct Funding Project illustrate widely used values and principles from the independent living movement.

These individualised funding projects intentionally weave together principles related to individualised planning, support, and funding. Individualised funding is seen as a mechanism to enhance these concepts and quality of life. In most projects, individualised funding is embedded in the language of community, participation, and social support. Projects stress concepts such as building support networks, person-centred planning, and community inclusion (Lord and Hutchison, 2003).

Policy frameworks are key to guiding change

Policy frameworks are important to guide planning and implementation of direct funding initiatives. In North America, there has been limited policy work completed in this area. The three case studies and the cross-site review were all based on policy frameworks related to self-determination, citizenship, and individualised approaches. In BC, capacity building is seen as the goal, together with service reform. In the multi-site review conducted by Lord and Hutchison (2003), creating a policy framework meant building mechanisms to strengthen choice and control of consumers, to develop social networks with individuals and families, and to expand community connections. As a few states and provinces are finding, a policy framework for individualised funding and direct payments must provide a direct funding mechanism and infrastructure support for individuals, such as by means of facilitators and brokers (Pedlar et al, 1999; Dowson and Salisbury, 2000; Ontario Round Table on Individualized Funding, 2000).

We find that a policy framework is important for building sustainable approaches to individualised disability supports. Some initiatives we studied have coherence between policy, principles, and practice. For example, the Ontario Direct Funding Project has well-understood principles, a blend of infrastructure supports for individuals/families, a direct funding mechanism, and a broad approach to accountability. In the case of the San Diego and BC projects, the lack of policy coherence remains a challenge to be addressed. Individualised funding projects must address issues of policy coherence in order to become more sustaining (Lord and Hutchison, 2003).

The power of independent planning support

The power of planning support for individuals and families that is independent of service provision has been gaining impetus in North America. What seems important here is the understanding that many individuals and families require unencumbered facilitation support over the long term. Independent planning support is an effective counterbalance to the truism that 'money doesn't think, people do'. The point is that individualised funding is not just about cash. As the San Diego case study showed, understanding this new role of planning and capacity building takes some time to learn and get used to. The project found that it is not only individuals and families who need time, but service providers must also learn to deal with their resistance to this approach.

While many families and individuals have traditionally experienced compliance and clienthood, an independent planner and facilitator act in very different ways – listening, assisting individuals to dream and express their own voice, supporting family involvement, and being skillful about planning and implementation of those dreams and goals. Most of all, a facilitator is conscious of the need to assist the individual with connections. John O'Brien (2001) challenges people with individualised funding to develop an array of 'agents' – people who provide broad connections and strategies in the community. The successful utilisation of a facilitator and the flexibility of direct funding expands the number of people and organisations in a person's life. These mechanisms build capacity and help people to begin to create a real life beyond services in the community. While this important insight comes from several local initiatives, many service systems in North America continue to resist the idea of independent planning support.

Non-bureaucratic, simple funding approaches

Creating non-bureaucratic, simple approaches to direct funding has been a challenge in many jurisdictions in North America. In San Diego, for example, SDRC had to learn in the first few years that it needed financial systems to successively allocate and track funding expenditures with participants or fiscal intermediaries. Without such systems, time delays and bureaucratic responses become the norm.

In the Lord and Hutchison (2003) study, most of the 10 sites emphasise the importance of accountability to the person and the state. Some sites stress that being accountable to the person and their plan is a very different way of working. Projects develop clear procedures and guidelines for tracking and utilising funds for disability supports. Our analysis showed the accountability mechanisms to be very effective. This finding is likely to be important for governments whose preoccupation with accountability can limit their interest in supporting individualised funding.

One of the benefits of direct funding occurs when the funding is portable. This means that recipients can use their funds for disability supports anywhere within a province, state, or country. Few programmes in North America have adequately addressed the need for portability.

The Ontario Direct Funding Project allows portability within the province, but not the entire country. This issue points to the need in North America to address direct funding and disability supports within both federal and provincial/state jurisdictions. Failure to do so limits citizenship because it does not see people with disabilities as needing flexibility to move for employment or personal reasons.

Small-scale change informs system change

Large-scale system change in North America is hampered by the entrenchment of traditional service systems, as well as by the fact that states and provinces have the right and responsibility to deliver social services. This complex array of policies and legislation makes system change very challenging and a patchwork approach to innovation is very common. As we have noted, small-scale change has benefits and, increasingly, smaller projects are demonstrating significant strengths and capacity-building expertise. Both the San Diego and Ontario case studies show the power of smaller projects with strong values, coherent policy, and effective infrastructure supports such as independent planning.

The paradox for North America, as it moves ever so slowly towards a new paradigm of disability and community, is to build larger service systems that reflect the values, principles, and wisdom that many small, local projects are showing. As we have seen in the case example from BC, this paradox will not be easy to resolve. Part of the challenge lies in transforming large, bureaucratic systems. The attempt in BC is showing that there must be structural changes in the supports that are available for citizens with disabilities and their families. So creating an independent unit for personal planning and community development can be seen as both insightful and essential. The BC experience also shows the need to find the right levers to transform the system. One lever has been to build in ways to stimulate innovation at the local and provincial levels.

At the same time, large-scale system reform clearly has its limitations. Some jurisdictions in North America are gradually learning that direct funding initiatives can be developed, separate from and parallel to traditional systems. These small-scale initiatives have been shown to be highly effective even though they may only serve relatively small numbers. The best research on this phenomenon is on the local area coordination and direct funding project in Western Australia (Lewis, 1996). This initiative has had great success in supporting the people who choose this approach while, at the same time, having very little impact on the broader, more traditional system.

Conclusion

What is the likely future of direct payments and individualised planning in North America? Current interest in paradigm change is very high among many consumers and family members, and among select professionals and service providers. However, despite an extraordinary amount of written material on person-centred approaches, implementation is often fraught with challenges, as many service providers and others with vested interests continue to dominate planning groups and policy development.

What will the 'tipping point' be in terms of a real paradigm shift? Will we have parallel systems for some time in the future? When will enough consumer and family demand ensure that paradigm and programmatic change become part of mainstream service delivery? These are difficult questions to answer, since the evolution of this work is painstakingly slow. Yet, today there are far more pockets of innovation and direct payments than there were 10 years ago. The fact that a small number of provinces and states are looking at individualised funding and independent planning as cornerstones of policy change shows that the work of the disability and disability family movements is beginning to pay off. Importantly, other sectors such as senior citizens and mental health are also beginning to explore the utility of more 'demand-driven' approaches to meeting individual needs. Demographics may indeed play a role in the future as well, since young adults with disabilities are the first generation to have experienced inclusion and community participation. As more and more individuals, families, and small-scale local projects become committed to citizenship and capacity building as the way to sustain the future, there can be hope that policy change and meaningful system change in North America will follow.

References

Americans with Disabilities Act, PL 101–336. 42 U.S.C 12101, et seq: Federal Registrar, 56(44), 35544–35756, 26 July 1990.

de Jong, G. (1979) 'Independent living: from social movement to analytic paradigm', *Archives of Physical Medicine and Rehabilitation*, vol 60, pp 435-46.

Dowson, S. and Salisbury, B. (2000) *Foundations for freedom: International perspectives on self-determination and individualized funding*, Seattle, WA: TASH.

Hulgin, K. (2004) 'Person-centred services and organizational context: taking stock of working conditions and their impact', *Mental Retardation*, vol 42, no 3, pp 169-80.

Hutchison, P., Pedlar, A., Dunn, P., Lord, J. and Arai, S. (2000) 'Canadian Independent Living Centres: impact on the community', *International Journal of Rehabilitation Research*, vol 23, no 2, pp 61-74.

Lepofsky, D. (1997) 'A report card of the Charter's guarantee of equality to persons with disabilities after ten years – what progress? What prospects?', *National Journal of Constitutional Law*, vol 7, pp 263-431.

Lewis, G. (1996) *Local area co-ordination and individualised funding: An evaluation of its operation and impact across disability types and geographic settings*, Perth, WA: Disability Services Commission.

Lord, J. and Hutchison, P. (2003) 'Individualised support and funding: building blocks for capacity building and inclusion', *Disability and Society*, vol 18, no 1, pp 71-86.

Lord, J., Hutchison, P. and Farlow, D. (1988) *Independence and control: Today's dream, tomorrow's reality*, Toronto: Ontario Ministry of Community and Social Services.

O'Brien, J. (2001) *Paying customers are not enough: The dynamics of individualized funding*, Syracuse: Syracuse University Centre on Human Policy.

Ontario Round Table on Individualized Funding (2000) *Individualizing supports and direct funding: Making money work for people*, Toronto: Individualized Funding Coalition.

Parker, I. (1995) *Self-manager's handbook: Self-managed attendant services in Ontario – direct funding pilot project*, Toronto: Centre for Independent Living Toronto.

Pedlar, A., Hutchison, P., Arai, S. and Dunn, P. (2000) 'Community services landscape in Canada: adults with developmental disabilities', *Mental Retardation*, vol 38, no 4, pp 330-41.

Pedlar, A., Haworth, L., Hutchison, P., Dunn, P. and Taylor, A. (1999) *A textured life: Empowerment and people with developmental disabilities*, Waterloo, ON: Wilfrid Laurier University Press.

Renwick, R., Brown, I. and Nagler, M. (1996) *Quality of life in health promotion and rehabilitation*, Thousand Oaks, CA: Sage Publications.

Roeher Institute (1993) *Social well being: A paradigm for reform*, Downsview, ON: Roeher Institute.

Roeher Institute (1996) *Disability, community and society: Exploring the links*, North York, ON: Roeher Institute.

Roeher Institute (1997) *Final evaluation report: Self-managed attendant services in Ontario – direct funding pilot project*, North York, ON: Roeher Institute.

Uditsky, B. (1999) *The erosion of individualized funding: Current issues*, Edmonton: Alberta Association for Community Living.

Wieck, C. and Strully, J. (1991) 'What's wrong with the continuum: a metaphorical analysis', in L. Meyer, C. Peck and L. Brown (eds) *Critical issues in the lives of people with severe handicaps*, Baltimore, MD: Paul H. Brookes.

Section 2
Policy into practice

FIVE

Direct payments and autonomy: issues for people with learning difficulties

Val Williams and Andrew Holman

"I think independence is to be what you are. Independence is about your life." (Kevin Smith, Swindon People First, 2000)

This chapter will focus on how people with learning difficulties have been able to gain access to direct payments, although in small numbers, and will explore evidence of the potential benefits for this group, especially in relation to the concept of independence. The chapter will draw on two main strands of work. One is an inclusive research project, in which people with learning difficulties did their own research about direct payments, with support from the Norah Fry Research Centre, University of Bristol. The other is the direct payments development and campaigning work, which was carried out by Values Into Action (Holman and Collins, 1997, 1999) from the time that the 1996 Community Care (Direct Payments) Act was first passed.

In the original draft direct payments legislation, people with learning difficulties were excluded, and this chapter will trace how and why this exclusion was challenged. The second part of the chapter will particularly focus on the two major problems for people with learning difficulties: one is to prove their ability to consent, and the other is to be able to manage the direct payment itself. As will be seen, people with learning difficulties and their supporters are exploring some innovative and effective solutions in both of these areas.

Background

From the very start of direct payments legislation with the introduction of the 1996 Act, the organisation called Values Into Action (VIA) was active in leading the way for people with learning difficulties. The series of 'Funding Freedom' reports and training resources (Holman, 1996; Holman and Collins, 1997, 1999) began with a conference on the eve of the passing of the direct payments legislation in 1996. Alan Milburn MP, shadow spokesperson on community care at the time, spoke at that first 'Funding Freedom' conference, addressing the question: 'Will Labour offer people with learning difficulties equal access to direct funding?'. His response was unequivocal:

> Labour believes that anybody with any type of disability may be suitable and should be eligible for direct payments rather than services. (Holman, 1996, p 26)

The Minister of Health, John Bowes, sent a written statement before the second 'Funding Freedom' conference, saying that people with learning difficulties were to be included in the direct payments legislation. Such a late inclusion was one of the first stumbling blocks that contributed to the lack of suitable support schemes and structures. Holman and Collins (1997) made a series of recommendations, based upon practice at the time, to ensure that direct payments support schemes took into account the needs of people with learning difficulties to have easy read information, support with consent issues, and continuing support to manage their direct payments. However, it would be true to say that these recommendations are still not universally incorporated into practice.

The Joseph Rowntree Foundation, which had funded the previous VIA work in 1997, remained committed to funding the work on developing direct payments for people with learning difficulties. A further development project (Holman and Collins, 1999) aimed both to map the current situation and to provide information to key players in each local authority area. To that end, an information and advice service was established, and a database of authorities making direct payments to people with learning difficulties and any accompanying support schemes was drawn up. The first easy read guide to direct payments was piloted by this project, and then produced, and the project also gave information, training and support to self-advocacy groups to enable them to support local people. The geopolitical mapping of authorities undertaken as a part of this work provided further information about barriers to implementation. There were clearly some local authorities that were reluctant to implement direct payments for people with learning difficulties for a variety of reasons. Sadly, this situation has still not been entirely resolved. As late as 2004, the government minister, Stephen Ladyman, said that "he was surprised that some councillors still did not know they now had such responsibilities [to offer a direct payment]" (Holman, 2004, p 114).

Following on from the work with VIA, there were moves from some of the self-advocacy organisations themselves to take a more active part in the campaign for direct payments. During 1999, Swindon People First made a successful bid for money to run its own direct payments support scheme. This was a pilot scheme at first, an attempt to show what could be done if a self-advocacy organisation was involved in providing support for its own members. At the same point, Swindon People First approached Ken Simons, at the Norah Fry Research Centre, who helped them to obtain funding from the Community Fund to run their own research project. This was the Journey to Independence project (1999-2002), in which Val Williams was involved as research advisor to the team.

The purpose of this research was to find the kinds of support systems that would enable this group of people to benefit from direct payments. The project was an unusual one in the way that it was run. Situated within a People First organisation, with support from the Norah Fry Research Centre, it employed three researchers who had learning difficulties themselves. The project did not make assumptions about what would work, and what was 'good for people'. The researchers with learning difficulties themselves went on a journey around the country meeting and talking with direct payments users, direct payments schemes, policy makers, social workers, family members and personal assistants. The final report (Gramlich et al, 2002a) is written in the words of the self-advocate researchers, and reflects the very broad and ongoing support that people with learning difficulties need in order to benefit from direct payments. That support often includes informal social networks, family and friends, as well as more formalised structures such as circles of support or trusts. The most successful direct payments schemes did not just deliver support and withdraw, but worked with individuals on a consistent basis, to enable them to take more and more control over their direct payments and over their lives.

Since the time of the research and development work mentioned above, a major force for change in learning disability services in England has been the White Paper, *Valuing people* (DH, 2001a). *Valuing people* aimed to improve the lives of everyone with a learning difficulty, according to the four key principles of choice, independence, inclusion and rights, and one of the tools for achieving these aims is direct payments. In the chapter on 'Choice and control', however, the White Paper recognised that "few people with learning difficulties receive direct payments". *Valuing people* set out to increase that number, for instance by setting up a development fund, by running regional workshops and by working with local authorities directly.

However, there is still a wide discrepancy between people with learning difficulties and other disabled people. There is evidence (CSCI, 2004) that the number of direct payments users is increasing rapidly, if all disabled groups are taken into account. There is also an increase for people with learning difficulties, from an estimated 216 (6% of the total number of direct payments users) in 2000 (DH, 2001a) to 900 (9.3% of the total) in 2002-03 (DH, 2004c). Statistics are notoriously slippery, but it would seem that people with learning difficulties still need to catch up with other disabled people, despite continuing support from the Department of Health (DH) (DH, 2004a, 2004b).

The primary purpose of direct payments for disabled people with physical or sensory impairments was to give them a new chance to control the support they received, usually in the form of personal assistance. They are the employers of their own assistants. The concept of someone with a learning difficulty being an employer, however, conflicts with conventional views of their *incompetence* to manage their own lives (Simpson, 1995). It is, as the argument goes, that very incompetence which means that they need a support service in the first place. The barriers between direct payments and people with learning difficulties, then, were inevitable and have been well documented (Ryan and Holman, 1998; Swindon People First Research Team, 2000), and fall largely within the frame of the twin issues of 'consent' and 'management'. We will now turn to a brief look at some ways in which individuals and their supporters are tackling these barriers.

Support to consent

One of the major barriers confronting people with learning difficulties is summed up in the slogan 'willing and able' (Ryan and Holman, 1998). The original guidance on direct payments said that local authorities could give direct payments to any disabled person who consented, and who was also "willing and able to manage them (alone or with assistance)" (DH, 1996, pp 10-11). The need to consent was included in the 1996 Direct Payments Act, after pressure from lobby groups who rightly wanted to make sure people were not forced into accepting direct payments. However, it has represented a major stumbling block for people with learning difficulties.

Having 'capacity to consent' is considered the legal and ethical right of the individual (BMA and The Law Society, 1995). In order to be able to consent, the person must be:

1. ... capable of taking that particular decision ('competent').
2. Acting voluntarily (not under undue pressure or duress from anyone).
3. Provided with enough information to enable them to make that decision. (DH, 2001b, p 3)

The right to consent is related to the fundamental human right of autonomy and choice. For most people, in most circumstances, this right is assumed without any need for tests of understanding or capacity. Indeed, the way in which most decisions are made involves a far from explicit mix of feelings, social influences and chance (Dye et al, 2004). However, prior to the introduction of the 2005 Mental Capacity Act, the right to consent lay exclusively with the individual. If a person was deemed to be unable to consent, for instance because they could not communicate adequately, then no one could do that for them. Additionally, the criteria used for assessing ability to consent were often far more stringent for people with a learning difficulty than for others. This led to the wholesale exclusion of people with learning difficulties from direct payments in many areas (Holman and Bewley, 2001).

Since the changes in direct payments guidance (DH, 2003), it is now a duty for local councils to offer all disabled people the choice of receiving their community care service as direct payments. This offer cannot arbitrarily exclude whole groups of people such as those with learning difficulties, even if they have a profound and multiple learning disability or 'high support needs'. These are people who may need help in many aspects of their lives, and traditionally services have had difficulty in arranging appropriate community-based services for this group. The increasing level of dissatisfaction, caused by the lack of appropriate services, has led people to turn to direct payments to see if this route offers better opportunities for the highly individualised support service which they need. People with high support needs, however, who can most benefit from a truly individualised service, are also the people least likely to be able to consent in any formal sense to direct payments.

For a few people labelled as having high support needs, some local authorities have agreed to accept the evidence of consent through what is essentially a supported decision-making process (Edge, 2001). As a result, these people are increasingly showing us the benefits of direct payments for all, often with well-developed and imaginative support systems such as advocacy, independent living trusts, circles of support, microboards or service brokers. One such person was a young woman whom the Swindon Team met:

> "Marie was a lively young lady who loved loud music and night-life with her friends. However, this had not always been so. She had a history of aggression, a very short attention span, and very little expressive language. She could be a very difficult person to be around. With the support of her parents, she had developed a circle of friends who had helped her to put together a person-centred plan. This was done with photographs, so that she could indicate who and what she liked doing. Additionally, if she decided she did NOT want to do something or to go somewhere, she was very good at refusing." (unpublished case study from Journey to Independence research: see Gramlich et al, 2002a)

Marie, like most of the people who participated in the Journey to Independence study, would not have been able to demonstrate an understanding of direct payments, in order to give 'informed consent'. What she could do was to indicate to those around her what she liked doing, and what she did not like. This is similar to the notion of 'assent' (Sachs et al, 1994), which is really a willingness to go along with something. Instead of measuring the capacity of the individual to understand, the focus turns to an assessment of the support and social systems around the person. If the *process* of supporting that person's decisions is a good one, then it is enough to recognise 'assent'.

However, there continue to be problems relating to consent, which hamper progress for people with learning difficulties. One possible solution is simply to withdraw the focus on consent by dropping that clause, and this is what happened in Scotland (Holman, 2002) where the decision was made to rely instead upon the supported decision-making process in Scottish capacity legislation. Despite this change, the numbers of direct payments recipients remain low. In England, work on the mental capacity legislation proposals that addressed the issues of how people with learning difficulties could legally consent, faced continued opposition from a variety of lobby groups. Many organisations raised concerns about how the legislation would work in practice. While it may help to clarify the legal position regarding direct payments, the general authority that allows decisions to be made for others was seen to be open to potential abuse. It remains to be seen how the new legislation will work in practice for potential direct payments users with learning difficulties of the future.

The minister Stephen Ladyman followed the example of his predecessors reiterating his commitment to people with learning difficulties using direct payments. When asked about the legal issues regarding consent he saw this as an "over strict interpretation of the law", stating:

> "… it is more often being used as an excuse for not making direct payments where the council is not really interested in pushing forward the numbers of direct payments in the first place, because there are ways that consent can be signified." (Holman, 2004, p 114)

This statement has not helped some people stuck in arguments over capacity to consent, and Ladyman has promised to look at the legal blocks again, saying, "we can fix the legislation and we can fix the guidance" (Holman, 2004, p 114). In the meantime, families as well as individuals may be left with long legal wrangles with local authorities:

> "My son, who has a severe learning disability, started getting direct payments two years ago. However, our authority have now decided that they should not have given him a Direct Payment as they say he cannot consent to one, nor does he have the capacity to manage one, even with assistance." (Learning Disability Forum, 2004)

Support to manage

Many people with learning difficulties, such as the young man quoted above, need higher levels of support with the practical management of direct payments. This is either through choice, not wanting to undertake some aspects of the administration, or ability. Local support schemes were often not equipped to provide the levels of support needed at first, and the Journey to Independence project found that many schemes were actively searching for solutions.

One of the ways to fill this gap is by formalising the concept of a circle of friends, to form a semi-legal structure such as a microboard or a trust, which can then be the formal recipient of the direct payments. Independent living trusts were developed and promoted from the beginning by the Funding Freedom project (Holman and Collins,

1997, 1999). The trust can put in place a framework for providing the support that the person with learning difficulties may need in order to fulfil their responsibilities as an employer. Early reports on independent living trusts (Holman and Bewley, 2001) showed the useful role such arrangements could play.

> The trustees of Clare's independent living trust manage funds from three different sources: the social services department, the health authority and the Independent Living (1993) Fund. The local authority pays Clare £200 a week as a direct payment. The direct payment agreement is between the local authority and the trust, and is signed by the trustees. The health authority, which provides the majority of funding, makes a payment under section 64 of the Health Services and Public Health Act 1968. The money is routed via a small charitable organisation that simply passes the money on to the trust as an indirect payment.
>
> All parties are happy with these arrangements because the processes for decision making, accountability and financial management are transparent. All decision making is discussed among the trustees and the circle of support, with one person acting as Clare's advocate, thus providing an extra safeguard for Clare. All financial records are kept. Clare's advocate manages her support arrangements. The trust feels that decision making about her support thus receives a high level of scrutiny. (Holman and Bewley, 2001, p 70)

Trusts, circles and boards, by their very nature, are voluntary bodies, and so for people with high levels of support needs, it is often necessary to insert a level of middle management. In some cases, trusts are hiring 'service brokers' to help to set up a highly individualised service for one person. That person can take over all the administrative tasks associated with being an employer, and can also fulfil to some extent the role of trainer, developer, and even service manager. For individuals with the highest level of needs, the cost-effectiveness of this option can be argued: all the money, including that to pay the broker, comes from the direct payment calculation for the service user. What is essential, with all these options, is to ensure that the individual service user remains 'in control' of the essential decisions – who should work with them, the pattern of their day, and how and where they should live.

Even with people with higher levels of independence, the Journey to Independence project found that the ability to manage a direct payment had very little, if anything, to do with the ability to manage the money itself. That aspect of things could be dealt with perfectly adequately by including in the direct payment an amount for a bookkeeper, for instance. However, people with learning difficulties clearly had many ongoing needs for support with their direct payments, and this support came from many sources. The final report from the project (Gramlich et al, 2002b) took a journey around all these various types of support, ranging from parents and friends, to self-advocacy groups and, of course, direct payments support schemes themselves.

One of the main messages was that people with learning difficulties need ongoing support to manage direct payments. It was not sufficient to arrange the direct payments, give some initial support, and then simply withdraw. People with learning difficulties needed a back-up system, where they could pick up the telephone and get advice or assistance immediately. For instance, this was most important if their personal assistant was sick, or if their usual arrangements failed for some reason. It was also important that they had someone they could call on if they had worries about any aspect of their assistance.

> David received direct payments, and employed two personal assistants to help him with his domestic chores. He suddenly had to travel to London for a hospital appointment, and did not know how to manage this, or whether he could use his personal assistants for this task. Luckily, he picked up the phone to the direct payments support scheme, based at People First, and they advised him to take a personal assistant with him to London. They also helped him to get a reassessment of his needs, when further hospital trips became necessary. (Example from Journey to Independence work, Gramlich, 2002a)

Although in this example, the direct payments support scheme was based within the self-advocacy (People First) movement, this is not usually the case. The project found many schemes that were run by disabled people's organisations, which were also providing very good individualised support. Local solutions have to be found, and developing good links between self-advocacy and the disabled people's movement can help both groups to share their ideas and further them. In one area, for instance, a leader in the independent living movement (a disabled man with a physical impairment) was working actively to set up a support group for direct payments users with learning difficulties at the local self-advocacy organisation.

A final theme in managing direct payments relates to easy read information. Direct payments support schemes were often acutely aware, in 2000-01, of the lack of good, accessible information about direct payments and about how to manage them. Many, indeed, were attempting to fill this gap for themselves. Since then, the Journey to Independence project has produced its own pack of resources and information for people with learning difficulties to use or adapt in order to manage each stage of their direct payments (Gramlich et al, 2002b). The DH, with Swindon People First, has also produced a new pack of easy read information to explain direct payments (DH, 2004b). Even when armed with such documents, people with learning difficulties are always likely to need appropriate personal support to work through the intricacies of becoming an employer. The reward for all this work, however, can mean a radically changed life, and this must make it all worthwhile.

Conclusion: the goal of autonomy

People with learning difficulties are not often used to having one-to-one assistance in their lives. Services have traditionally been delivered to them in groups. People are assessed for a generic 'need' which they may share with others (for example, the need to go out during the day, the need to have help with their shopping or cooking) and are then grouped together in day centres or residential homes in order to receive those services. Therefore, direct payments not only give them a new way of obtaining their assistance, but also offer them a whole new type of life. Both the VIA work and the Journey to Independence project found that people with learning difficulties often need considerable and ongoing support to manage direct payments, but that with the right support, their lives can be turned around. Where previously they felt controlled entirely by others' expectations and demands, direct payments give them a unique chance to gain some real autonomy by controlling their own service.

There is clearly a difference between the kind of assistance needed by people with learning difficulties and the help with physical or care tasks that may be necessary for other disabled people. Most of the participants in the Journey to Independence project felt that, prior to direct payments, their lives had been controlled by the staff who supported them. It was the staff who made decisions for them, and who taught them independence skills, and measured their progress.

The ability to employ one's own personal assistant, then, offered the opportunity to break out of this system. With the right one-to-one assistance, people could actually learn to be more autonomous, and to start making decisions for the first time.

> Ellen and Sue were two friends since schooldays. Now in their late twenties, their families had helped them to move in to a flat together. With parents and support staff always around them, they had previously enjoyed very little freedom to really control their lives. This means that they often wait for other people to tell them what to do. But now, when their personal assistant comes in to work with them, the first thing she does is to sit down and ask them 'what is it that YOU want to do today?'. (Unpublished case study from Journey to Independence research: see Gramlich et al, 2002a)

Providing for 'choice' has been a key theme in services for people with learning difficulties for decades, and direct payments now open up a new avenue for developing everyday decision-making capacity. Paradoxically, however, people with learning difficulties can literally work their way out of eligibility for a service, since the basis for their need for support is to do with lack of independence, autonomy and the ability to manage their life. Social services departments are setting eligibility criteria with tighter and tighter qualifications, and so only those people with learning difficulties who have the highest levels of need are likely to receive a community care service. Several participants in the Journey to Independence project would have liked to use direct payments, but were in dispute with their local authority about whether or not their assessment made them eligible for a service. It would seem that this is a classic example of a catch-22 situation: if people are not independent and autonomous, then they are considered not able to consent to direct payments. However, as soon as they become more autonomous, they may not receive a service at all.

At the end of the Journey to Independence project, the team looked back at all the people they had met who used direct payments. Compared with other people with learning difficulties, these direct payments users certainly seemed to have better opportunities in life, more involvement in their communities and a richer social life. Direct payments offer people the opportunity to escape from assumptions about group service provision:

> "When we are labelled as people with learning difficulties, we are put inside a special world. When we are in residential homes, they keep us shut off from the real world. We are all put in crates. But direct payments can help us get into real life." (Gramlich et al, 2002b, p 85)

Getting into real life, it could be argued, is a direct result of individualised planning and individualised support, rather than direct payments themselves. Any truly individualised support system, as promoted by the In Control programme (see www.selfdirectsupport.org), could work, and it could indeed be argued that the very changes promoted by *Valuing people* are providing better life opportunities for all people with learning difficulties. People with learning difficulties have generally turned to direct payments through dissatisfaction with existing services, but in fact there is some evidence that individualised choices are improving for all people with learning difficulties. Person-centred planning is now promoted as a way of listening carefully to what every person with learning difficulties really wants (DH, 2002).

Despite this, the Swindon People First research team felt that direct payments did make an important difference: the one key factor for direct payments users (Gramlich, 2002a) was the changed relationship between the person with learning difficulties and their staff. Instead of being controlled by support staff, direct payments gave people the opportunity to 'be the boss'. This is such a dramatic and complete reversal of roles, and is probably a key to other changes in people's lives. In the words of the Swindon People First research team:

> In the past, care staff have always told us what to do. They may do this by suggesting: "do you want me to do this for you, or that for you?"
>
> Now we are the bosses. We can sit down with the PA and say, now this is what needs to be done. She listens to us. (Gramlich et al, 2002b, p 84)

As Ken Simons remarked in the Journey to Independence report (Gramlich et al, 2002b), 'facilitating' and 'enabling' require some very specific skills. In some circumstances, they will require some complex balances between the safety and well-being of the individual, and the need to respect autonomy. If the relationship between personal assistant and direct payments user is at the heart of the matter for people with learning difficulties, then we need to know more about how this is achieved, and a forthcoming research study (see Williams and Kelly,

2005) aims to do just that. Although we know in general terms what is considered to be a good personal assistant from the point of view of disabled people, there is a gap in our knowledge of what people with learning difficulties really want, and what skills are required of their personal assistants. Funded by the Big Lottery, the Skills for Support project is a partnership venture with the West of England Centre for Inclusive Living and the Norah Fry Research Centre, and will support people with learning difficulties to focus on this topic.

We started this chapter with the insight of Kevin Smith. 'Being what you are' and having 'your life' may seem like ordinary ambitions for most of us. For years, however, these human rights have been effectively denied to most people with learning difficulties. We trust that, in this chapter, we have been able to demonstrate how vitally important direct payments can be for people in this situation. Despite the many barriers facing people with learning difficulties, their lives can be completely altered by direct payments. No tests of capacity should be necessary to grant people the right to benefit from direct payments; instead, we should continue to concentrate on an improved structure of support that will enable people with learning difficulties to escape the traps of not being able to 'consent and manage'.

References

BMA (British Medical Association) and The Law Society (1995) *Assessment of mental capacity: Guidance for doctors and lawyers*, London: BMA.

CSCI (Commission for Social Care Inspection) (2004) 'Social services performance assessment framework indicators', (www.csci.org.uk/publications).

DH (Department of Health) (1996) *Community Care (Direct Payments) Act 1996: Draft policy and practice guidance*, London: DH Publications.

DH (2001a) *Valuing people: A new strategy for learning disability for the 21st century*, London: DH Publications.

DH (2001b) *Seeking consent: Working with people with learning disabilities*, London: DH Publications.

DH (2002) *Planning with people – towards person centred approaches*, London: DH Publications.

DH (2003) *Direct payments guidance: Community care, services for carers and children's services (direct payments) guidance, England 2003*, (www.dh.gov.uk/assetRoot/04/06/92/62/04069262.pdf).

DH (2004a) *Direct choices: What councils need to make direct payments happen for people with learning disabilities*, London: DH.

DH (2004b) *An easy guide to direct payments: Giving you the choice and control*, London: DH.

DH (2004c) 'Referrals, assessments and packages of care for adults', in *Community care statistics 2002-3*, (www.publications.doh.gov.uk).

Dye, L., Hendy, S., Hare, D. and Burton, M. (2004) 'Capacity to consent to participate in research – a recontextualization', *British Journal of Learning Disabilities*, vol 32, pp 144-50.

Edge, J. (2001) *Who's in control? Demonstrating control of decisions by adults with learning difficulties who have high support needs*, York: Joseph Rowntree Foundation.

Gramlich, S., McBride, G. and Snelham, N., with Williams, V. and Simons, K. (2002a) *Journey to independence: What self-advocates tell us about direct payments*, Kidderminster: British Institute of Learning Difficulties (BILD).

Gramlich, S., McBride, G. and Snelham, N., with Williams, V. and Simons, K. (2002b) *Journey to independence: How to run your life with direct payments*, Kidderminster: BILD.

Holman, A. (1996) *'Funding Freedom' conference report*, London: Values In Action.

Holman, A. (2002) 'Help with consenting to and managing direct payments', Factsheet 10, Edinburgh: Direct Payments Scotland.

Holman, A. (2004) 'In conversation with Stephen Ladyman', *British Journal of Learning Disabilities*, vol 32, no 3, pp 113-14.

Holman, A. and Bewley, C. (2001) *Trusting independence: A practical guide to independent living trusts*, London: Values Into Action.

Holman, A. and Collins, J. (1997) *Funding freedom: Direct payments for people with learning difficulties*, London: Values Into Action.

Holman, A. and Collins, J. (1999) *Funding freedom 2000: People with learning difficulties using direct payments*, London: Values Into Action.

Learning Disability Forum (2004) online message forum run by Foundation for People with Learning Disabilities, 14 December.

Ryan, T. and Holman, A. (1998) *Able and willing? Supporting people with learning difficulties to use direct payments*, London: Values Into Action.

Sachs, G.A., Stocking, C.B., Stern, R., Cox, D.M., Hougham, G. and Sachs, R.S. (1994) 'Ethical aspects of dementia research: informed consent and proxy consent', *Clinical Research*, vol 42, no 3, pp 403-12.

Simpson, M. (1995) 'The sociology of "competence" in services', *Social Work and Social Sciences Review*, vol 6, no 2, pp 85-97.

Swindon People First Research Team (2000) *Looking at people's lives*, Bristol: Norah Fry Research Centre.

Williams, V. and Kelly, J. (2005) *Skills for support*, (website as link from: www.wecil.co.uk).

SIX

"It's meant that, well, I'm living a life now": older people's experience of direct payments

Heather Clark

Most studies on direct payments have focused upon the experiences of younger disabled people, and little is known about how older people work with direct payments and the benefits they derive from them. This chapter seeks to address this gap in knowledge by presenting partial findings from a study (Clark et al, 2004) undertaken with older direct payments recipients in three local authorities in England. The study, with Helen Gough as research assistant and Ann Macfarlane as consultant, involved 41 older people, and sometimes their partners, receiving direct payments and was conducted between January 2002 and July 2003. The ages of the older participants ranged from mid-sixties to early nineties. Six older Somali women, all of whom were refugees, were among the participants. Although 32 local authority care managers, 11 team managers, five senior managers, and 10 direct payments support service workers also participated, this chapter is based mainly upon the experiences and perceptions of the older people.

Loosely structured individual interviews and discussion groups were used to gather the data. We met with an informal advisory group comprised of three older women, all of whom were receiving direct payments, at the onset and on three further occasions during the course of the research. This helped ensure that our focus and the questions we asked remained firmly fixed upon the things important to older people. Two of the women, together with an older couple from another local authority area, also served on the national advisory group to the research. The Somali participants took part in two group discussions, hosted by a Somali community centre and facilitated through interpretation by community workers attached to the centre. It was the women's preference that we use known and trusted community workers to interpret for us.

Background

In February 2000, the scope of the 1996 Community Care (Direct Payments) Act was extended to older people in the UK. This followed sustained pressure by organisations such as Age Concern and the National Centre for Independent Living (Glasby and Littlechild, 2002) and calls by older people themselves. When the Act had first been implemented in 1997, local authorities were not allowed to offer direct payments to people aged 65 and over. This was widely perceived as discriminatory, but it has also been conjectured, as is suggested in the Introduction to this book, that the exclusion of older people marked the government's concern about opening the floodgates should direct payments have proved a costly mistake (Means and Smith, 1998). Older people are the biggest group of service users and should direct payments have proved an expensive experiment there would have been "major implications for public spending" (Glasby and Littlechild, 2002, p 77).

The Labour government has made it clear that it wishes to increase the uptake of direct payments by older people. By 2003 there were estimated to be 2,700 older people getting direct payments in England marking a threefold increase on the previous year (DH, 2003a) but still representing only a very small proportion of all older service users and far from the "tens of thousands" envisaged by the Health Secretary in 2002 (DH, 2002).

Routes into direct payments

Having access to clear and timely information is paramount to older people's ability to make choices about direct payments. As Hasler says, older people "are not going to choose something they know nothing about" (2003, p 23). Direct payments are only very slowly becoming part of the 'mindset' of social services care managers working with older people and so direct payments are rarely offered as a mainstream option (Clark et al, 2004). This means, as was the case with many of our older participants, that older people may be denied the opportunity to exercise control over their support arrangements and avoid the onset of crises brought about as a result of feeling controlled by them. These issues will be discussed later in the chapter.

Information

The experience of the older people involved in this study was that getting information about direct payments could be rather haphazard.

Some felt that there was either a deliberate strategy of withholding information or that their care managers were insufficiently aware of direct payments. While care managers were the single most common source of initial information, many of the older people first heard about direct payments from other sources: friends, care assistants, resource and community centre workers, hospital staff, district nurses and, in one instance, a public talk on the subject by a direct payments support service. Furthermore, it appeared that where care managers had introduced the option, this was usually as a problem-solving strategy – for example, where older people had expressed extreme dissatisfaction with conventional services, relationships between user and provider had broken down, or direct payments presented the only way of providing an appropriate service – rather than introducing direct payments more proactively within a framework of independent living.

Consequently, many older people first heard about direct payments when they had reached a crisis point. They wished that they had been able to access this option earlier:

> "It is so important for us to know what is best for us from the beginning, not to wait until I collapse and go into hospital ... not to wait until I get so upset I have got to go into hospital."

> "I only wish I had known about it at the beginning. It's almost as though it's a secret."

One older woman told us that she had been at the point of 'giving up' and was considering residential care. Hearing about direct payments from a neighbour came in the nick of time and enabled her to get some control back over her life. Without the intervention of her neighbour who put her in touch with the local direct payments support service, she would never, she said, have found out about this option.

Choosing direct payments

The majority of older people chose direct payments because they wanted more control over their support arrangements. Most commonly this stemmed from dissatisfaction with conventional home care services. Care assistants, they said, were 'too rushed', 'came when they wanted to', and often did not stay for the allocated time. Some older people said that they could not be sure 'who would turn up' and that this meant they constantly had to explain what needed to be done and how. The older people often could not, however, get their care assistants to do what they wanted. The lack of flexibility, continuity and reliability caused some older people sleepless nights. It also undermined feelings of independence because they felt that they had lost control of their lives and their homes:

> "You didn't feel as though you were in your own home.
> You felt as though, like, they were in charge."

Regaining control over their lives by taking control of their support was then the major reason for choosing direct payments. For some, however, it was more a matter of *retaining* control. This was particularly the case for those who would otherwise have been reluctant to accept support. Mr Fowler[1], for example, was worried that having services when he came out of hospital meant he would lose control over his life. Direct payments made acceptance of help more palatable:

> "It makes me feel that I'm running things and not somebody
> else running them for me."

Mrs Fontwell, a retired nurse in her eighties, realised she needed help supporting her disabled husband. She was, she said, "coming to the age that I am now, and feeling the strain, very much, looking after Fred 24 hours a day". But she also wanted to stay in charge in order to ensure the quality of her husband's support:

> "I wanted to choose my own as it were. Or at least be able
> to be the boss and to say how I wanted things done ....
> And so this seemed such an ideal thing for me so that I
> could actually go and buy myself a help."

For a small number of older people, opting for direct payments was the only way that they could get appropriate support. Miss Dixon's support requirements straddled the health and social care divide (see Glendinning, in Chapter Eighteen, for a detailed discussion of this issue). Agency nurses were reluctant to meet her personal care needs, seeing these as the province of home care, while some of the more intrusive elements of Miss Dixon's health care needs were beyond the remit of home care staff. The local and health authorities had also failed to reach agreement upon their respective responsibilities for long-term funding. Until direct payments became available to older people, Miss Dixon had self-funded much of her support arrangements but had also relied heavily upon her sister. Direct payments enabled Miss Dixon to employ her own staff and protect her dwindling savings.

Direct payments were the sole means by which the Somali older participants could have 'care' workers who spoke their language. Statutory and independent agencies in the locality simply did not have Somali-speaking care assistants. The Somali women told us that language rather than other cultural issues was key:

> "I think it is more important to, um, the worker, she doesn't have to share the culture but the more important thing is to understand the language. If you cannot understand you cannot communicate it, what you're going say to your carer or your worker then? No, you're just going look at each other."

It seemed, however, that direct payments were the major route to receiving social services in the first place for these older women. Community workers reported that there had been an 'information gap' between social services and the Somali community. When direct payments became available to older people a line of communication was opened with the direct payments support service. The community workers referred individual older people to the support service and this became the bridge to social services.

Recruiting and managing their own staff

Being able to recruit and manage personal assistants, or alternatively to find agency support that meets requirements, are key issues facing direct payment users. While the personal assistant option clearly accords more direct control over support arrangements than does the agency option, some older people – and noticeably older carers as will be shown below – prefer to use agencies because it presents less onerous tasks. Most of the older people, however, preferred to choose and manage their own workers.

Choosing their own workers

One of the major perceived benefits of direct payments was that the older people could choose whom they wanted to work for them. Most opted to employ personal assistants and some looked for specific skills but, generally speaking, most wanted someone they could get on with, who was trustworthy and who would respect them, their home and belongings.

Many older people reported that finding personal assistants was difficult – a problem shared with other age groups (see, for example, Vasey, 2000; CSCI, 2004). It can, however, be particularly difficult for people who have only a small number of hours of employment to offer – as was the case for many of the older people involved in the study. Older people tend to be allocated fewer hours when being assessed for a community care service and therefore less money when opting for direct payments.

Advertising locally so that travel time and distance would not be barriers was one strategy to ease the difficulty; another was to share personal assistants. There was also a widespread call for direct payments support services to maintain registers of actual or potential personal assistants to assist older people in finding someone and in a way deemed safer than other forms of recruitment. Otherwise, a range of methods was used: advertising in a local university, putting cards in shops and post offices, and using the local job centre, although some degree of personal recommendation was preferred.

The Somali older women experienced few difficulties in finding personal assistants. They recruited younger women from their own communities and on the recommendation of other community members:

> "I ask the people … I say I need a nice lady whose care will do me well."

Managing the relationship

The majority of older people saw handling the relationship with their personal assistants as one major key to managing direct payments successfully. Most indicated that the relationship was friendly and some described it as like an extended family relationship. The majority of the older people had transferable skills from their past employment and home lives. Some had managerial or supervisory experience; one had been a foreman, another a shop steward. However, it was also clear that, while such skills were useful, the fact that the relationship took place in their own homes rather than the public sphere of work made a difference. Mrs Robinson articulated this most clearly. In her past career she had been responsible for 16 staff. That, however, was:

> "… a very different relationship, because that was a professional relationship. Here, they are in our home, they are sharing our lives. That was sharing my work."

For some older people, being able to have a friendly relationship with their personal assistants was of paramount importance. Mrs Fox told us that she had let one personal assistant go because although she was pleased with the standard of work the relationship did not gel and it had been awkward, while for some others being able to have a laugh and a chat with their personal assistants was part of the benefits of direct payments. Most appeared able to combine a friendly relationship with the maintenance of appropriate employer/employee boundaries. This meant, as some put it, that they were still 'the boss'. Only one participant reported keeping a strictly employment relationship with his personal assistants. His concern was that if he allowed his personal assistants to become friendly they would 'try to take over', which, he said, was 'a very big problem'.

A minority of older people used their direct payments to purchase agency services. In all instances this was where an informal carer – usually a partner, was providing significant amounts of support and undertaking the bulk or all of the administrative tasks involved in managing direct payments. Purchasing agency services was seen as preferable as it removed worries about holiday and sickness leave, reduced the paperwork and other administrative demands, and enabled support to be found quickly. For some older carers, finding personal assistants would simply have been too onerous a task. As one woman said:

> "I just haven't the time. I'm still very, very busy as it is."

Personal recommendation was again important in choosing an agency, as was cost, although some older people were prepared to pay a bit more to ensure quality of support. This came, of course, from their own pockets. Without personal recommendation, it was more difficult to find an appropriate agency, and there seemed to be little support available. This meant:

> "… a lot of hit and miss, because it takes a lot of getting it right."

Using and benefiting from direct payments

Negative experience or having no other option were not the sole reasons for choosing direct payments. Mrs Young had attended a public talk given by the local direct payments support service and was enthused by the message she heard:

> "She wanted us to feel that we could live our lives as near to how we were before we had this stroke or what have you."

Mrs Young had been dissatisfied with her earlier agency carers – particularly because "they wouldn't do housework" – but what she really wanted was "somebody to take me out":

> "I just used to get suicidal stuck in that flat all the time."

Mrs Young realised from the outset that direct payments could be "like a magical door opening" and she has been able to continue to pursue her lifelong interest in the arts from which she still gets 'a buzz'. She uses some of her money to employ a personal assistant/ driver who takes her to shows and exhibitions. Another personal assistant now keeps the flat tidy, although "you can't look in the corners". Mrs Young summed up the benefits of direct payments:

> "It's meant that, well, I'm living a life now."

Going shopping

Mrs Young was not alone in recognising one major advantage of direct payments over conventional services – that support need not be confined to the home. Some of the older women talked about the benefits of having someone to take them shopping. Shopping has been recognised as a quality issue for older people (Henwood et al, 1998; Raynes et al, 2001), but is one that is rarely met by conventional services. Shopping is, as Godfrey et al (2004) recognise, not simply a functional event but a social occasion – providing, for example, the opportunity to meet friends and acquaintances. But it was also important to the older people to choose their purchases themselves. For one woman with a vision impairment, being able to buy birthday and Christmas cards and presents, and outfits for outings with her husband was essential to the maintenance of her self-identity as wife, mother and friend. This, and having her personal assistant assist her in cooking the evening meal one afternoon per week – a task that her husband had otherwise taken over – enabled her to feel, she said, that she had:

> "… an identity apart from my husband."

For the Somali older participants, having help with shopping enabled them to meet their cultural requirements, which language and literacy barriers, as well as mobility difficulties, otherwise made difficult:

> "Sometimes I don't understand. I will … choose some food that I don't eat. I get confused and end up eating something with alcohol or pork, which we cannot eat, by mistake."

Support within the home

Direct payments enabled the older people to direct their support to achieve the things that were important to their quality of life. For Mr Robinson this was about being able to watch a football match on television to the end without being put to bed in the middle, while Mrs Robinson had her "home ticking over so that it's comfortable".

Many older people chose to use some of their personal assistant's time in maintaining the appearance of their home, illustrating once again the high value of such help to older people (see Clark et al, 1998). However, in one of the local authority areas such use was under critical review, as the authority was seeking to cut costs by reducing as many care packages (including direct payments packages) as possible. Consequently some older people were too afraid to contact social services if they felt they needed more hours in case the reverse happened and their hours were reduced, while others were afraid they would lose the flexibility to choose what was important to them.

Inflexible policy and practice over the use of direct payments goes against the underpinning ethos of the 1996 Community Care (Direct Payments) Act. It also neglects the dynamics of the couple relationship. For example, where partners could provide support with more intimate tasks, some of the hours allocated for 'personal care' were swapped for help with housework. Retaining privacy was the preferred option for those older couples who wanted to keep their 'personal selves' to themselves for as long as possible. For others, providing support was exhausting and, while a bit of help around the house would have protected dwindling energy resources, there were simply not enough hours allocated for this. None of the older partners involved in the research had been offered direct payments in their own right, as may have been their entitlement under the 2000 Carers and Disabled Children Act, and one older couple were paying for extra hours out of their own pockets to get a bit more help with housework.

Enhancing personal safety and health

Safety was a particular issue for the older Somali women. In discussion groups it emerged that part of the isolation typically experienced by the older people emanated from their fear of crime.

The Somali participants lived in a relatively deprived and high crime area where mugging and burglaries were common experiences. The women and the community workers told us that local 'gangs of youths' sometimes followed the Somali women when they were collecting their pensions, and that their distinctive cultural dress made them a 'soft target' for verbal abuse. The older women were too afraid to counter as they might have done in Somalia – but where, we were told, they would also have been treated with more respect:

> "I can't go out because it is frightening because of the teenagers, they have the dogs and they are harassing me."

Respect from their personal assistants was then crucial for the older women; they appreciated that their personal assistants spoke to them as they would to their own mothers and this enabled them to develop a friendship based on mutual respect. But the personal assistants also made them feel safer by collecting their pensions for them or accompanying them to do so, going shopping with them and making sure their home were safely shut at night.

Getting direct payments did not, of course, solve all the problems of isolation the older women faced. They remained afraid to go out at night and missed the more sociable life they had enjoyed in their home country. However, their family relationships did improve, as having personal assistants meant that they no longer moaned at their adult children for practical support, which in itself made them feel more independent:

> "It makes it easier for me … every day I get everything I need, I got it. That is my independence. No moaning anymore for me, that is independence."

Feelings of personal safety were also enhanced for many older people in relation to the more 'personal care' elements of their support. The lack of consistency and reliability of the care they had received from conventional home care services not only undermined their sense of well-being, but may have also endangered their safety. Mrs Cavanagh, for example, has severe back problems. She told us the agency care assistants had 'no idea' how to handle her. Being able to employ her own workers meant she could train them herself. Others felt safer with already trained workers than they had with care assistants – for example, Miss Turner used some of her payment to employ staff who worked in the local hospital and who knew "how to take you out and put you in the bath". Safety was enhanced also for other older people who required help or simply needed to have someone around when showering or bathing. We were told that they had sometimes felt rushed by care assistants and that this was a particular issue for those who suffered bouts of dizziness.

Some of the older people would have liked to use their direct payments to purchase chiropody services. These, however, were deemed to be health rather than social care needs and were disallowed. As one older person put it, "feet are not in the formula". Many found this restriction ridiculous, pointing to the importance of chiropody in maintaining their mobility and some had specific medical conditions which meant that their feet could easily become infected if cut. They therefore overcame this inflexibility by having their personal assistants cut their nails.

More generally, many of the older people reported improvements in their general sense of well-being since receiving direct payments. They said they felt more motivated, were able to get out and about more, felt freer than before, were more relaxed, and able to do more for themselves. These factors were central to the greater sense of independence they reported as a result of being in control of their support arrangements.

Alternatives to conventional respite care

Respite care costs could cause difficulties for some older people using direct payments. Although direct payments continued to be paid during periods of respite, personal assistants still had to be paid at least a retainer and some older people felt they needed to pay in full. Mr Clarke explained that if you had good personal assistants you wanted to keep them but you could not expect them to lose a week's pay while you were in respite. So the costs, as he said, were double. On the other hand, direct payments could be used to develop alternatives to traditional institutional respite care or at least make it more palatable.

Like some other older people involved in the study, Mr Clarke had disliked having to go into a residential care home for older people during periods of respite for his wife. He therefore developed an alternative when his wife next took a much-needed break. He went on a fishing trip accompanied by his personal assistant. He paid the personal assistant £100 for three nights away and 24-hour support. He had to put in extra of his own money to cover the costs, but as he said:

> "It's brilliant; it beats staying in an old people's home. But you see you'd be paying about £170, for an old people's home. Well we couldn't afford it."

Mr Robinson loved to watch football on the television. A vision impairment meant that he had to sit very close to the screen to see it. This was not possible when he was in respite care. Like Mr Clarke, Mr Robinson entered respite during those times his wife was away on holiday. The couple therefore arranged for Mr Robinson's personal assistant to bring him home from respite when there was a match he wanted to see. The couple was considering respite at home for the future with personal assistant support.

The importance of direct payments support services

Established direct payments support services are vital to the successful implementation of direct payments schemes (Hasler et al, 1999; DH, 2003b). Certainly for the older people involved in this research, this was the other key factor (along with managing relationships with personal assistants) in making direct payments work for them.

The tasks older people most commonly sought help with were recruiting personal assistants, drawing up contracts of employment and managing the financial and administrative demands set by the local authority. This last task seemed to be what worried the older people most, and the help they received with this from direct payments support services was highly appreciated. One woman managing this for her husband told us:

> "It's like a weight lifted. It would worry me. I've never kept books, I never kept accounts … I'm just weary. All I want to do is just flop in the chair."

For another woman, such help stood between her and residential care. She had considered residential care to be her only option before hearing about direct payments, but when the information pack arrived she was 'terrified' that she would never manage. Support and encouragement by the support service coordinator persuaded her, however, that "with a bit of gumption" she could work successfully with direct payments.

The older people generally found making telephone contact with their support worker on the phone much easier than with their care managers. But some older people had no named care manager and without the support service would have felt 'alone'. As Miss Turner said:

> "It's frightening when you're on your own and you've got nobody to turn to."

Older people who had aged with a disability and who had been in receipt of direct payments prior to their 65th birthday found it particularly disconcerting when they no longer had a named care manager but had to rely on the duty system. They found care managers from older people's teams relatively inexperienced at working with direct payments. They were also worried that their hours would be reduced as their needs would be perceived differently from those of a younger person.

This worry was not misplaced. Older people's needs are seen differently, and their independence accorded lower priority (Henwood, 2002). When we asked senior managers in social services departments why older people got fewer allocated hours than younger disabled people, we were told that older people tend to have 'less complex needs'. However, a number of care managers pointed out that care packages for older people tend to be aimed at minimal physical maintenance and that they had great difficulty in finding the resources to meet the social, emotional and leisure needs of their clients. Financial restraints and lack of community facilities, beyond day centre and institutional respite provision, precluded the inclusion of such needs in care packages, while concerns about equity between traditional service users and direct payments users, coupled with financial restraints, meant that few care managers felt able to allocate hours to meet these needs.

The fragmented approach, whereby services are designed and provided separately for older people and younger disabled people, was also an issue for many older people who had aged with a disability.

They now had to shift to day care centres and respite facilities for older people, which were deemed to meet their social, leisure and holiday needs. This meant that some were cut off from long-term friends and most certainly from important sources of peer support and information. Assistance and back-up from direct payments support services were important to older people affected in this way.

Many support service workers reported that, with the right level of help, older people could manage direct payments well. However, they also pointed out that older people sometimes needed more intensive and ongoing support than younger disabled people who had more experience of direct payments. Resources, however, can be a difficulty for support services. With no mandatory duty upon local authorities to provide and/or fund support services and a lack of government guidelines about the appropriate level of funding, there is wide national variation in the level and duration of support available (see Clark et al, 2004). This can provide another barrier to the take-up of direct payments and reduce the ability of support services to adapt to the needs of different user groups.

Peer support, together with information, advice and/or advocacy, and training, are core elements of a support scheme (Hasler et al, 1999). It is widely recognised that peer support is a highly effective way to share experiences and information, to solve problems, to support others to take up direct payments and to inspire others to realise choice, control and opportunity in their own lives (Joseph Rowntree Foundation, 2004).

It was not clear in this study, however, just what 'peer' in 'peer support' meant. Very few older people were involved in peer support groups. Some did not want to attend meetings because the seating provided was too uncomfortable, others did not have personal assistant cover at the time of the meetings, but many regarded such groups as being for younger disabled people whom they simply did not identify as their peers.

While, therefore, the majority of older people involved in the study were appreciative of the support they received with the practicalities of managing direct payments, only a few were fully benefiting from being part of a wider community of direct payments users. This suggests the need for adjustments by support services to ensure both that older people can provide positive role models for other older people and that their own service does not replicate the fragmentation of statutory provision.

Conclusions

There can be little doubt that the older people involved in the study benefited greatly from the greater choice and control offered by direct payments. This was over and above solving the difficulties many had experienced with traditional home care services. Nobody suggested that working with direct payments was easy but the majority voiced the view that direct payments were a positive option well worth the effort. The help and back-up they received from support services was vital, but they themselves were a largely untapped resource in terms of providing information, positive role models and peer support to other older people. Yet as Mr Clarke said:

> "I would recommend it to anybody ... it's the best thing I've done, because you've got quality of life, which I didn't have before."

Notes
[1] This and other names are pseudonyms to protect the anonymity of participants.

Acknowledgements
The Joseph Rowntree Foundation supported this project, but the material presented here represents the findings of the author, not necessarily those of the Foundation.

Thanks to Ann Macfarlane for her helpful comments on the draft of this chapter.

References
Clark, H., Dyer, S. and Horwood, J. (1998) *'That bit of help': The high value of low level preventative services for older people*, Bristol/York: The Policy Press/Joseph Rowntree Foundation.

Clark, H., Gough, H. and Macfarlane, A. (2004) *'It pays dividends': Direct payments and older people*, Bristol: The Policy Press.

CSCI (Commission for Social Care Inspection) (2004) *Direct payments: What are the barriers?*, London: CSCI.

DH (Department of Health) (2002) *Expanded services and increased choices for older people*, Press release reference 2002/0324, London: DH.

DH (2003a) *Community care statistics 2002-03 – Referrals, assessments and packages of care for adults, England*, London: DH.

DH (2003b) *Direct payments guidance: Community care, services for carers and children's services (direct payments) guidance, England 2003*, London: DH.

Glasby, J. and Littlechild, R. (2002) *Social work and direct payments*, Bristol: The Policy Press.

Godfrey, M., Townsend, J. and Denby, T. (2004) *Building a good life for older people in local communities*, York: Joseph Rowntree Foundation.

Hasler, F. (2003) 'Making choice a reality', *Care and Health*, no 34, April 23 – May 6, pp 22-3.

Hasler, F., Campbell, J. and Zarb, G. (1999) *Direct routes to independence: A guide to local authority implementation and management of direct payments*, London: Policy Studies Institute.

Henwood, M. (2002) 'Age discrimination in social care', in Help the Aged *Age discrimination in public policy: A review of evidence*, London: Help the Aged.

Henwood, M., Lewis, H. and Waddington, E. (1998) *Listening to users of domiciliary care services: Developing and monitoring quality standards*, Leeds: The Nuffield Institute for Health.

Joseph Rowntree Foundation (2004) *The importance and availability of peer support for people with learning difficulties accessing direct payments. Findings*, December, ref: D64, York: Joseph Rowntree Foundation.

Means, R. and Smith, R. (1998) *Community care: Policy and practice* (2nd edn), Basingstoke: Macmillan.

Raynes, N., Temple, B., Glenister, C. and Coulthard, L. (2001) *Quality at home for older people: Involving service users in defining home care specifications*, Bristol: The Policy Press.

Vasey, S. (2000) *The rough guide to managing personal assistants*, London: National Centre for Independent Living.

SEVEN

"Direct what?" Exploring the suitability of direct payments for people with mental health problems

Julie Ridley

This chapter considers direct payments made to people with mental health problems. It examines this in the context of findings from a study commissioned by the Scottish Executive involving the author (Ridley and Jones, 2002), which explored the feasibility of direct payments to people labelled as 'mental health service users' (including those with dementia). The research investigated the implementation of direct payments across Scotland, and whether mental health service users were being encouraged to access them. It explored mental health service users', carers' and professionals' opinions about the idea of direct payments, any concerns or perceived obstacles, and the support that might be needed. Take-up of direct payments by people with mental health problems was found to be minimal in Scotland, as in the rest of the UK, although the work of the National Pilot in England and development work commissioned by Direct Payments Scotland (DPS) has started to change this. A degree of flexibility will clearly be required of direct payment schemes and support organisations, both initially to establish willingness to accept payments, as well as to manage the responsibilities of, for example, being an employer, if direct payments are to become more widely available.

The term 'mental health service users' was used in the research and was intended to cover disability from mental illness including dementia. In this chapter, the term 'people with mental health problems' is also used to cover a vast array of conditions as diverse as depression, anxiety, phobias, eating disorders, schizophrenia, and also dementia. Terminology in this field is fraught with difficulties, particularly in light of changes in legislation and understanding of mental health problems, and especially with respect to the notion of 'incapacity'. In Scotland, the

2000 Adults with Incapacity (Scotland) Act incorporated into law for the first time the notion that 'incapacity' is not a fixed state. Echoing this, Hasler et al (1999) have argued that being 'willing' or 'able' to accept and to manage a direct payment are not fixed states but rather these are determined by the amount of support (that is, information or assistance) available to the individual.

Research background

Previous research had found that direct payments are rarely offered to mental health service users and that the majority of direct payments are made to people who are physically disabled. In particular, an earlier Scottish Executive study (Witcher et al, 2000) had found no such individuals to be in receipt of direct payments during 1999/2000. They found just 13 of the 32 Scottish local authorities were operating a direct payments scheme and most failed to give much serious thought to the low take-up among mental health service users. The research referred to in the rest of this chapter was commissioned to investigate further Witcher et al's findings, and over a year later found evidence of only two such recipients (Ridley and Jones, 2002). By 2004, the picture had improved only marginally. While the statistics showed an overall 70% growth in direct payments in Scotland, the number of mental health service users who had taken up direct payments compared with other disability groups remained low: only 16 out of 912 recipients of direct payments in 2003/04 were mental health service users (Scottish Executive statistics quoted in DPS, 2004).

Research methods

The study carried out during 2001/02 was a qualitative study in three different local authority areas in Scotland to examine the factors inhibiting direct payments being offered to mental health service users and examining ways to promote them. The three areas were chosen to represent the geographical spread (urban/rural/mixed) across Scotland and included one area that was operating a 'third party' or 'indirect payments' scheme, as this included some mental health service users. In-depth qualitative interviews and focus groups were the main research methods used.

The research was in three parts: first there was a telephone survey of all Scottish local authorities to establish whether they were operating a direct payments scheme, how many recipients were mental health service users, and what future plans they had to extend provision of direct payments to people with mental health problems. The second comprised a broad exploration of the nature of home-based services received by people with mental health problems as well as exploring different perspectives of the perceived suitability of direct payments and the practical support that would be required. The third stage focused on individual experiences and views and consisted of a case study approach with nine mental health service users, their carers and care manager or equivalent.

A total of four focus groups were carried out with:

- mental health service user groups (two groups);
- a support group for younger people with dementia; and
- a carers group.

In addition, 23 individual interviews were carried out with:

- three senior social work managers;
- three senior care managers or equivalent;
- three voluntary sector organisations supporting people with mental health problems;
- three voluntary sector organisations supporting people with dementia;
- two independent advocacy organisations; and
- nine mental health service users, including two people with dementia.

Oliver (1992, 1996) and others have made powerful arguments for disability research that ensures that the views, perceptions, direct experiences, and definitions of knowledge of those receiving services are incorporated and valued and for the research process to be acknowledged as a political act. With this in mind, it was intended to work in partnership with disabled people as far as was practicable within the timescale and resources for the project. Experts from the Scottish Personal Assistance Employers Network (SPAEN) were involved as advisors on the design of the study and directly with the focus groups and case studies. A disabled co-facilitator was employed to explain about direct payments in the focus groups and a research advisory group was set up comprising individual mental health service users, representatives of user and carer organisations, and representatives of relevant national voluntary organisations in the fields of mental health, dementia and advocacy, as well as DPS.

Existing support for independent living

To help identify the kinds of support that mental health service users might use direct payments for, the research started out by exploring people's experiences of formal (paid) community care support. Although professionals in the three areas were aware of an array of support services provided by the statutory and voluntary sectors, the reality for the majority of mental health service users included in the study was that they received little, if any, support to enable them to live independently in the community. Many relied solely on informal (unpaid) support from members of their families, relatives and friends with back-up support from the psychiatric health services.

The main gaps or shortfalls identified in services were that they lacked flexibility and were not tailored to individual needs. Day care was very often segregated and thus served to further isolate people. There were few vocational or employment opportunities. There was a chronic lack of out-of-hours support and there were insufficient holiday or short breaks opportunities. All of this placed a strain on individuals and their families in the community. Professionals acknowledged shortcomings in terms of a generalised lack of choice in mental health services, especially over who provides support, when it is provided and how. The biggest gap was undeniably in the provision of social support to ensure that people with mental health problems were socially included and had opportunities to participate fully in the life of the community.

Confusion over eligibility for direct payments

There was a great deal of uncertainty about eligibility for direct payments. This confusion arose partly out of what was perceived to be the complexity of designing appropriate community support for people with mental health problems, and partly out of ignorance of direct payments legislation and guidance. The 'medicalisation of mental illness', which prevented social support needs from being identified in the first place, let alone met, was further highlighted as a reason why people with mental health problems might not be considered for direct payments. A survey of the 32 Scottish local authorities found only 10 out of 16 that actually had direct payments schemes were planning to include mental health service users.

Care managers in the local authority tended to assume that most mental health service users would, by default, be ineligible for direct payments. For instance, one individual's care package was said to be "so minimal" and the level of support that would be needed to manage a direct payment so great, that it would "not be cost-effective". It was assumed that others would be excluded because they would require "such a high level of support to manage", or they would simply be excluded under mental health legislation. Care managers also highlighted "poor motivation" among mental health service users as a key reason why direct payments would not be a suitable option for their clients. In contrast, many of the service users expressed an interest in the scheme. This highlights how professionals' lack of awareness and understanding of direct payments, especially of the eligibility criteria and that as much support as is needed to manage can be offered, exerts a strong influence over whether direct payments are even considered for mental health service users.

Individuals with mental health problems had trouble relating to key terms used in relation to direct payments; for example, there was a mismatch between the term 'disabled people' as used to describe the recipients of direct payments and how people who had experienced mental health problems perceived themselves. When it was explained in focus groups that a basic criterion for eligibility was that a person must be disabled, participants had great difficulty relating this concept to their own situation. Referring to someone with mental health problems as a 'disabled person' is uncommon both among service users and professionals in the field. Although it should not follow from this that people with mental health problems be excluded from consideration about direct payments, it is clear that such a perception will have a bearing on whether individuals themselves seek access to, or agree to, direct payments if offered.

Chronic lack of awareness of direct payments

A main finding of the research was the pervasive lack of awareness of direct payments among users, carers and mental health service professionals in local authorities and voluntary organisations. The only exception to this was in the area where there was an active support organisation managing the direct payments scheme and providing information and training support. In all other places, there were few training opportunities about direct payments for care managers or operational and senior managers within the local authority sector. In addition, the response to a question about whether clients with mental health problems or dementia who are assessed for community care services are routinely told about direct payments was a resounding 'No'. Even where there was an understanding of what direct payments are and what they can be used for, they were perceived to be something 'mainly aimed at those with physical disabilities'.

Mental health service users themselves and carers were the least informed about direct payments. The characteristic response when asked what they thought about direct payments was "direct what?". Although some said they would know to approach social work departments or centres for independent living first to find out more, most, especially those with early onset dementia, did not know that direct payments was an option they might consider or whom they should ask for more information should they want it. Voluntary organisations supporting people with mental health problems and dementia, not local authorities, had been the most significant sources of information on direct payments for the few users and carers who had any knowledge of this option. This dearth of information for users and carers in one person's view was reflective of a general lack of user involvement in mental health services:

> "The information people generally have given to them is abysmal. The care managers do assess the users' needs then it goes to the local authority to decide which services are to be offered. The user is not informed about the different services available, including direct payments." (Voluntary organisation manager)

Advantages of direct payments

Mental health service users generally reacted positively to the idea of direct payments. Some were hesitant because they did not yet know enough about them, while others said, "it sounds brilliant". The anticipated benefits bore close resemblance to advantages identified by existing recipients of direct payments in previous research (Witcher et al, 2000). They felt direct payments would afford them greater say and control over who provides them with support, what they do and when they do it. The term 'independent living' represented 'freedom' for one person, and for others it meant in-built flexibility to change patterns of living to suit themselves. Others highlighted potential intrinsic benefits:

> "It would be higher self-esteem to think that you were now in control of your services."

One person envisaged buying the services of a "sort of life coach to help organise your time". Echoing the work of Stainton cited in Maglajlic et al (2000), who highlighted the imaginative use of direct payments by users pooling resources to create new services, one person commented:

> "I can see a possibility where you got around with other people and imagined what you wanted and we've got enough people here to finance it."

The following case study (in Box 7.1) provides further detail of the kinds of advantages identified by people with mental health problems.

Box 7.1 : Case study 1

Bob, a male in his fifties, lived in a ground floor flat with his wife. He had a diagnosis of schizophrenia and 'mild physical disability'. Bob was happy with the support workers he had coming in to check on him once a week, to organise trips out and to do art activities with him, but he felt that the home help told him and his wife what to do and this caused him a great deal of stress. He had complained to the community mental health team who organised the service, and asked for a change of worker but nothing was being done. In his opinion, the home help did not do enough work and sat about chatting too long. Bob wanted the home help to clean the bathroom and kitchen because his wife did these tasks and she found them increasingly difficult. Overall, Bob thought a direct payment would be a 'good idea' as it had the potential to give him more control over making sure the worker did what he or she was supposed to do, over defining what tasks should be done, and the times when the worker came.

The range of potential benefits identified by carers was similar. In addition, carers felt that being able to choose the nature of the support to fulfil an ambition such as securing a job or getting out more would mean that direct payments had great potential to tackle the social exclusion of people with mental health problems and increase social inclusion. Professionals from local authority social work departments and voluntary sector projects working with mental health service users anticipated increased choice and control, more flexible and tailor-made services, increased independence, user empowerment and increased self-confidence. They were aware that "to have choice in how you rely on the state would be more dignified". Direct payments had the potential to "get people off the mental health treadmill" and increase their personal horizons. Advocacy organisations thought direct payments might address the power imbalance between users and professionals and provide a "healthy challenge to services".

Disadvantages of direct payments

Several disadvantages were also imagined. Having to manage the financial arrangements directly was perceived as the most significant. All types of participant in the research were concerned that people's fluctuating or worsening mental health problems would mean that they would be unable to manage the financial arrangements independently. One person commented that having direct payments would be like "taking on a bit more of the bureaucratic problems of life" at a time when he or she might find it difficult to cope, thus adding an extra burden and creating unwanted stress. Another concern was that due to some people's mental state, they might misspend the money:

> "With my manic depression I shoot high where I'm totally delusional and I go so low where I can't get a thought into my head and you know this happens randomly all over the place.... The thing with hypermania is when you go manic you can go off on a huge spending spree, so I could quite easily go off and blow the money on something else."

Many service users were anxious about becoming employers and dealing with these responsibilities when they felt unwell. The complexities of being an employer and the additional responsibilities were daunting to some as there was little or no awareness that recipients could receive assistance to manage payments or that they could chose to pay a support agency to act on their behalf. Professionals and carers highlighted potential difficulties in the complex relationship with personal assistants and were also concerned about payments being misspent, vulnerable people being exploited and the potential for fraud. Professionals were also worried that if individuals employed their own personal assistants, the system would lose an 'early warning system'. Case study 2 in Box 7.2 below illustrates some of the perceived disadvantages from a user perspective.

Box 7.2: Case study 2

Simon was a young man in his twenties who had mental health problems, and had experienced drug and alcohol problems in the past. He had a tenancy with a supported housing agency in a rural area and support from a care manager, a community psychiatric nurse, an occupational therapist and two support workers. Simon was very happy with the service and level of support he received and, when asked, did not think a direct payment would be something he would want.

He did, however, think a direct payment could be used to employ someone to clean his house or support him to take part in more social activities. But he felt he might have a problem "spending the money on services" rather than on other things, and would need support with paperwork and "someone who kens what they're on about" to help manage the money. Simon was unsure what would happen to a direct payment if he became unwell and had to go into hospital as "everything stops when you go into there". Consequently, he envisaged periods of time when his employees would have no work and he wasn't sure how this would work out. His care manager did not think he would be motivated to take responsibility for a direct payment and would have difficulties being committed to his role as an employer.

Obstacles to direct payments

The study identified significant attitudinal and practical barriers to the implementation of direct payments to mental health service users. As with previous studies, it found perceived threats to the funding or future development of local authority and voluntary sector services, anxiety about people's ability to manage payments and concerns about the support available.

A fundamental obstacle is that many people with mental health problems will not be in receipt of community care services, like the research participants were. The research participants presumed this automatically made them ineligible for direct payments. Further, both mental health service users and carers felt that community care assessments sometimes underestimated the needs of people disabled by mental illness as their needs were "not so obvious on a good day" and as such would subsequently not be met. Another criticism of existing community care assessments was that often assessments were not person-centred. It was claimed that a lack of involvement in decision making was a common feature in mental health services and that many people had thus become passive recipients, "grateful for anything they get". Professionals contrasted this with the philosophy of 'independent living' and direct payments.

Lack of knowledge and understanding of direct payments among users emerged as a major obstacle. Witcher et al (2000) previously found a clear correlation between having experience and knowledge of direct payments and a positive attitude towards them. Absence of information was a fundamental barrier to progress and may well have been symptomatic of other obstacles such as prejudicial and judgemental staff attitudes. Service users felt that if professionals were not in favour of, or did not even know about, direct payments, then information would simply not reach them and there was even less chance that they be encouraged to apply. Taken together with misunderstandings about eligibility, lack of information was indeed a formidable barrier. Professionals were generally ill informed about eligibility and assumed wrongly that most mental health services users would be ineligible.

The practical obstacles to implementing direct payments included concerns about people's ability to manage the payments. A recurring concern was about giving cash payments to people whose judgements might be impaired either temporarily or permanently, for instance to someone who has severe dementia. Although ways of supporting people who require assistance to manage the payments have been demonstrated in other parts of the UK, particularly in relation to people with severe learning disabilities (Holman and Bewley, 1999), there was limited or no awareness in the mental health services field that this could be the case. As mentioned earlier, the bureaucracy and paperwork required to monitor a direct payment were perceived as a significant obstacle. Additionally, it was suggested that the employer–employee relationship might be compromised in situations where, to be effective, an individual needs supporters to be directive and authoritative, when it was imagined that "an employed carer wouldn't have that authority".

There were concerns about the impact direct payments might have on the workload of existing paid workers in both the voluntary sector and local authorities. It was suggested there would be a negative impact on the range and quality of specialist mental health services available as "there's an efficiency in aggregating a pooled pot of money and staff". One local authority manager suggested that "there may be a critical point when we cannot manage services properly if more people become employers". There was fear that implementing direct payments would change the 'balance of services' for the worse. Areas with well-developed specialist mental health services felt most threatened. On the other hand, as users suggested, increasing choice through direct payments might force existing services to 'smarten up their act' or face going out of business.

Support required

Although research participants were in most instances imagining a hypothetical situation rather than one they had direct experience of, clear ideas emerged about the kind of support they would require to consent to and manage a direct payment. The first theme was about the need for better person–centred assessment. Professionals argued that the cornerstone of direct payments was 'good assessment'. Further, Hasler et al (1999) suggest that assessment for direct payments requires a different kind of relationship to be developed with users as well as a new approach to allocating community care resources. Care managers were in a unique position to present direct payments as an option as part of the community care assessment process, but clearly were not routinely informing mental health service users about them and to increase uptake, this would need to change. It was suggested social work staff needed training about direct payments so that they could 'spread the word' more effectively.

Promoting awareness among people with mental health problems, their relatives and other carers and professionals in the field is an obvious first step to take in addressing the inequity in direct payments. A key message from the research participants was to tell mental health service users about direct payments. This, they suggested, could be achieved through media campaigns, producing information on cassette, leaflets, and organising roadshows that involve existing recipients of direct payments who are themselves mental health service users. Participants identified the need for "nuts and bolts" information as, once the concept was grasped, users needed to know how local systems work, how to apply, and what assessment consists of, as well as how payments will be received and what systems will be in place for monitoring. They also need information about sources of support and advice.

Good local support organisations will be critical to promoting direct payments to mental health service users. They need to provide practical expertise on direct payments, including information about what is involved in becoming an employer. They also need to provide training on practical issues, advice and advocacy on support arrangements and potentially to be there to "step in when you're down and don't feel particularly able or capable to do things". Such organisations need to be independent but, importantly, to be staffed by people with expertise in mental health problems. The process of the research, in that it involved a user expert on direct payments in the focus groups, showed that having someone "in the same situation" with whom to discuss direct payments and how they might be used, is an essential element of the support package for people with mental health problems:

> "I think for someone who's actually experienced this, who's gone through it, the experience you have, I think is the person I would speak to rather than a helpline or read leaflets."

Mental health service users were concerned that there might be times when they would not manage a direct payment, and some form of advance planning or advance directives would alleviate their concerns. This would ensure that the individual retained as much control and choice as possible while ill, and regained full control once well again. Advance planning with personal assistants has been shown to ensure direct payments work for people with fluctuating illnesses including people with mental health problems (Heslop, 2001, 2002), and this was a familiar concept to the research participants, albeit in relation to health care rather than community care services.

Participants were concerned that procedures set up to ensure that the money was used for the purpose intended might become overly bureaucratic and therefore off-putting. To be successful, there would need to be flexible ways found for managing the money that addressed service users' fears about paperwork and bureaucracy, while remaining true to the spirit of the Direct Payments Act. As Holman and Bewley (1999) have argued in relation to people with severe learning disabilities, any procedures need to be accessible, easy to understand and straightforward. This will require meaningful involvement of mental health service users, including people with dementia, both at local and national levels, advising on the setting up of schemes. It was also suggested there should be a transitional agreement in relation to services, effectively freezing agency-provided services while individuals tried out direct payments, but entitling the individual to return to previous levels of service in case things did not work out.

Conclusions

The spread of direct payments continues to be inequitable. Many people with mental health problems have still never heard of them although this is changing slowly. Research discussed in this chapter shows that direct payments are far from being a 'first option' for all disabled people, as advocated by the Community Care Minister for England (DPS, 2004), and certainly not for those with mental health problems. The perceived obstacles found in the research persist as more recent development work commissioned by DPS shows (Scottish Development Centre for Mental Health, 2003). Wider take-up will clearly not be achieved without first overcoming obstacles such as:

- ignorance about direct payments especially among service users and carers, but also among professionals;
- misunderstandings about eligibility and wrong assumptions that all mental health service users are ineligible;
- the lack of a person-centred planning approach in community care assessments in the mental health field;
- perceived threats to the funding or future of mental health services;
- major concerns about people's ability, or rather inability, to manage payments in view of fluctuating or worsening mental health;
- a lack of adequate support organisations which understand both direct payments and mental health problems.

The information deficit found by the research was so acute that it would be misleading to conclude that a lack of demand from people with mental health problems for direct payments equates in any way with lack of interest. In a small way, the development work being carried out by DPS in one area of Scotland goes some way to addressing the information gap.

There was general antipathy towards mental health service users having direct control over money when there was potential, at least in some people's eyes, for misspending, exploitation and mismanagement, especially during periods in people's lives when they were ill. What was plain from the research was an almost universal lack of accurate knowledge about direct payments, including who is eligible, what is meant by 'consent and control', and what support arrangements could be made available to individuals to help them to manage.

The research discussed in this chapter found gaps in community living support, especially in terms of promoting the social inclusion of people with mental health problems. Direct payments have the potential to offer the flexibility, choice and control that service users seek, and the national mental health pilot scheme in England (Coldham, 2004) has ably demonstrated that this can be turned into reality. The pilot schemes report increased access to non-stigmatising mainstream activities, greater independence and flexibility in support arrangements, gains in self-confidence and self-esteem, and a knock-on positive impact on mental health: all of which the research participants imagined might be the advantages of direct payments. A clear context of choice, control and supported decision making is therefore crucial, as is the need to start from an assumption of competence when considering individuals' ability to decide on, as well as to manage, a direct payment (Dawson, 2000).

Consent and ability to manage direct payments was often interpreted as an 'all or nothing' concept. It was commonly assumed that direct payments equated with becoming an employer of personal assistants, as well as having direct management of the financial arrangements. Few had thought in terms of individuals exercising choice on an agency basis or of using indirect payments. The possibility of benefiting from having more say and control over support arrangements in this way, or of using indirect payments to third parties such as a council for voluntary service, should not be ruled out. While indirect payments are never a substitute for direct payments, they might be used as a legitimate option, even if only as a temporary measure.

The benefits of user-controlled trusts (see Holman and Bewley, 1999) and other proxy arrangements could usefully be explored as part of the solution to anxieties over handling the financial and employee responsibilities. User-controlled trusts mean the individual does not have to handle the money directly while retaining ultimate control on how it is spent. The individual can choose to appoint someone to act on their behalf. This would provide the in-built flexibility to take account of life changes and fluctuating conditions.

In short, if people with mental health problems are to have better access to direct payments they, their relatives or carers and health and social care staff who support them, need to be told about direct payments and to have access to schemes and support organisations that understand mental health problems. Community care assessments need to become more person-centred and there needs to be scope for self-assessment. Safeguards, such as advanced directives for independent living, will have to be built in at the outset in recognition of the fluctuating nature of mental health problems. The potential of direct payments to increase choice and control and to empower those with mental health problems has yet to be realised. The fact that direct payments resonates with the central government agenda on patient choice and the recognition that offering choice is fundamental to mental health recovery (George, 2004) is, however, promising.

Acknowledgements

Many thanks to Richard Brewster at DPS for his helpful comments on this chapter.

References

Coldham, T. (2004) 'Mental health pilot supports the positive impact of direct payments', *Direct Payments News*, June, pp 4-5.

Dawson, C. (2000) *Independent successes: Implementing direct payments*, York: Joseph Rowntree Foundation.

DPS (Direct Payments Scotland) (2004) *DP news*, Issue 14, October.

George, C. (2004) 'What chance choice?', *Mental Health Today*, September, pp 12-13.

Hasler, F., Campbell, J. and Zarb, G. (1999) *Direct routes to independence: A guide to local authorities implementation and management of direct payments*, London: Policy Studies Institute.

Heslop, P. (2001) 'Direct payments for people with mental health support needs', *The Advocate*, May, pp 8-9.

Heslop, P. (2002) *Direct payments for mental health users/survivors: A guide to some key issues*, London: National Centre for Independent Living.

Holman, A. and Bewley, C. (1999) *Funding Freedom 2000: People with learning difficulties using direct payments*, London: Values Into Action UK.

Maglajlic, R., Brandon, D. and Given, D. (2000) 'Making direct payments a choice: a report on the research findings', *Disability & Society*, vol 15, no 1, pp 99-113.

Oliver, M. (1992) *The politics of disablement*, London: Macmillan.

Oliver, M. (1996) *Understanding disability: From theory to practice*, Basingstoke: Macmillan.

Ridley, J. and Jones, L. (2002) *'Direct what?' – A study of direct payments to mental health service users*, Edinburgh: Scottish Executive Central Research Unit.

Ridley, J. and Jones, L. (2003) 'Direct what? The untapped potential of direct payments to mental health service users', *Disability & Society*, vol 18, no 5, pp 643-58.

Scottish Development Centre for Mental Health (2003) *The development of direct payments in Scotland for people with mental health problems: A project working in two different areas*, Edinburgh: Scottish Development Centre for Mental Health.

Witcher, S., Stalker, K., Roadburg, M. and Jones, C. (2000) *Direct payments: The impact on choice and control for disabled people*, Edinburgh: Scottish Executive Central Research Unit.

EIGHT

Overcoming barriers to the take-up of direct payments by parents of disabled children

Jeanne Carlin and Christine Lenehan

The 2000 Carers and Disabled Children Act extended the power of local authorities to offer direct payments to people with parental responsibility for disabled children and disabled young people as an alternative means of providing a service. In October 2003 this power became a mandatory responsibility for local authorities, and this chapter explores the factors, which may be holding local authorities back from fully exploring the opportunities offered by direct payments, and the reasons take-up by parents has remained relatively low. The chapter will draw on two main sources of information, *Direct payments: What are the barriers?* (CSCI, 2004) and *Direct experience: A guide for councils on the implementation of direct payments in children's services* (Carlin and Lenehan, 2004).

The implementation and take-up of direct payments for parents and disabled young people has varied considerably across the country and is extremely low in some areas. The figures collated by the Commission for Social Care Inspection (CSCI) at the end of September 2003 found that there were only 875 parents of disabled children receiving direct payments. Some areas such as Norfolk, Essex and Cheshire have relatively high numbers (between 50 and 100) of families receiving direct payments (source: personal communication), while in other areas direct payments had not yet been set up as an alternative means for providing services.

The CSCI report identified seven barriers to successful take-up of direct payments across all user groups. This chapter considers these barriers in the light of the work by the Council for Disabled Children (CDC) with 13 local authorities (see Carlin and Lenehan, 2004).

The CDC was keen to work with local authorities as direct payments developed and to highlight both the critical success factors and any significant barriers. Utilising a grant from the Department for Education and Skills, the CDC selected a group of 13 local authorities at differing stages of development and within different settings. The selection was made on the basis of local authorities having a particular interest in developing direct payments or because the CDC felt a local authority represented a particular political or community perspective. A group was formed and met six times over a period of 18 months, with additional written information provided. Local authorities were asked to share their concerns, successes and developments and to look at whether these were specific to an authority or transferable.

Barriers to direct payments

This section will explore the following areas and their role in creating barriers to the successful take-up of direct payments:

*   differing ethos or philosophy;
*   becoming part of the main commissioning strategy;
*   responsibility to safeguard and protect the welfare of the child;
*   role of the 'champion' within children's services;
*   developing a strategic approach across client groups;
*   positive independent information;
*   advice and support services appropriate to children's services;
*   developing a person-centred perspective;
*   responsibilities of becoming an employer;
*   developing a children's marketplace;
*   financial resources.

One of the greatest challenges posed by direct payments is that they are based on a very different philosophy or ethos from other aspects of children's services. Over the past 25 years, children's services have seen an increase in the amount of monitoring and regulation that apply to its services. Direct payments are based on the philosophy of parents becoming the commissioners of their own services. The underlying assumption is that generally people are responsible parents, and they will make responsible arrangements for their disabled children in the same way that they would do for non-disabled children. This means that local authorities have to hand over control and decision making to parents of disabled children, while, at the same time, local authorities retain their duty to safeguard and protect the welfare of children.

It is important not to underestimate the sharp contrast which now exists between direct payments and other directly provided services.

For example, many parents use direct payments to purchase a variety of short break services. These services are regulated, and some may argue over-regulated, to a significant degree. Short break services, provided directly by the local authority, are registered and regularly inspected against a set of national standards by the CSCI. This can lead to social workers perceiving direct payments as under-regulated when compared to directly provided short break services, and this perception leads to anxiety and a lack of trust in the process. Many local authorities have struggled to find the middle path between these two seemingly opposing philosophies. It is therefore not surprising that it has been identified that local authorities were reluctant to devolve power away from themselves to families (CSCI, 2004)

In its recommendations the CSCI argues that not only should local authorities remove the barriers to the setting up of direct payments, but once this is done, direct payments should stop being viewed as an 'add-on' scheme and become part of the local authorities' main commissioning strategy for providing support. For children's services this provides a particular challenge. The eligibility thresholds for children's disability services tend to be set at a very high level, and consequently the children eligible for services are only those with the most severe disabilities. This may be due to the changing profile of disabled children, for example the increasing number of disabled children in the population with multiple impairments and additional health needs (Glendinning et al, 1999). Therefore, in general, families who are entitled to receive services are either those experiencing a range of problems, those with children with multiple impairments or those with disabled children with complex health needs.

This latter group of children, while presently small, although increasing, in number (for example, a report to the Department of Health (DH) estimated that there were 6,000 children in Britain dependent on assistive technology), have support needs that are expensive and require services that are not always easy to provide. One local authority, for example, awarded direct payments to a family of £8.50 an hour to obtain support. While this was in keeping with other local arrangements, the child in question had a complex medical condition, that required trained nursing staff at night. The cost for this service was £14.50 an hour in the particular locality (source: personal communication). See Chapter Eighteen in this book by Glendinning, where health issues are discussed.

One of the practice areas that caused difficulties for many local authorities and front-line social work staff is that the direct payments regulations state that the decision whether or not to seek a Criminal

Records Bureau (CRB) check on the person being employed is that of the parents (DH, 2003). On the other hand, it is left to the discretion and interpretation of local authorities to define their responsibility for child protection. When approving a direct payment, local authorities must be satisfied that the payment will safeguard and promote the welfare of the child and may set 'reasonable conditions' on the direct payment (DH, 2003). Despite the wording of the legislation, many local authorities have insisted on a CRB check being carried out as a condition of approving the direct payment. Other local authorities have discharged their responsibility to safeguard the welfare of the child by strongly advising that a CRB check should be undertaken, and if parents do not want this check they require parents to sign a statement accepting the risks of their action. This statement is not legally binding, but local authorities feel that it is evidence that the issues have been explored with the parents (Carlin and Lenehan, 2004).

From the work undertaken with the 13 local authorities, we found that one of the key factors in attaining successful take-up of direct payments was the role of a 'champion' within children's services. It is important that there is a middle or senior manager in children's services to take on the role of direct payments champion. This person needs to hold a position within the local authority with the power and responsibility to make things happen and needs to be able to resolve issues of difference and make policy decisions, which enables clear policy to develop.

In order for direct payments to become a part of mainstream services, local authorities should develop a more strategic approach to direct payments. One way of achieving this is for authorities to develop direct payments boards or steering groups across all user groups. A benefit of working across children and adult services is to resolve some of the transition issues for young people using direct payments who wish to continue into adult services. This may become more difficult to achieve with the introduction of children's trusts and the separation of children and adult services. These issues include having the same payment rates so that personal assistants will remain with the young person during the move from children to adult services. Having consistent eligibility criteria allows young people to continue using direct payments into adulthood. This has been an issue for particular groups of service users, for example, adults with Asperger's syndrome.

Local authorities with joint steering groups have also used this forum to develop promotional material across all their users groups, for example, the development of a promotional video in Enfield. This can be particularly important, as the CSCI report found that the lack of clear information for potential users of direct payments was one of the main barriers to successful take-up. The use of direct payments in any area is dependent on the local authority consulting with parents, parent groups and voluntary organisations in order to promote direct payments and ensure that parents have a realistic understanding of what direct payments can offer.

A study by Scope asked parents, young people and adult users of direct payments how they had heard about direct payments (McMullen, 2003). An interesting finding was that there was a clear difference in the experience of accessing direct payments between those people who had heard about them through social services and those who had heard of them from other sources. When people heard about direct payments through social services, the process of access was relatively smooth. However, when information came through other sources there then followed a process of having to convince social services of the existence of direct payments and their own particular eligibility. This study found that parents of disabled children were the only group who had heard about direct payments from their friends. The following quote from a parent sums up the issues of culture and access well.

> "I then had trouble convincing social services that direct payments existed.... My social worker was scared, didn't really know what to do. It was early days and they just kind of put the brakes on it." (McMullen, 2003, p 19)

In order to address the information gap, local authorities should consider producing leaflets and other publicity material that detail how to access direct payments in their particular area. Many local authorities have already started to produce their own information in a variety of formats. On a national level, Scope has produced an information resource for parents (Scope, 2004). Scope also offers information on direct payments to parents on its website (www.scope.org.uk/issue/directpayments).

The CSCI report also found that staff were often not fully committed to the use of direct payments and tended to overemphasise the difficulties rather than promoting the positive opportunities of direct payments. In some cases, front-line staff had not been adequately trained to understand direct payments and therefore did not give accurate information to families. It is essential that all staff promoting direct payments or assessing families should receive basic training in order to understand the legal basis, the philosophical context and the practical arrangements of offering direct payments.

An evaluation study of direct payments by Cheshire County Council

(2003) highlighted the role in the training programme of 'product champions' to promote direct payments by relating the positive impact direct payments have had on their own lives. Another important element of the training is that staff should be given sufficient time to ask questions and express their concerns about the different philosophy which underpins direct payments. A report on the training offered by Norfolk highlights this:

> The issues of the social worker not being responsible for choosing the carer was the most difficult to come to grips with. Social workers need to be reassured that it was OK for parents to take responsibility.... (Carlin and Lenehan, 2004, p 29)

A training programme for front-line staff needs to give clear guidance around other areas of child care legislation and regulations and how these impact on the interpretation of direct payment regulations. The guidance on direct payments still reads from an adult perspective with children's issues added on and this can lead to some difficulties. One such example is that of childminding regulations and using direct payments to provide a service for a disabled child under the age of eight years. The direct payments guidance states that under "Section 79D of the Children Act 1989 anyone caring for a child under eight years for over two hours a day and for a payment in their own home has to be registered as a childminder" (DH, 2003, p 33). Although the direct payments guidance does not specifically stipulate that parents purchasing this type of service must only use registered childminders, it appears to be implied by the guidance.

The final aim of any training programme for front-line staff is to give them the knowledge to promote direct payments in a way that gives families real choice. Staff need to develop a realistic understanding of the positive benefits of direct payments from the viewpoint of families.

One way of assisting families in understanding and using direct payments is by supplying independent advice, support and advocacy services. The CSCI report found that the support and advice offered was often inadequate and varied considerably from one part of the country to another. When direct payments were extended to families of disabled children many children's services utilised the expertise of their adult services counterparts. This frequently led local authorities to contract with the same organisation to provide advice and support to families as already used to provide these services to adults using direct payments.

Generally, a number of these organisations with a mainly adult focus have adapted and developed to offer an excellent service to parents. However, local authorities need to consider carefully the essential differences between offering direct payments to families and offering them to adult service users and ensure that the independent advice and advocacy organisations with whom they contract are flexible and robust enough to understand these differences and offer services with an appropriate focus to parents and children.

One of the main differences in this focus is that in children's services the direct payment is not being provided to the person who is the service user, in other words, the child. Therefore, the needs of both the parents and the disabled child must be taken into account during the assessment. The support organisation must be aware that the needs of the parent may be different from those of the child, and staff should be trained to recognise and work with this difference. If the support organisation is assisting in the recruitment of the personal assistant there needs to be clarity as to whose needs are being met so that an appropriate person is recruited and employed. In addition, unlike adult services, where if a direct payment is made to a carer, the person employed cannot undertake intimate care tasks, this is not the case, when a direct payment is made to a parent (DH, 2003).

Some support organisations have set up and developed peer support groups for direct payments users. Given the discomfort many adult disability groups have with the role of parents (as the needs of parents may conflict with those of disabled direct payments users), it may not be appropriate for parents to become part of the same adult support groups. However, parents need to be offered the opportunity to use peer support and have a place to discuss the practical issues involved when using direct payments, as well as their changing role as parents when their child approaches adulthood.

In order to empower families, front-line staff should be given the freedom to explore creative and flexible services that will meet the unique needs of families. The CSCI found that some local authorities have very strict and rigid policies determining how direct payments can be spent. This serves to undermine the potential flexibility that makes a direct payment different from a direct service. Within children's services some local authorities feel that there is a lack of clarity in the direct payments guidance as to whether or not children are 'looked after' if an overnight break is purchased using a direct payment, and therefore local authorities may be reluctant to approve direct payments for this type of service. Most direct payments in children's services are still narrowly focused on the provision of domiciliary care, although a small number of local authorities have now gained the confidence to approve overnight placements. There is little evidence so far of flexible usage of direct payments and this tends to be because of council policy rather than the will of individual direct payment officers (source: personal communication).

Within the assessment process social work staff have become accustomed to trying to fit the needs of the family into the direct services provided or contracted by the local authority. Direct payments require practitioners to think very differently when developing a care plan to meet the recommendations of an assessment of need. Social workers are required to take a person-centred perspective, with the needs of disabled children and their families becoming the primary focus. Additional training may be needed for practitioners to embrace this fundamental change in thinking.

The work by the CDC with local authorities found that the provision of direct services is dominated by waiting lists or lists of unmet need. Many assessments lead to a place on a list, rather than to a service. Over 90% of short break schemes operate a waiting list and 60% of the children on the list have waited for longer than one year before service is received (Prewett, 1999). For some children, particularly those with complex difficulties, being on a waiting list is a semi-permanent state with little real chance of service. Waiting lists for family-based short break services may be the result of services being unable to recruit sufficient or appropriate carers. Within the area of direct payments, one of the first queries discussed by the group of local authorities was whether or not they could operate a direct payments waiting list. The answer is that many local authorities have already started to do this, as there is insufficient funding to support all the direct payments requested. Thus, direct payments may well become dominated by waiting lists in the same way as direct services have been, although it is important to stress that the guidance for direct payments clearly states that "problems with internal budget management procedures may not be used as a reason to refuse or deal the offering or start of a direct payment" (DH, 2003, p 9). Local authorities operating 'waiting lists' for direct payments may be open to legal challenge.

CSCI (2004) identified that one of the main barriers to the take-up of direct payments is the responsibility of becoming an employer. The DH has produced a guide for parents, which takes them through the process of recruiting and employing a person via direct payments

(Carlin, 2003). However, many parents do not wish to take on the responsibility of working out tax, national insurance and wages. As a number of parents in the Essex review of direct payments stated:

> "Trying to sit down and work out PAYE, then making sure the right stuff gets sent off … is a responsibility that I wouldn't really want."

> "I didn't want anything to do with the money side … I just want life made easier."

However, this is not always the case:

> "It's only four hours a week, it's not big money…. I find it very straightforward, but then again I quite like figure work…. For me it's been writing out a cheque and filling in one form every quarter." (Pountney, 2003, pp 21-2)

In order, to make this situation as easy as possible for parents and therefore to improve the take-up of direct payments, many local authorities offer a payroll system run by a voluntary organisation which will take on the routine employment responsibilities without undermining the control and commissioning role that direct payments give the parents. For parents who wish to deal with these tasks themselves, it is essential that local authorities keep the paperwork as simple as possible. While there needs to be clear accountability in terms of the use of the money, the system of monitoring this should reflect the size of the amount given.

Discussions with local authorities found that a further barrier to the successful take-up of direct payments in children's services is the lack of a children's 'marketplace'. Unlike adult services, the 'marketplace' of service providers in children's services is relatively underdeveloped.

Parents can use direct payments to purchase care from an individual or from a voluntary, not-for-profit or independent organisation, not managed by the local authority. Parents can purchase from voluntary organisations which have contracts with the local authority as long as the service purchased using a direct payment is outside the amount of service the voluntary organisation is contracted to provide to the local authority. There has been a lot of confusion and muddled thinking in this area. While it is important that local authorities are not paying for the same service twice, it is also important that voluntary organisations should be given the flexibility and freedom to develop services which can be purchased by families via direct payments. The encouragement to do this is in the interests of all parties. If there are no services available to be purchased from voluntary and not-for-profit organisations in the long term, the market will be developed by private, for-profit organisations, and this may result in local authorities having to pay higher rates for direct payments.

Most parents used their direct payments to purchase support from an individual already known to their child – someone in the disability network or a family member. This is a 'positive' for the child; however, the use of existing care staff has been seen as a threat by a number of providers of services. Many service providers have found that their staff have been approached to work on an individual basis with children using direct payments. This is particularly problematic in the area of fostering and short break services, where foster carers are paid an allowance. It has long been recognised that this allowance is relatively low for the work they are required to undertake. The carer can offer the same service to a disabled child using a direct payment at a far higher rate of pay.

A further barrier to the successful take-up of direct payments is that of local authority financial resources. According to Leece (2002), introducing direct payments into children's services presented a very different challenge to that in adult services. Following the implementation of the 1990 NHS and Community Care Act in 1993, local authorities had to spend 85% of the grant to fund community care in the private, independent or voluntary sector. Many local authorities started the process of transferring services to the independent sector. Thus paying adults to purchase their own services instead of paying an outside contractor in the independent sector was a relatively straightforward matter. However, children's services have not developed in the same way, and most local authorities have their financial resources tied up in residential provision or committed to in-house providers. It has not been easy to alter this situation and change these resources into the cash to provide direct payments.

In addition, the levels of unmet need in children's services are significant and the introduction of direct payments has only served to highlight these further. A number of families who had not previously used direct services have come forward to request direct payments. In Essex, for example, 40% of families using direct payments in the first year had not previously used direct services (Carlin and Lenehan, 2004). Therefore the total number of service users has increased, thus having an impact on the limited resources available to local authorities.

The original assumption behind direct payments suggested that, as children transferred from direct services into direct payments, this would release money to expand direct payments. This assumption was too simplistic and has not held true. For the reasons given above, local authorities are having to find new resources on overstretched budgets. The 20% of the Carers Grant[1] allocated for children's services has proved useful but has often been spent a number of times over. A number of authorities have already closed the option of direct payments to new families or not developed this option at all for reasons of financial cost. Financial challenges in children's services are compounded by the fact that Fair Access to Care Guidance (a framework introduced in 2003 to assist local authorities to decide on eligibility for social services provision for adults) does not apply. A number of local authorities are now looking at charging for children's services, but they are reminded that direct payments for children's services are part of section 17 of the 1989 Children Act and they would need to bring in a charging policy to cover all services under this statute. While the 1989 Children Act gives local authorities the power to charge, previous attempts at charging have not been sustainable as revenue income has always been much lower than the administration costs incurred in its recovery.

Conclusion

In conclusion, a small number of authorities have seen direct payments as a positive development for children's services and delivered excellent results in a short time. However, the rest are held back for two main reasons. The first is that direct payments represent a significant change to the philosophy or underlying ethos of children's services. This barrier is key and councils are going to need significant reassurance that they really can let go and trust parents with direct payments. The second reason is that of finance. Some creative financing is needed in order for direct payments to expand. Even in successful authorities, financing has become a crucial issue. There is little doubt that direct payments have the potential to transform the lives of disabled children and their families. As this potential begins to be realised, the financial impact is likely to be significant. The extension of performance indicators[2] to direct payments for those under the age of 18 years may operate as a key lever to unlocking finance within local authorities.

The road to direct payments has only just begun for children's services; the next few years will see many twists and turns and, hopefully, horizons we have yet to dream about.

Notes
[1] The Carers Grant forms part of the government's strategy for carers, set out in *Caring about carers*, 8 February 1999 (unpublished report).

[2] Performance indicators are measures of performance set by the departments in central government. They came into effect under the 1999 Local Government Act.

References
Carlin, J. (2003) *A parent's guide to direct payments*, Written on behalf of the Council for Disabled Children (CDC), London: Department of Health (DH).
Carlin, J. and Lenehan, C. (2004) *Direct experience: A guide for councils on the implementation of direct payments in children's services*, London: CDC.
Cheshire County Council (2003) *Review of direct payments*, An evaluation study, August (unpublished report).
CSCI (Commission for Social Care Inspection) (2004) *Direct payments: What are the barriers?*, London: CSCI.
DH (Department of Health) (2003) *Direct payments guidance: Community care, services for carers and children's services (direct payments) guidance, England 2003*, London: DH.
Glendinning, C., Kirk, S., Guiffrida, A. and Lawton, D. (1999) *The community-based care of technology-dependent children in the UK: Definitions, numbers and costs*, Research report commissioned by the Social Care Group, Department of Health, Manchester: National Primary Care Research and Development Centre.
Leece, J. (2002) 'Changing direction: direct payments and disabled children', *Representing Children*, vol 14, no 4, pp 215-25.
McMullen, K. (2003) *The direct approach: Disabled people's experience of direct payments*, London: Scope.
Pountney, K. (2003) *The use of direct payments in Essex by families with disabled children*, Written on behalf of Essex Social Care, October 2003 (unpublished report).
Prewett, B. (1999) *Short-term break, long-term benefit*, Sheffield: University of Sheffield Joint Unit for Social Services Research.
Scope (2004) *In the driving seat – direct payments for your child*, London: Scope.

Section 3
Voices of experience

The views and experiences of people using direct payments and the people they employ to provide their support are of immense importance, and this book would not be complete without them. Chapter Nine includes a number of contributions from direct payment users, and personal assistants who were asked to write about their personal experiences of direct payments. Their words bring direct payments to life: they are the voices of experience.

NINE

Voices of experience

The freedom of direct payments

Louise Smyth

Life so far has showered me with opportunity. Following secondary education I was rewarded with three brilliant years of partying – ehm, I mean studying – to further my professional development, at university. I then invested a few years doing voluntary work for the Red Cross as a trainer and community worker around first aid and humanitarian work. I gained some valuable insights into life, met some wonderful people and made fantastic friendships. Recently I completed my second degree and moved to Kent to live with my fiancé and take up full-time employment with social services. Looking back I know that the past nine years would not have been possible without direct payments and other funding for personal assistance.

When I was born I came with an instruction book that said I was 'special' and to 'handle with care'. My parents were guided through the pages by the authors – educators, medical and social welfare professionals – who claimed to know what was in my best interest. I too followed the book, which amazingly also told of my future (or lack of one). At first I believed in the book; now I believe in myself. Aged 19, I threw this manual away and began my life. It was the best thing I ever did.

Starting university in Hertfordshire, miles from my home in Wales, I entered an alien world I had only really seen on the TV. I had never seen anyone outside of school or socialised in a pub for example (but I soon got the idea!). Buying my own clothes and shopping for food was a new experience. Items I saw in supermarkets just bowled me over! I'd never had a bank account or written a cheque and had no experience of money. I used to feel incredibly stupid studying the coins in my purse to see what their value was before paying for things. With some creative thinking my social worker came up with 24-hour assistance and a system of cash payments in the absence of any Direct

Payments Act. She helped me look into getting a car, guided me through the benefit maze and was a strong advocate.

When I left university I rented a flat and for a few months had agency carers sent by social services. They were often nameless people who arrived late (if indeed at all), let themselves into my house, rushed me through the prescribed 'routine' and disappeared 30 minutes earlier than expected. A few hours later another person would make an appearance and do the same. And so it went on, day in day out. One person left me a hot drink and when they left I discovered to my amazement they had left a length of spaghetti in my cup instead of a straw: what a 'mistaka to maka'! My friends were getting jobs, still socialising together and many were getting married. I couldn't even get out the house because most carers the agency sent couldn't drive. My friends helped out when they could but it made me feel indebted to them and I became more and more isolated.

Then I remembered my social worker in Wales mentioning something called direct payments that were being introduced. I dug out the information and made contact with my local personal assistant support services (PASS) scheme. A few phone calls and a couple of visits from PASS and social services was all it took for me to get set up. At first I found the monitoring forms too complicated, but PASS helped me out and after that they became a necessary chore! Still, a small price to pay for freedom! At first I used an agency then recruited my own personal assistants after a few months. Having independent advisors was invaluable. They didn't judge me when things went wrong, they just helped me make informed decisions to get back on track. For the first few times, PASS helped me out with all the recruitment side of things until it became all too familiar! I often recruited badly in the beginning which I put down to inexperience and the area I lived in. However, the main thing is that each time I become a little wiser and gain new ideas to make the process more successful.

The personal assistants who have never done 'care' work are always the best. They have been respectful, responsive and have a whole different attitude about their work, and I get better quality assistance. I have had bad experiences but I feel it's more about how you deal with such situations, feeling confident to discipline staff or be assertive and talk over problems. Also knowing who to go to for advice and guidance and moral support, like a support scheme and other users. This is essential to make the most of the freedoms these payments can offer.

How direct payments changed my life

Angie Stewart

Getting the job that I had always dreamed of meant moving out of the small town where I had grown up. Just like most people in their early twenties it also meant that I needed to start thinking of buying my first home. There was one major difference, though. While all my friends were considering nearness to their family, friends, work, public amenities and a good pub, my top priority was living in a local authority area where direct payments were well established.

This was my first experience of using direct payments and truly being in control of the support that I receive. I didn't realise just how much control I would have until my social worker supported me to complete a self-assessment of my needs. I kept a diary over one week of all the things that I needed support with and also what I could have been doing that week, had I had support! Doing this made me realise how much I was missing out on, but also made me think of the times of day where I might want to spend time on my own. This gave me a good indication of what I would use direct payments for and my social worker reassured me that I would be in control of the hours that my personal assistants worked.

From there everything happened very quickly and I was amazed how fast things moved. Opening bank accounts and clearing a corner of my wardrobe to keep all the paperwork in order was probably the hardest part!

I placed a job advertisement in the local newspaper asking for people to apply who thought that they could support me with personal care, domestic tasks and partying! The completed application forms came flooding in, which meant the next step was interviewing people. This would have been a daunting task had I not had support from my local direct payments support scheme. They introduced me to people who had been employing their own staff for years and I found the experience that I gained from them invaluable. I was able to acquire ideas of the qualities and skills that I was looking for in my new personal assistants.

It wasn't too difficult to put two personal assistants into post. It was at this point that I really noticed the difference in my life. It was amazing to be able to go shopping, out for a meal or a drink with friends, without having to rely on my dad to drive or a friend to support me to go to the toilet. I have a wonderful relationship with my family and friends, but having to rely on them to do things like this for me always left me with a feeling of guilt. The relationship with personal assistants is different, as they are paid to provide the support that I need.

My personal assistants also support me with domestic tasks in my home. This was the first time that I had ever had a place of my own and although I try to do as much around the house as I can there are some things that I physically cannot do. As I am the employer, I am able to set the ground rules and one of them is not to assume that I can't do anything for myself; I sometimes just need a helping hand. My personal assistants respect this and are supportive of my need to maintain my independence.

This was only the beginning of the advantages of being on direct payments. Writing contracts, job descriptions and organising time sheets has introduced me to many new skills. Being an employer comes with a lot of responsibility, but having good support means that the advantages far out weigh the disadvantages. I know that having direct payments to employ personal assistants has increased my confidence, enhanced my management skills and for the first time ever put me in control of my life and my future.

Being a guinea pig for direct payments

Jackie Gelling

I was among the first people in Cambridgeshire to receive direct payments and also one of the first to receive the money for direct payments in the county. For the first year I was a guinea pig for the scheme, it was very interesting. I was a trainer for social services, which is how I became involved in the first place. Asked by the person who was to oversee the introduction of direct payments if I was interested, I didn't need asking twice.

My care coordinator carried out my assessment and the help I needed was described as being to relieve my husband of having to do all my care. At the time my husband was unwell, since then he has become disabled himself with multiple sclerosis. I have arthritis, spinal nerve damage, diabetes and renal failure (on dialysis).

The assessment identified my needing three hours' home help a week, five hours' personal care and two hours' shopping. Also, on a need basis, a driver: this was identified as eight hours a month. I was also given one day a month as an outing with one of my carers, either for shopping or any other outing I might require. I think it was identified as 12 hours per week, and five weeks' respite a year for both myself and my husband.

The direct payment was due to start in February 2000, I think, but social services pay office could not get the idea of paying us money, so February passed, March passed, and I was now getting quite frustrated. Finally in April the first cheque arrived. I rang the office of our care coordinator, and we could hear the whole office cheering. The pay office could still not get the idea of paying us, so for some months the payment had to be raised manually every month and if someone went on holiday the system still failed. This has all changed now, of course, and the payments are as regular as clockwork (I probably shouldn't have said that!).

The difference it has made to my life, even during the pilot period, was nothing short of miraculous. I was lucky in that the people working with me from agencies were not on contract to their employers so I was able to employ them as my carers. I have three carers and a driver, as needed. Being able to choose my days and times, where and when I wanted to and best of all being able to choose when and where we went for respite.

Direct payments have revolutionised my life (and many of the people I know are also in receipt of direct payments). The pilot period was really a wonderful trial for me and we were worried that at the end of it Cambridgeshire might not agree to start direct payments. Fortunately they did decide to go ahead with it and so I became one of the first people to officially receive direct payments.

The start was very much a DIY period. I had to employ my own staff, do all my own paper work, tax and insurance. When I had to advertise I had to be so careful with the wording. Being aware of the pitfalls was all very well, avoiding them was another matter. Fear of the taxman was another matter again. Social services did arrange for us to have a half-day training session at the Inland Revenue and they were very helpful, but it was all down to me to do my best to make or break how I did things. Eventually the Rowan Organisation was brought in as the support agency for Cambridgeshire, and many more people are now being encouraged to undertake direct payments, feeling far more confident with Rowan there to support them.

As I said at the beginning I was a trainer for social services, and when training co-coordinators and others who might be involved with people receiving direct payments, I met with varying degrees of hesitancy. Many of the care co-coordinators were reluctant to let go of their traditional role of providing the care they thought people needed and some even voiced the opinion that it would not be safe to let clients choose their own staff. Even now, although it is a legal requirement, some care co-coordinators are not publicising direct payments as much as they should and I do know of some clients who have to really push to get what is now their legal right. On the whole the system now works very well and more people are being won over. For those who hesitate I do my best to ensure they are aware of the facts and that it really isn't as hard as it sounds, and it is improving all the time

Direct payments: the heart of independent living

Jane Campbell

For decades disabled people have demanded citizenship and full participation in our communities. One of the greatest barriers to this involvement is an absence of human support. One can have all the access to public transport, housing, education and employment in the world, but there are some people, given all this, who will never benefit unless they have personal assistance.

As chair of the Social Care Institute for Excellence (SCIE) and a disability rights commissioner, I have a demanding daily schedule of meetings, conference presentations, and national negotiations. My personal assistants get me up for those breakfast meetings and they put me to bed after midnight when I am required to attend networking dinners. They patiently type as I compile briefings and drive me to meetings and conferences up and down the country as I promote the work of my organisation.

There is not a statutory service in this country that would offer me the flexibility and type of personal assistance I need in order to do this work effectively. Personal assistance via direct payments is at the heart of independent living. For the disabled people's movement in this country, the Direct Payments Act was the culmination of a 20-year campaign to legalise our direct control over personal care/assistance arrangements. Direct payments were, in fact, conceived, developed and largely executed by disabled people. Therefore, the intention behind this legislation is not new to us.

In the last 15 years we have created support infrastructures called Centres for Independent Living (CILs), which are vital to the success of any direct payments scheme. Sadly these centres remain chronically underfunded, as they are not substantially recognised as part of mainstream community care provision. However, things are changing. There has been a steady increase in the diversity and numbers of disabled people wanting to take up the option of controlling their own personal activities, and they look to other disabled people for guidance. It is commonly recognised that learning from the experience of others is the easiest way to develop your own personalised package. In addition, disabled people can consider from a range of options what suits them best, for example, by purchasing their own service, by becoming an employer or taking the control with the help of advocates, trusts or perhaps circles of friends. The elderly, the young, people with learning difficulties, disabled parents: there is no one type or age of person that direct payments does not potentially suit.

This brings me to my role as an employer, an aspect of my role as a user of direct payments that I think needs to be understood more fully. My eligibility to receive direct payments involves a responsible commitment to manage my own care in a business-like manner. Many people who have resisted the new community care ethos of independent living fail to recognise the positive shift that results through more creative and emancipatory approaches to disabled people's personal assistance needs. With my personal assistance needs met, I am able to focus my attention on the needs of others. Independent living goes hand in hand with direct payments and allows me to contribute more broadly, benefiting society as well as myself.

Evidence-based direct payments practice needs to recognise that the knowledge comes from disabled people's endeavours. This will help statutory providers to not only offer a direct payments option, but also support local organisations of disabled people to provide the information and guidance. Placing the Act within its disabled-led historical framework ensures we do not deviate from the original intention of the legislation. This was to create a community care option for those of us wanting more choice and control, first, over who assists us, and ultimately, over our lives. It is important to link these two concepts inextricably.

The time is right, the expertise is available and the case has been made not only for direct payments but also for its greatest intention – independent living. It is now up to us all, across professions and interest groups, to work together for it to become reality for all disabled people regardless of impairment.

A direct route to a career and independence: this is what direct payments means to me. For others it will be a different life plan. However, what is probably common to all direct payments users is that they start us on the road to participating in society as equal citizens.

A disabled mother's story

Simone Baker

I am disabled as a consequence of the drug Thalidomide, which resulted in my being born with my arms shortened to elbow length, three fingers on each hand, and legs (femurs) shortened by about 20 cm each side.

The main difficulties I experience as a result are reduced mobility, reach, dexterity and stamina. I am able to do most things, although everything takes me that much longer (washing, dressing, meal preparation, etc).

Throughout the first 34 years of my life, I coped independently with a very small amount of help (mostly provided by family members and a cleaning lady I employed). I worked full time as a secretary and lived on my own for nine years and met and married my husband John in 1991.

In 1996, I gave birth to a baby daughter, Lois. I coped independently until my daughter was two, with a lot of support from my husband. I did find that the additional time required to care for my baby ate into the additional time I required to remain self-caring and to manage the house (laundry, meal preparation, etc). I was becoming quite exhausted trying to keep on top of all of these quite basic things.

Once my daughter became mobile, things were really hard. One day in desperation, I contacted my local social services department to ask for some support in my parenting role. I wanted help to take my daughter out to toddler groups and to go swimming – both of these things to reduce isolation – and to socialise my child with other children.

I was assessed as needing 10 hours of help a week. However, after just one day of direct services, it became apparent that it wasn't going to work out. The agency worker who arrived wanted to take my daughter out for a walk to give me a break, even though I had never set eyes on her before! I didn't want someone to take my daughter off my hands. I wanted help with the everyday tasks which were becoming a struggle with a small baby toddling about the place – things like ironing, changing beds, hanging washing. My one day's experience was so inappropriate that I cancelled the arrangement.

In 2002, following a serious car accident in which I broke my ankle, I was left requiring a substantial amount of assistance following my return home from hospital. I needed help with everything, from toileting, to washing and dressing, to meal preparation. I was unable to climb the stairs as I was non-weight-bearing and my leg was in a cast. The only toilet in our home was on the first floor.

My general practitioner contacted social services, and I was given an emergency care package. Once I had made a partial recovery (I am still recovering more than three years on), I was offered the choice to move onto direct payments. I now receive eight hours' assistance a week and employ two personal assistants. One helps every morning for an hour with the morning school routine, such as getting my daughter ready for school (packed lunches, uniforms, putting her hair up) and some laundry and meal preparation. My second personal assistant works three mornings a week assisting me with household chores (housework, laundry, ironing, shopping).

As a result, all of our lives have been changed. I am less tired, experience less pain, and feel more in control of things. My husband has regained time to do things he wants to do rather than having to come in from a day's physical work to start on preparing meals and hanging up laundry. I am left with enough energy at the end of the day to do things with my daughter that she wants me to do, such as watch a video together, go to the park, or have her friends home for tea.

I wish that when she was younger I'd had access to direct payments. Without the assistance I needed, there were days when I couldn't face leaving the house because I just didn't have the necessary energy. I would struggle to get us both up, washed and dressed and try in vain to keep on top of basic household tasks such as laundry and food shopping.

The first ten years of direct payments: a personal experience

Simon Stevens

I actually started using indirect payments back in 1993, although direct payments were enacted in 1996. I am now 30 and chief executive of Enable Enterprises, a leading provider of disability consultancy and training, which has included for many years independent living and direct payments. My greatest achievement in direct payments so far is when I made a presentation at a big conference in July 2000 in Seattle, US.

I have cerebral palsy, which affects my speech, coordination, balance and general ability to perform practical tasks. Employing personal assistants and having the control to do this under direct payments has been essential to the quality of my life. As someone who works from home but travels a lot, I have no fixed routine as I juggle my many work and leisure commitments. I have had care agencies before which simply do not understand that the term 'care' has anything to do with caring! The quality of agencies has deteriorated so much in recent years, I could never possibly consider using one under any circumstances.

Employing staff can be one of the most empowering things when it works and the last few years it has worked well for me. I think this has been partly good luck and partly good management skills. But things have not always been plain sailing and I wish to explore two major disadvantages of direct payments and employing staff.

The first is the paperwork involved in employing staff. Since Labour came into power in 1997, the amount of paperwork and forms has increased dramatically. It is no longer just a case of doing PAYE and all that is involved in that, including online annual returns. You now need to check the legal status of new staff, do police checks, work out holiday pay, issue contracts, implement a disciplinary procedure and then keep watching your back just in case you are taken to a tribunal for unfair dismissal! Direct payments users also have a hard task being accountable to all their funders: in my case three social services, access to work and the Independent Living Fund. This is why I have set up my own payroll service to help other direct payments users with the minefield.

The second major issue is trusting staff and this is more difficult than you may realise. Over the years I have seen everything from persistent lateness to someone coming once, taking my key and never returning! Here are three bad examples which make you just wonder if you can trust anyone ever again.

The first was a female personal assistant who did not drive and, at that time, I was using a taxi account heavily to avoid using cash. I also found out my personal assistant was using the same account heavily without my permission or me realising! I had to sack her straight away.

The second case was very unusual. I employed the guy and, just after three days, he gave me the creeps and had made it very clear he was unable to perform the simplest of tasks. So I let him go with immediate effect and thought nothing of it! A few weeks later, I received paperwork to inform me I was being taken to an employment tribunal! He eventually dropped the case but it was not a very nice experience.

The third and most awful case was at the very start of 2000. I had a young man working for me who went to Devon for a New Year break with my bankcard and PIN number, and over a four-day period, he managed to take £2,600 cash out of my account. As you may have expected, he did not return to work and has never been caught! If I ever catch up with him, I would simply rugby tackle him to the floor, and sit on him until the police arrive!

These are, however, extreme, but still true stories. Gut reaction plays an important part in deciding how far you can go with people. Direct payment has been a liberation which still needs developing and let's hope the next 10 years builds on the success of the first.

Supporting disabled children with direct payments

Helen Lee

My name is Helen Lee and I am 17 years old. I work for an organisation called Sharecare, based in Stockport. Sharecare specialises in providing respite care for children with disabilities and their families. I got involved with Sharecare about a year ago when they were looking for help with play schemes. Before being able to work for Sharecare, I had to do 18 hours of training, spread over six weeks. I also had to go through the ordinary interview process and have a CRB (Criminal Records Bureau) check, because I would be working with children.

Supporting children with disabilities at an organised event, such as the play schemes, gave me the confidence to be able to support disabled children outside the group environment. So I got involved with another section of Sharecare called specialised childcare, which is support given to the child out in the community or local area. Specialised childcare is aimed more at older children and teenagers, who want time away from their parents and to have fun with other young people.

The Linkcare workers at Sharecare linked me with a child according to what the child wanted to do and my time availability. A lot of the support workers are of a similar age to myself, and have to juggle busy academic schedules so sometimes a compromise has to be reached between the support worker and the child's family. Often the families will accept any time the support worker has to offer as they are so desperate for the help.

I am linked with a girl of 13, Emily (not her real name), who has diagnosed cerebral palsy. She is partially sighted and has difficulty with coordination and focusing. She also has difficulty judging distances when crossing roads; this gives her a lack of confidence when crossing.

In the past, Emily has had some difficulty in the local community and can be easily led by other young teenagers.

It was decided that Emily would benefit from support to go out at weekends and do things that most teenage girls enjoy, such as shopping, going to the cinema, going swimming, and so on. The service is paid for by direct payments. Sharecare sends Emily's family a bill for the service which they then pay with the money they receive from direct payments.

Emily and I go out for four hours, three Saturdays a month. We take the bus into Stockport and home again. I encourage Emily to plan her time, for example what time we have to get the bus home to be back for a certain time. Every time we go out, Emily keeps all the receipts from anything we do, such as buying cinema tickets or receipts from swimming so her family can claim the money back.

Working with Emily through Sharecare rather than being directly employed by the family is definitely an advantage. The Linkcare workers at Sharecare are always there, with support for when Emily's family or I need it. At the first meeting with Emily, one of the Linkcare workers from Sharecare came with me to Emily's house to meet Emily and her family. There were some forms to fill in about insurance, risk assessments, and so on. Every child is different, whether they have disabilities or not, so the risk assessment gave me an idea of what Emily would find hard or what she would be like in certain situations, based on past experience.

The first time I took Emily out into Stockport, I had only met her once before and therefore did not know her very well. A Linkcare worker from Sharecare, Kate, came into Stockport town for the time I was supporting Emily. Kate did not stay with us, but it was reassuring to know that I could just ring her mobile if I had any problems. Kate also met us at the end of the session to check everything had gone well.

I very much enjoy working with Emily, especially as I know it is making such a positive difference to her and her family. Just a few hours away from her mum each week gives Emily the independence she craves and allows her to have fun, while being under the supervision of someone a little older. This gives her mum peace of mind that Emily will be safe. While Emily and I are out, Emily's mum has a few hours to do something she wants to do, or spend the time looking after the baby, so Emily's time with me is also of benefit to the rest of the family. I think that being only four years older than Emily is an advantage in this particular situation, as she is at an age where she doesn't want to be going out with adults any more and prefers the company of other young people. I think that this enables me to relate to Emily a little better than if I were much older than her; I am also able to understand her better, being not much older than her, and hopefully know what she would enjoy.

The professional shadow: a personal assistant's account

Antony Clayton

I have worked in the health care profession for 14 years both in the UK and abroad. During that time I have worked with many disabled people and supporting agencies. Personally I believe that being a personal assistant is a profession rather than a job and for that reason I spent four years gaining a Bachelor of Arts degree in social studies. This, combined with up-to-date first aid, manual handling, health and safety certificates plus my commitment to professional development, allows me to offer a quality service and request a wage that reflects my abilities. I have always struggled to make certain sections of the health care profession believe that carers should be treated and trained as professionals, although thankfully things are beginning to change for the better. The days of those who believe that the only qualification for being a carer is to have brought up your own children are numbered! I recognise that parenthood is a difficult occupation, but there is a world of difference between offering services to a broad-based group with a variety of needs and making the personal choices and decisions which go toward shaping a family.

Nearly four years ago I answered an advertisement, which requested the services of a personal assistant to support a young disabled man. I answered that ad and began the familiar process to me of understanding the individual and his family and then beginning to help them to create structures in their lives that would allow for their greater independence. Although I am not focusing here on the specifics of my 'manager' and his family, it is worth noting that the man in question, with support, has now created a successful business and an independent life of his choosing. Similarly, family members have helped to create something for their son which will hopefully last beyond their lives. Social services, supporting agencies and the family all agree that direct payments have been a success in this case.

The question is: what is it like to be part of that successful team? The success of my manager and his business belie the fact that a lot of patience, hard work, listening and routine work has had to go on in the last four years for us to reach this success. However, I never once believed that I was setting my employer up to fail. My experience allowed me to recognise his potential and my qualifications have allowed me to draw it out and help him to develop himself as a credible member of the workforce and an individual with real choices. This is the beauty of being a personal assistant with professional 'tools'.

I have been disappointed with the support that my employer and his family have received from supporting agencies and wonder at times what would have happened had I not had management experience with which to teach my boss how to be my boss! It seems strange to me that, while most of us learn the hard rules of managing a team over many long years, direct payments users, or at least the ones that I have had contact with, are expected to have this knowledge almost instantly. I have heard some horror stories in the last four years from friends and colleagues who have seen unscrupulous personal assistants matched up with inexperienced managers. I *am* hopeful that these are isolated incidences but it does reinforce my idea that personal assistants and carers should be professionally screened before they are allowed near vulnerable people, especially now that direct payments are available for children with disabilities.

Being a personal assistant is a bit like being a shadow in as much as you have to learn to move with your client while not blocking the sun from their face. Your job is not 'to steal their thunder' but rather to allow them to build the confidence that they need to live their lives the way they want to. If that means leaning on you then it should be managed with dignity and with as few people watching as necessary. A colleague of mine calls this 'invisible support'; I call it professional care.

Thoughts of a personal assistant

Christine Erskine

I have always been interested in helping youngsters with learning difficulties and, although it has never been my full-time job, I have known quite a few over the years. I was lucky enough to be recommended by a local contact as a possible personal assistant for a young man whose family now has direct payments.

Having just retired from running my own commercial business I was not sure I wanted to take on further commitment but I cautiously agreed to give it a go. How glad I am that I did. I have been a part-time personal assistant to Michael (not his real name) for a year now and I love it.

For the first few meetings I went to Michael's house to get to know him and his family. I also accompanied his mother on outings and met the other personal assistant. Finally, I started to work with Michael and have never looked back. Our regular time started as three hours on a Saturday, with two of us taking him to a trampoline centre, followed by lunch out. This has now been our pattern for the last year. As we have all got to know each other better, confidence all round has increased. We now spend four hours out on Saturdays and have expanded to a few extra hours during the week, whenever convenient. I now take Michael out on my own to any suitable local activities, and he comes visiting to my home for a meal.

Michael's family have a professional administrative organisation to help and give advice on such matters as interviews, contracts, salaries and holiday pay, and so on. They run and recommend courses such as: 'Becoming a Personal Assistant', 'Health and Safety', 'Lifting and Handling' and 'First Aid', for which we were paid our usual hourly rate. Michael's mother and his two personal assistants attended together and this helped us bond as a team, as well as meet other personal assistants. It is important not to feel isolated, just because of working in a one-to-one situation, and the knowledge gained on these courses has given us confidence in what we are doing.

Although Michael employs me, a company manages all finances. We fill in time sheets and our salaries are paid directly into the bank. I chose to be employed and receive holiday pay, (which is calculated by the company), while my colleague chose to be self-employed. There is no problem in this and the financial process is excellent.

The matching of client and personal assistant is very important as both people need to be comfortable together but also enjoy the same sort of activities. I am far too old for disco dancing and football matches and, as Michael is a wheelchair user, he gets pleasure from a musical sing-song, a ride in the car or a walk to feed the ducks, all of which I enjoy as well. In time, Michael will also need a younger personal assistant who is happy to join in younger activities, so expanding his experiences.

Looking to the future, when Michael leaves school and needs more assistance, I have already learnt that two or three regular sessions a week is sufficient for me as I have grandchildren of my own and a full social life. At present I really enjoy my time with Michael and would never want to feel it was a chore. He complements my life and I hope I complement his.

"Not just an assistant, but also a friend"

Lyn Tidder

I decided to have a complete career change five years ago, after doing the same job for 35 years. I went for an interview as a carer in a home for elderly people. I loved the work; most of the elderly people were very grateful for the help that they were given. The shock came when I saw and heard how some of the staff treated them. There seemed very little respect or dignity given to these people who had once been young and independent themselves, and through no limit of their own were old, and could not manage a lot of daily tasks unassisted. Needless to say I only stayed for three months.

One day I went to the job centre. Looking through jobs vacant I found a vacancy for a personal assistant for a disabled gentleman. Not quite knowing what the job would entail, I phoned up to find out a bit more about it. An interview was arranged.

Feeling very nervous I knocked on the door. I was greeted by the disabled man's wife. I was offered a drink and introduced to him and his other personal assistant. I was told that I would be employed to assist with all aspects of his daily life. This would include showering, dressing, cooking, cleaning (his wife was out at work all day). It also meant helping him in his work, which was mostly done at home, although he did go to a lot of meetings. We would also go shopping and visit his friends.

As time went by I started to understand the role of a personal assistant rather than being a carer. When I was working with elderly people in a care home they often got help when the carer had time. This often meant waiting to get up or go to bed, among other things. Working as a personal assistant means that you are working for one person, you are employed by them to do things when they want to and how they want it done. They also choose who they want to do it for them.

Disabled people may have two personal assistants, working on a job-share basis. This way, time off for holidays and sickness could easily be covered by the other personal assistant, rather than agency staff. I worked three days one week and four days the next. This could vary according to the disabled person's needs. It is important to have a good working relationship with the other personal assistant as you would sometimes be working together on the same day. Also to put things away in the same places so that things could be found and used easily. Because our personalities were so different, he would sometimes arrange his days according to which one of us was working.

The role of a personal assistant is not just to be an assistant. It is also to be a friend and confidant, to give support and respect. There were times that I was asked to do things that I may do differently myself, but when you are in someone else's home you do things the way that person has asked for them to be done, and in some cases this could mean having respect for somebody's religion and culture – all the time having respect for their home, their family and belongings.

I have learned a lot being a personal assistant. Not only human rights and such things, but also that disabled people can live independent lives. Independence does not mean being able to do things yourself (after all, don't we all pay people to do things for us?). Independence is having choice and control over your own life. The choice to do what you want, when you want to do it and how you would like it done. Why spend an hour or more trying to get dressed, then because you are so tired you haven't got the strength or energy to do the things that you want to do?

Employed as a personal assistant I had only one person to please; employed in a care home I had lots of people to keep happy. I do not work any more, but if I did I would go back to being a personal assistant. It is a very worthwhile job, I know, I was with him for three-and-a-half years.

My job as a personal assistant

Hilary Sparkes

I have been working as a personal assistant for just over a year now. The client that I work for is a 25-year-old lady who has a severe learning disability. She lives in her own house on a small housing development in a small Essex town. She needs 24-hour care seven days a week, and I am part of a small team that cares for her. I am one of three ladies who are employed on a direct payments basis; the other hours are covered by a care provider who supplies staff on a full-time basis.

I work on my own. I work evenings and do sleep-ins, with the occasional day shift when needed. My previous care experience is wide ranging. I have worked with older people, with people who have terminal illness, and also for Mencap for several years. I have an NVQ level III in care and have also attended many training courses over the years, including first aid and Makaton.

I feel that my role is one of great responsibility: because I work on my own I am in a position of great trust. There are many positives about my job. It is a one-to-one service, which is always a positive. The service is totally client-focused; communication is good with care planning followed and precise.

My client's parents are very much involved in the day-to-day running of the house and I feel that I have a good relationship with them. They are supportive employers but they have not had the courses and training that I have had, so they see care as more personal to my client, rather than the professional approach, which can lead to dilemmas regarding age-appropriate behaviour and so on.

Because I work on my own I do at times feel vulnerable. I do not have the structure of a large organisation to protect me. I do not have a complaints procedure that I can refer to. I do not have supervision or career development meetings. I have in effect stepped off the career path, but this is not in any way a negative statement as it was very much my choice to have a change and I enjoy what I am doing.

There is a great difference from working with someone who has a physical impairment who needs a personal assistant to help them with day-to-day living, who is able to direct the personal assistant and tell them exactly what they want compared to the role that I have, which I feel is very specialised and does need staff who are totally trustworthy and trained to a good standard. I do at times wonder if this is the way forward for care in the community: who is going to police the system? I feel that both clients and staff are vulnerable and, as care has never had a very high profile and wages remain low and the job is seen as not having status and professionalism, I just wonder what the future will be.

Section 4
Reporting from the field

TEN

Implementing direct payments: a support organisation perspective

Etienne d'Aboville

The legislation to enable direct payments as an alternative to service provision was a prize long fought for by disabled people and their organisations during the 1980s and 1990s. Nearly 10 years after the initial permissive legislation was introduced, how has the actual implementation of direct payments been experienced in practice? This chapter briefly reflects on some of the key issues from the perspective of an organisation run by and for disabled people.

First, a little background information. Glasgow Centre for Inclusive Living (GCIL) is a user-controlled organisation committed to promoting inclusive living by assisting disabled people to challenge barriers and make informed choices. Established in 1996 with a remit initially to support disabled people using indirect payments, GCIL now provides a range of inclusive living support, training, housing and employment services. With a total staff of around 30 and an annual turnover of over £950,000, GCIL is a genuinely user-led organisation – three quarters of the staff and directors are disabled people.

In 2004 GCIL secured the contract with Glasgow social work department to provide a support service to disabled people and others in Glasgow in receipt of direct payments. This supplemented existing contracts with two adjoining local authorities to act as an interim direct payments support organisation and to develop local user-led alternatives.

By and large the implementation of direct payments in Scotland has been much slower and more difficult to achieve than appears to be the case south of the border (see Witcher et al (2000); Pearson (2004); and Pearson in Chapter Three of this book). GCIL's own experience certainly bears this out. Until recently, the emphasis in Glasgow has been on the indirect scheme which supported around 100 disabled people, but which has effectively remained frozen since 1996. Apart from a relatively small-scale pilot project with approximately 15 participants, which began in 2000, no new direct payments were issued in Glasgow until 2004. This, it must be remembered, despite the introduction of permissive legislation as long ago as 1997 and despite the availability of an existing user-led support organisation – GCIL (formerly the Centre for Independent Living in Glasgow) – which was ready, willing and able to provide the necessary support.

The reasons for this are open to a variety of interpretations. Some might highlight the severe pressure on social work budgets around that time and the lack of any bridging finance from the Scottish Executive. Others of a more cynical bent might point rather to an entrenched political and organisational culture fundamentally committed to public sector provision and inherently unenthusiastic about the prospect of giving up power and control to service users.

Either way, when the legislative imperative did finally bite, all was by no means plain sailing. Contract negotiations took around 12 months to conclude. The crux of the problem lay in the differing priorities and expectations of the commissioners (the social work department) and the prospective provider (GCIL). For GCIL, after several years of either static or reduced grant funding, the main concern was to secure stable, long-term funding for the organisation as a whole. This meant recognising and valuing the broader role of the CIL as a focus for user involvement and, effectively, community development among disabled people. This would enable the organisation:

- to continue to identify and respond to perceived gaps in services, as it has done, for example in developing new housing and employment services;
- to take on specific time-limited projects such as developing an accessible transport strategy for the city;
- to support the development of a variety of local and national user-led initiatives; and
- to build disabled people's capacity to contribute to the planning process.

Indeed, this had been the original vision when first funded. For the social work department, however, the priority was simply to commission a specific service – support for people using direct payments – in response to a specific legislative requirement. Existing commissioning structures and procedures did not lend themselves well to GCIL's aspirations, although, fortunately, an acceptable compromise was reached in the end.

It could be argued that this tension within the commissioning process reflects a wider problem in respect of the implementation of direct payments generally. The focus of many initiatives seems to be on implementing direct payments almost for their own sake rather than on exploring the many ways disabled people can be empowered to develop flexible forms of support and take control of their lives – an obsession with process, perhaps, at the expense of purpose.

As we have noted, having an existing user-led organisation of disabled people with the capacity to provide support is no guarantee of the speedy implementation of direct payments. However, the lack of such an infrastructure can clearly act as a barrier. The temptation for some authorities in this position is to go for the quick fix and either fund an existing voluntary sector organisation – but one which is not accountable to service users – or simply to provide support 'in-house'. Neither of these options is likely to promote the development of a genuinely empowering service model as envisaged when direct payments were first conceived and pioneered by disabled people themselves. In practice, they may just lead to 'more of the same', with disabled people the all-too-often passive recipients of services rather than being active agents in taking control of their own lives. Indeed, either option may actively inhibit the development of more accountable alternatives later on.

There is clearly an enormous tension between the desire to take advantage of the benefits direct payments have to offer and the need to ensure that the way they are implemented is properly accountable and genuinely empowering. There are no easy answers. At the very least, however, the Scottish Executive should employ an independent living framework in evaluating the *quality* of any given scheme, rather than merely focusing on the number of individuals receiving direct payments.

The commissioning process and the need to be accountable to service users raise a further thorny issue for disabled people's organisations. As direct payments are rolled out to a wider range of community care service users, such as asylum seekers or people fleeing domestic violence, then mechanisms to involve service users will have to adjust accordingly. Because new support organisations tend to be commissioned on the basis of supporting direct payments for all service users, rather than supporting independent living for disabled people, it may be harder than before for them to exist as, or develop into, organisations *of* disabled people, for example CILs. GCIL's current position is that it will provide a service to a wider range of direct payments recipients and encourage participation through a stakeholders' forum, but it will not compromise disabled people's ultimate control over the organisation. Should this arrangement no longer be sustainable, for instance if the number of non-disabled service users were to grow dramatically, then GCIL would work towards assisting those service users to establish their own support systems.

Fortunately, the number of direct payments made in Glasgow has now started to rise (there were approximately 40 in place in January 2005, with a further 30 or so in the pipeline), and the infrastructure is now set up to ensure that quality is not sacrificed for the sake of quantity. Clearly, there are a number of challenges ahead for the social work department and support organisations alike. There are training and assessment issues to address and, for support organisations, there are potential tensions between service delivery, advocacy and campaigning roles.

This brief chapter has focused on some of the key issues facing disabled people's organisations as they take on the task of supporting the implementation of direct payments. Although the emphasis has been on problem areas, we should not lose sight of the fact that the implementation of direct payments, however tardy, still offers disabled people and others unparalleled opportunities to improve the choice and control they have over the support they need, and ultimately their quality of life. It is important that disabled people's own organisations continue to play a key role in enabling that to happen.

References

Pearson, C. (2004) 'Keeping the cash under control: what's the problem with direct payments in Scotland?', *Disability and Society*, vol 19, no 1, pp 3-14.

Witcher, S., Stalker, K., Roadburg, M. and Jones, C. (2000) *Direct payments: The impact of choice and control for disabled people*, Edinburgh: The Scottish Executive Central Research Unit.

ELEVEN

The Direct Payments Development Fund

Frances Hasler

Background

The Direct Payments Development Fund is £9 million of Department of Health (DH) money, allocated over three years, for the purpose of improving the take-up of direct payments, through encouraging investment in direct payments support services.

Unlike other special funds set up to support policy initiatives (the Carers Grant, for example) it was decided to spend it through grant aid to voluntary organisations, rather than allocating directly to local authorities. To qualify for the grant, organisations had to show they were working in partnership with their local authority, and that there was a local implementation plan for direct payments. Crucially, given the short-term nature of the funding, they also had to have an exit strategy.

The DH hoped this would enable voluntary organisations to play a significant role in the development and promotion of direct payments.

It decided to make the grants in two rounds, giving each project 18 months' worth of funding. A key condition of funding was that the organisation had the commitment of its local authority, to support the project, and work in partnership on it.

Projects had to show they had a workable, innovative plan to increase take-up, either for all users or for a selected group. They had to say how they would promote the project and disseminate its findings, and how they would work with a local multi-agency implementation group.

The grants

Before grant making to local organisations started, a single national grant was made, to the National Centre for Independent Living (NCIL), of £280,000 for each of three years. One of the conditions of this grant was that NCIL would evaluate the other projects supported by the Fund.

In round one, 43 grants were made. They ranged in size: the largest single grant was to the Rowan Organisation (£400,574) for work in eight authorities. There were 19 grants of just over £100,000, including three to one organisation, Choices. Of the others, the smallest grant was £40,408.

Round one grants ran from September 2003 to March 2005. It was decided to overlap the grants for round one and round two, starting round two projects in September 2004, so that they would be finished by the end of March 2006.

In round two, 42 grants were awarded. The largest, to Penderels Trust (£374,086) was for work in nine authorities. The smallest grant was £55,180. There were 23 grants under £100,000 and 17 grants just over this amount (most in the region of £106,000). Three organisations, the National Development Team, the Shaw Trust and Choices, received more than one grant, and six Age Concern groups received a grant.

Steering group

As a support to the work of the fund, the DH created a steering group. This group comprised significant contacts in government and the voluntary sector. It was chaired by the chief executive of the independent think tank, the King's Fund. The aim was not only for the steering group to advise the DH, but also to become 'champions' of direct payments in their own organisations.

The projects

In round one, more than a third of the grants were made to general projects, not targeting a specific group. Of the other successful projects, several targeted people with learning difficulties, mental health service users, older people and 'under-represented' groups. Just three targeted black and minority ethnic users, two focused on children and young people, two on carers and one on blind people.

The methods were varied, too. All projects included some plans for information, half were planning training, nearly a quarter were offering peer support and the same number were planning some sort of personal assistant register or other work on personal assistant recruitment. Eight projects were planning to introduce a payroll service; seven were focused on advocacy. Three were examining the barriers to direct payments use.

In round two, the projects were even more varied. Six specifically targeted older people, 13 targeted a range of 'under-represented groups'. Four focused on people with learning difficulties. None was solely targeted on black and minority ethnic disabled people, although two had this as part of their focus. Five targeted children or young people, and one specifically targeted disabled parents among a range of groups. Three were aimed at carers. One was focused on deaf-blind people.

A new theme for round two was brokerage, with seven projects mentioning brokerage or circles of support. Five planned to increase the capacity of independent living organisations. Five were working on personal assistant recruitment or personal assistant career development. Two included direct payments for equipment as part of their focus.

There was a range of imaginative ideas, including user cooperatives, peer mentoring and electronic tools for users.

External evaluation

The Personal Social Services Research Unit (PSSRU), based at London School of Economics and Political Science, was chosen to provide an overarching evaluation of the Fund. (This was in addition to the evaluation of individual projects, being carried out by NCIL.) The PSSRU role was to examine how well the Fund had met its objective of increasing take-up and whether the method of distributing development money via the voluntary sector had succeeded. It looked in detail at how take-up was being extended among older people, black and minority ethnic people, and mental health service users. At the time of writing (late 2004) this work is ongoing.

NCIL evaluation

That NCIL would undertake an evaluation as part of its core funding was agreed before any grants had been made, indeed, before the number of grants to be made had been decided. The methodology of the evaluation had therefore to be evolved to suit the available resources. NCIL decided to work in three ways – e-mailed questionnaires to organisations; one-off visits to projects; and national or regional meetings for funded projects, where experience could be shared. A website forum for projects, where queries could be shared, was also set up.

Although, like the PSSRU evaluation, this work is ongoing, there have been some tentative findings, which are now set out.

Small is beautiful

The larger projects had more difficulty than the smaller ones in getting going. One, which required some matching funding, never got started. So, one suggestion from the evaluation might be that where funding is short term, just 18 months, smaller projects are preferable.

Some of the smaller projects had very well-designed methods, and had already identified staff for the work before the project began. They were confident of reaching their targets within the allotted time, and already knew what they would do to continue the work after the project ended.

... but short is not always best

Eighteen months is quite short for a development project. Where new staff had to be recruited, they often took several months to settle in, as they needed to learn about direct payments before going out to users. Staff from a number of projects were dismayed that they were not able to apply for a second tranche of money in round two.

Plans change

Some projects had to redesign their methods, when initial recruitment failed. This involved splitting jobs, using secondments, using partner agencies, or extending the life of the project. It was noticeable that all the organisations produced revised plans very quickly and effectively.

... but practitioners change slowly

A number of projects reported that their biggest barrier had been the unwillingness of care management staff to make referrals for direct payments. This was particularly a problem in projects focusing on mental health. The way projects tackled this was to find ways of approaching users directly, without the intervention of care managers.

Perhaps in the light of this, some of the projects in round two were specifically focusing on training care managers.

Councils do not always understand the word 'partnership'

Although local authorities had to sign up to support the project in order for it to be funded, their actual support for the work was highly variable. Some were enthusiastic and helpful, some neglectful, and a handful positively unhelpful. One council was failing to invite the funded project to its local direct payments implementation group. Another failed to send any representation to the project steering group. In a number of places, plans to continue the project at the end of the grant period were hazy, with the council not making any firm commitments. This contrasted with a few where the council had pledged (and identified) funding to keep the project going after the Development Fund money ran out.

... and do not adapt their budgets to facilitate direct payments

A number of older people's projects reported difficulties in getting referrals, because the local authority provision was tied up in block contracts, and care management staff would simply say they had 'no money' for direct payments. The guidance makes clear that this is not an acceptable excuse, but some projects encountered it nonetheless.

Working with sketches, not maps ...

A number of projects are looking at innovative ways of supporting people to manage direct payments, including trusts, cooperatives and circles of support. Many have appealed for information on these via the NCIL website forum, but little has been forthcoming. A finding from the NCIL, DH-funded 'Wider Options' project is that, although the potential of these methods is widely acknowledged, there is very little actual use of them. So projects are truly innovating, and having to bear the risk and responsibility associated with that.

... and getting conflicting directions

Some personal assistant register projects had encountered difficulty over the legal status of what they were doing. The Care Standards Commission (now the Commission for Social Care Inspection (CSCI)) had given unhelpful and inconsistent advice about the requirements to register one project as an agency. Although this was subsequently sorted out, it delayed the start of the project.

Local implementation groups

Although the existence of a local implementation group (LIG) was expected by the DH, not every project had one. Where such groups did exist, most projects found them very helpful. They were a useful mechanism for formalising user input. They also served as a way of coordinating work on direct payments across the council. Most projects reported that their LIG would be strengthened by more input from the local voluntary sector. Some also wanted more input from certain social work teams, where there was felt to be a lack of engagement with direct payments.

Peer outreach works

A number of projects were targeting 'under-represented' groups. Several reported difficulty in reaching black and minority ethnic users. In contrast, some had recruited outreach workers with backgrounds in the target communities, who spoke the community languages. In these areas, take-up from minority ethnic users was growing quite fast.

Some projects used people with learning difficulties as part of the outreach team; often this involved some sort of drama presentation as a way of explaining about direct payments. Although this succeeded in generating enthusiasm for direct payments, projects reported delays in getting formal referrals for people with learning difficulties.

One project had recruited an older disabled person to act as outreach worker. This was proving very successful, not just in spreading the word about direct payments, but also in raising awareness about independent living for older people in general.

It's about independent living

The projects reporting the biggest success were all in organisations that identified themselves as user led, and had a pre-existing commitment to independent living. Some projects run by more traditional voluntary sector organisations were having difficulties. In one, just one new direct payments user had come on to the scheme, after 12 months of work.

... and good quality support

Another success factor for projects was being based in an organisation where other colleagues supported the work. For example, some projects worked in tandem with their organisation's information team, providing roadshows, information fairs and similar initiatives. This helped to maximise the impact of the project.

A good way to give away money?

For many projects supported by the Fund, this was their first experience of using the DH's 'section 64' funding. A few expressed surprise at the comparatively 'hands-off' approach of the DH compared to local authority grant makers. This has good aspects – there is no monitoring for its own sake: once the grant has been agreed, paperwork is kept to a minimum. There are downsides, too. The DH does not have the same stake in the local organisation as a local authority does, and some groups felt that there is not the same opportunity to build relationships with the funder as exists at local level. This was not true for all groups; some had been in regular contact with DH staff.

A good way to invest money?

It is clear that the dozens of projects supported by the Fund have been making generally good use of the money. This funding has been completely transparent. Projects have been proud to say how they are spending the money. (This might be contrasted with some previous government grants to local authorities, in particular the Independent Living Transfer money, where users sometimes asked in vain to find out where the funds had gone.) Even where projects are not meeting all of their targets, they are adding to our store of knowledge about good and bad practice on direct payments. The Fund has reached 109 local authorities across England (some projects work in more than one local authority area).

Without wishing to pre-empt the findings of the PSSRU evaluation, the Fund seems to be a good way of investing public money to support direct payments. The voluntary sector, in particular the user-led part of the sector, has risen to the challenge of the Fund.

A good way to support grant making?

The creation of a steering group to oversee the fund has had mixed success. Participation in the group has been variable and the extent to which individual members felt themselves to be 'champions' of direct payments is hard to gauge. Some, who were already enthusiasts, have been able to use the group as a networking opportunity. Members of the group helped to choose the evaluation consultants. But the group has had no influence over which projects got funded.

A good way to achieve independent living?

The NCIL evaluation has been asking the projects to assess whether direct payments have resulted in independent living outcomes for the participants. This has been hard to track, as it involves individual interviews with users, a time-consuming process. Some projects had given considerable thought to independent living outcomes. One reported that they had spent several months renegotiating existing direct payments packages, to make them more focused on independent living, before moving on to recruiting new users. Another is working to empower users to take over management of the support scheme.

The next steps

NCIL is continuing to evaluate the Fund, and continuing to hold networking events for projects. It has appointed a lead consultant to coordinate the work. NCIL plans to visit most of the projects. The Fund officially ends in March 2006. This is also the date at which NCIL's current core funding expires. It is hoped that a final report will be ready some time in 2006.

By then, we will know how many of the local authorities involved have picked up the project funding and enabled the work to continue. We will know the total of new users coming on to direct payments in the project areas. We will have gathered the learning on what worked and what did not work. It should all help to make direct payments a real option for more people.

Conclusion

The Direct Payments Development Fund is small beer compared to some other government initiatives for involving the voluntary sector, notably Futurebuilders (an investment fund to support the infrastructure of the voluntary sector. But it does represent a large investment in direct payments support organisations. At the time of writing, the Fund is just over halfway through its life, so making firm judgements on its success is a speculative activity. There are, however, some conclusions that can be made from experience to date.

The first is that the voluntary sector and in particular user-controlled organisations have a major role to play in the future expansion of direct payments. This is hardly surprising, given that it was user-controlled organisations which pioneered and campaigned for direct payments.

The learning from the Fund is mixed. It has plugged gaps in some places, for example setting up payroll schemes or peer support groups. For some places, it has allowed a long-cherished project to be implemented – advocacy in Sussex, a personal assistants register in Hull, and so on. The learning in these cases is mainly about applying what we already know, but doing it better. There have been places where work has been truly innovative, for example the approach to paying for the support scheme trialled in the Wirral. But much of what feels 'new' is based on expanding a small-scale idea (for example, circles of support, trusts) into a more organised system.

A frustration with the Fund has been the difficulty of sharing the learning effectively. Schemes where work is going well are happy to talk about it. But schemes where progress is slow are understandably reluctant to advertise the fact. And, as the national body charged with synthesising the learning, NCIL (which is itself a very small agency) has been stretched by the demands of trying to support and to track more than 80 projects at the same time as carrying out its own programme of work.

The Fund has highlighted the state of partnership arrangements between local councils and voluntary organisations. The competition model applied in tendering for support contracts does not always lend itself to the most productive working relationships. The hope that the Fund would foster better partnerships was in part frustrated by the speed with which the first round of grants was made. In some areas, the Fund was able to cement partnership arrangements, in others rather hasty and weak commitments were made.

Despite difficulties, the Fund has made a real contribution to the development of direct payments support. It has shown once again the key role played by disabled people's independent living organisations. It has also shown up the difficulty of implementing good practice without real commitment within the local authority. Peer support, outreach, payroll services, advocacy, help with recruiting staff, are all obvious and necessary parts of direct payments support. Without them, the numbers of those attracted to direct payments will not grow. The Fund has underlined what many veterans of independent living already knew. The hope for the future is that this knowledge becomes accepted wisdom, as a result of the Development Fund.

TWELVE

An experience of the Direct Payments Development Fund

Rob Wilson and Kathryn Gilbert

In July 2003 the Rowan Organisation was awarded a grant of £400,574 from the Direct Payments Development Fund. On the face of it this was a major achievement and at the time was very exciting for the organisation, giving the opportunity for funding a major project in the field of direct payments. However, gift horses should always be looked in the mouth, and this is an opportunity to consider some of the issues to emerge out of our experience of bidding for funding, setting up the project and working in partnership to increase the use of direct payments as a means of empowering disabled people.

The Rowan Organisation is an organisation of disabled people, which has been providing direct payments support services since direct payments were introduced in 1997. Prior to that it had supported the use of indirect or third party payments (the pre-runner to direct payments) in a local authority in the Midlands since the early 1990s. The initial development of a third party payment scheme came about because disabled people in the area were desperate to find an alternative to the inflexible and often unreliable services that were their experience at that time. The Rowan Organisation now provides direct payments support to 13 local authorities nationally, including three in Wales, and supports nearly 2,000 direct payments users, employing over 70 independent living advisors. In addition to the support provided directly by the advisors, the organisation also provides a national information service and a comprehensive payroll or salary service to direct payments users.

Bidding for funding

At the end of April 2003 the Department of Health (DH) published its criteria for applications to the Direct Payments Development Fund. A fund of £9 million, spread over three years, had been anticipated for almost 12 months and was seen as offering the potential for moving direct payments forward quite significantly. The voluntary sector was aware that the funding was targeted at them as lead agencies and there was a great deal of excitement at the potential of running major projects with secure funding for at least three years. Local authorities were keen to be involved as partners, because this represented the first new money to be made available since the introduction of direct payments six years before. However, the structure of the funding was not quite as anticipated and at the launch the fund was split into two rounds of £4.5 million each, for projects of 18 months.

The whole complexion of the nature of bids had to change quite dramatically, since it was now apparent that the fund could not be used to bankroll support schemes as many local authorities had anticipated. It was made clear that support to direct payments users was the responsibility of the local authorities and that the new funding was specifically to stimulate and increase the uptake. There was still, however, a great deal of pressure on organisations such as ourselves to submit bids so that the local authorities could get their share of the cash. This was, after all, still a sizeable amount of money and, while it may not have been intended, there was a sense of expectation that, as the lead partners, we would be able to put together a successful bid.

This then was the start of our problems: we worked with 10 local authorities in England and the majority expected us to make a bid in partnership with them. The dilemma for us was that we could not agree to submit a bid with one local authority and refuse others without risking upsetting them, always a problem for voluntary organisations, particularly with the present contract culture and the pressures on local authority budgets. It was also clear that the DH wanted to spread the funding around and had limited bids to £120,000 for the 18-month period and it was therefore unlikely that multiple bids would be successful. Our problems were compounded by the very short timescales for submissions, with the closing date being mid-June 2003, giving around six weeks. The thought of preparing up to 10 bids within that timescale was, to say the least, daunting. In the end we identified what we considered at the time to be the perfect compromise: one large bid in partnership with all the interested local authorities with which we worked. At this stage, with the benefit of hindsight, the phrase 'fools rush in …' springs to mind. Eight of the local authorities that we worked with were interested in a partnership bid and we agreed to ask the DH to consider a submission on that basis.

Surprisingly, the DH agreed that we could submit a collective bid as if it was eight individual bids. This meant that we could bid for up to eight times the individual funding limit of £120,000, or £960,000 in total. However, as always, there was a downside to this because it took the DH four weeks to make a decision, which left only two weeks to complete the application.

From our own observations of the use of direct payments, it was clear to us that certain groups of potential users of direct payments were substantially under-represented in the uptake. These were: people with learning difficulties; people with mental health problems; older people; children and young people; and people from black and minority ethnic communities. The statistics collected by the DH annually confirmed this as being the case and the aim of the project that was formulated was to stimulate the use of direct payments by these groups.

The main focus of the project was to be the identification of the barriers that limited the take-up of direct payments. The project was to be run on an action research basis, with the intention of enabling potential service users to find their own solutions to the problems that they encountered. This was then to be written up as practice guidance so that the experiences and solutions identified could be shared across all direct payments schemes. It was recognised right from the start that some of the people who we would be working with would require support in order to be fully included in the process of consultation, and an element of the bid was for specific training to be provided particularly for people with a learning difficulty. The need to provide information in fully accessible formats and languages was also recognised and was part of the strategy for making this project fully inclusive.

In addition, it was noted that it was becoming increasingly difficult for direct payments users to recruit suitable personal assistants, particularly in areas where the direct payments schemes were most successful and the available pool of potential employees was rapidly being used up. Anecdotal evidence suggested that, because there were no recognised qualifications for personal assistants or a potential career structure, being a personal assistant was not considered in the same way as other employment opportunities. It is not promoted as a job through colleges or by career advisors and therefore was not gaining credibility despite being a massively expanding employment market. The project would therefore also look at the means of promoting the role of personal assistants as a real and positive career opportunity.

The overall aims and objectives of the project were listed as:

- to increase access for under-represented groups;

- to identify the barriers which are currently limiting access to direct payments for some groups of potential service users;
- to create regional/national liaison in pursuit of best practice for direct payments users, local authorities and other organisations;
- to create local, regional and national training directories to improve employer/employee access to high quality training, thus improving employers' ability to offer competitive development opportunities to staff and increasing the pool of competent potential employees;
- to work in partnership with our existing information service, to consult with users and to develop appropriate strategies that would improve access to information;
- to ensure that information is available in formats that are fully accessible to all potential service users;
- to encourage proactively local, regional and national peer support groups for new and existing users;
- to enhance the training and development of local authority staff in recognition of their 'gatekeeper' status.

The practicalities of completing the application with eight partner local authorities, which were spread all over the country, were immense and the letters of agreement and final copies of the submission were still being emailed and faxed backwards and forwards at 5pm on the evening before the deadline. Thank goodness for courier services and fast motorcycles.

The final proposal was for two project teams, one to work in the north and one in the south of the country. Each project team would have a development worker for each of the target groups and an additional training and development worker, with an overall project manager who would manage both teams. The final bid amounted to £778,664.99, well within the budget limits that had been set, and all we had to do was wait.

The results of the first round of bids were announced on 31 July 2003 and our award of £400,500 looked very impressive, being nearly 10% of the total fund. Not surprisingly we were initially very pleased with ourselves until we stopped to consider that we had to reduce the original budget by over 45%. This was coupled with the added complication that there was an expectation that the projects would commence in September 2003.

To say the least, there was a very hurried re-costing of the original submission and the outcome was that the initial proposal for two teams was rapidly reduced to one. This had to be re-submitted to the DH and the implications considered by the partnership. What was eventually agreed was that there would be a single team that would not work with all the local authorities, but each team member would work with four of the eight, with each local authority specifying which three priorities they would have for their area. The results of the research and the practice guidance would still be available to be shared and so the benefits to the partners were not necessarily reduced overall. We also managed to convince the DH that January 2004 was a more realistic starting date, given the need for recruitment and so forth, and that it had been October 2003 before the details were finalised.

So a brief view from the horse's mouth reveals that from the anticipated starting point of £9 million over three years the final situation was that we had half the number of staff to do the same amount of work in half the length of time with half the budget that we had hoped for. For anyone who has worked in the voluntary sector for any length of time this will be very familiar territory and, as they say, 'the impossible we can do at once but miracles may take a little longer'. This then was the start of the project in earnest but the delivery of this project has been a revelation in more ways than one.

Setting up the project

A great many lessons have been learnt throughout each stage of the project for both the Rowan Organisation and for the partner local authorities. Even before the project team was recruited, there was evidence of the gap between the vision that we had crafted into the bid and the reality of delivering. To some extent, we knew from previous experience that this gap would exist but had not anticipated the nature of some of the issues. The adverts for development workers were placed but the response was surprisingly low. Indeed, throughout the life of the project we have battled with at least one vacancy, which has clearly had a major impact on the workload and capacity of the project manager who has had to absorb the unallocated workload. There is work still to be done on exploring the reasons for these posts not being filled, but it is likely that the temporary nature of the contracts was a contributing factor. Due to the tight timescales of the project, we needed to find specialists in both direct payments and a particular service user group (so they could hit the ground running, as there was so little time available for 'catch-up training'), which is a very small pond in which to be fishing in a very short space of time!

After the initial (costly) recruitment round, we decided that salary was another of the contributing factors to the poor response rate. We went back to the DH and sought agreement to increase the salary beyond the scale in the original bid. Of course, the increase had to be offset somewhere, and the compromise was to drop one of the posts (service development worker for personal assistant training and development) and amalgamate the unallocated work into the project manager role.

The vacancy issue was further compounded by successfully recruiting people who later chose to leave the project: one for personal reasons; one who was promoted internally within the organisation (great for the individual and the Rowan, but not such good news for the project!); and one who did not fulfil the contractual requirements of the post. This led to further delay, spiralling recruitment/advertising costs (from an already overstretched budget) and yet more time invested in inducting new team members.

Covering these gaps has led to the core team working very long hours and finding it almost impossible to claw back the time they are entitled to. This additionally created a difficult management situation for the Rowan Organisation in ensuring that our commitment to health and safety could be balanced with the needs of the project. We have been incredibly fortunate to find a team of committed and dedicated people who have worked tirelessly to ensure that the timescales do not slip. As an organisation, we probably could not have written the bid any differently to address this situation but the impact has been none the less stressful.

Like all teams we have a variety of strengths and experiences, including a social worker (seconded to the team from a local authority partner), a communication aids expert, a supported employment advisor, an advocate for people who use mental health services and a direct payments advisor. This has led to a supportive team environment, with someone usually knowing the answer to any queries we may have. However, nothing is perfect and despite having made the travel expectations clear at interview, there has been some reluctance to travel so extensively among team members. Travel is always the main query that applicants to the team have and remains the main gripe of the team.

The management of a geographically diverse team is a situation that the organisation has many years' experience of delivering, and this team has presented no surprises in terms of the issues that this brings (including isolation of individuals and creating time to meet as a whole group), and yet the project manager has introduced some innovative solutions to the issues such as telephone conferencing and maximising time by meeting near train stations as two people cross paths on their way to opposite ends of the country. In a complex management environment, this team has been able to bond and form as a unit, which has significantly benefited the delivery of this project. The level of support between the team members is self-evident and has been essential when facing some unanticipated opposition to the project.

Focusing on the project aims, the team has undertaken research and identified the barriers that are faced by the target groups. Although we are aiming to conduct robust qualitative research, we appear to have conducted one of the largest pieces of research into barriers to direct payments to date, with the experiences of over 260 direct payments recipients, local authority and primary care trust staff and personal assistants being collected by the team. As we are a non-academic team, much time has been spent looking at existing research into direct payments and the known barriers that the different target groups face when trying to access them. There is a lot of research available for some groups, reflecting recent investment in certain areas such as people with learning difficulties. However, for other groups such as disabled people from black and minority ethnic groups there is little research into barriers to direct payments, although much study has been done on the lack of engagement with statutory services by people from black and minority ethnic communities.

In order to complete the research as outlined in the original bid, the team felt that training was needed in action research. Recommendations from the partners were requested but there seemed to be limited experience of this specialist field and so training was commissioned from an already tight budget. It was important to the team and to the bid writers that we conduct valid and robust research that would have sound methodology. The first obstacle that we faced was that we were advised that we were not actually doing action research, but a realist evaluation. True action research would have meant that the service development workers would have coordinated a group of people from each of the target groups and supported them to go out and do the research, or to support local authority staff to conduct research into their working practices in order to remove barriers. However, this was not realistic within the timescales and budgetary restraints of the project (although it may have been what was hoped for and the team would have enjoyed doing this type of research). We received training from a professor of action research on how to conduct a realist evaluation/gap analysis instead. This allows us to assess the values and attitudes that interviewees have, and how things should work ideally and how they actually work in reality. The aim of this realist evaluation is to identify solutions that are meaningful to those who are currently denied access to direct payments so that there are clear strategies to address the barriers that they encounter.

The halfway point in the project was reached when the data gathering was completed, having collected the information mostly through semi-structured interviews either face to face, by telephone or via postal/email questionnaires. This is quite an achievement bearing in mind that other national projects looking into the barriers to direct payments have interviewed very small samples. For example, the recent Commission for Social Care Inspection (CSCI, 2004) report on barriers included feedback from 52 people (32 direct payments recipients and their carers and personal assistants, 20 professionals) and is seen as representing the national viewpoint. As a team we probably wish that we had only interviewed 52 people, because the work involved in analysing data from over 260 people has been very time consuming. This represented another lesson learnt in translating the 'dream' of the bid into the 'reality' of delivering – the logistics of collating information from such a huge number of people had potentially been underestimated by all involved in this partnership: consequently, there has been limited patience and understanding of the subsequent inevitable slippage in timescales.

Most of the existing research found common barriers to direct payments, and these barriers are also the common themes in our research (for example, lack of accessible information, negative attitudes towards direct payments by social workers and lack of training). So did we need to do our research in order to confirm that this is the situation? Possibly the research stage of the project could have been avoided and all barrier removal work could have been done based on known barriers, but this would have resulted in asking people for their solutions to barriers identified by someone else. What the research has shown is how far each of the eight local authorities has progressed in promoting direct payments in their areas to the target groups and the differences between them. For example, some local authorities have comprehensive professionally delivered mandatory training on direct payments for their staff and run regular training sessions, while some have not offered any regular training to their staff on direct payments. Needless to say our research has found that staff training is more of a need/barrier in the latter authorities. Other areas are struggling to pay for a direct payments support service for disabled children and their families who want direct payments, whereas others overcame this issue some time ago. There are also common themes, such as all local authorities grappling with block funding, and issues relating to eligibility, and what the direct payments guidance (DH, 2003) outlines as uses for direct payments.

Working in partnership with local authorities?

As with most research into direct payments, we have included local authority and primary care trust staff, staff from voluntary organisations who work with the target groups, direct payments recipients and potential direct payments recipients from the target groups, and personal assistants employed by personal assistant employers. This has been an interesting process, as local authority partners have been inconsistent in facilitating access to interviewees within the local authorities.

Finding interviewees was difficult as we were focusing on the under-represented groups and almost by definition they were not known by the partners. Local authority staff were also hard to book time with, as direct payments were not always seen as a priority area in their work, which in itself tells us something about the reasons direct payments are not being promoted.

One thing that was underestimated in the bid was the extent of the concern that would be experienced by the partnership local authorities and the degree of personal criticism that officers would feel. This is despite a basic assumption in the original bid that, regardless of how many steps have been taken, the statistics show that what is being done to promote direct payments does not work for some groups. If it did, then there would not be such a low take-up of direct payments by people who were, on the face of it, eligible and willing to receive them.

However, when we presented the first draft of our interview findings, the reaction of some local authorities was one of personal indignation and denial that anything could be improved. While it was not the intention of the development team to cause offence, the spirit in which the research findings were offered was not always how it was received. With hindsight, this is an important lesson for all partners (including the DH): communicating with a local authority inevitably means communicating with an individual who has a personal and professional interest in ensuring that work done is acknowledged. Unfortunately, the project was only ever meant to highlight barriers: if you substitute the word 'barrier' for 'failing', we can begin to empathise with the reaction of some individuals. The time that has been invested in attempting to clarify this and repair the partnership relationship was not accounted for in the original bid.

To be fair, some local authorities reacted positively to research findings and are keen to take these issues forward, making best use of service development workers' time to remove the identified barriers. They recognise that, although they are working hard to increase the take-up of direct payments, there is little measurement of progress other than dry statistics. However, others may have seen the report as an attack on their work and feel that it does not give them credit for the efforts that are currently being made. It has been difficult to invest time in reminding partners that the perceptions of both their staff and service users are relevant even if they do not reflect the level of commitment that the local authority feels it is making. We have needed to remind our partners that the project was about identifying the barriers: highlighting what is not working rather than what is working, and to restate the underlying assumption that what is being done is not working, however positive all may feel.

There is possibly a lesson here for the DH: where a partnership has a complex and potentially volatile relationship it is essential that an external monitoring organisation is constantly available to 'referee' the situation.

The impact on team morale was massive. Possibly the impression that the local authority partners manage the project team and can dictate our research findings is historic, since in most situations, they control the process because they provide the funding. The relationship between local authorities and the voluntary sector is complex: supposedly equal partners but one has the power of purchasing and the other does not.

It is understandable that people will feel concerned at criticism but this project was always going to be critical of current practice, and the challenge is to recognise this as an opportunity rather than 'shooting the messenger'. The focus should be on positive development rather than defending what is already being done and predominantly there was an acceptance that the second part of the project, although not reported here, would be the more rewarding. We are now approaching the stage where solutions will be identified and tried out, but the route to this point has been difficult.

One issue that has arisen throughout the project is that we need to prove that giving the money to a voluntary sector organisation such as ourselves is a better use of the Development Fund money than giving it directly to the local authorities. Not something for this project to determine, but it does appear that there is a great deal of repetition with other groups that have funding from the Development Fund, working on the same issues and reinventing the wheel in their locality. It is left to each project individually to network with others to share information, and this is something in a time-limited project that is very resource-intensive. It may have been helpful for the DH to allocate resources for a post that would pull this information together and share it with all the beneficiary projects. The DH does offer support by phone or email, but it is hard to know how much the support staff understand about our project. The monitoring role has been delegated to the National Centre for Independent Living (as discussed by Hasler in Chapter Eleven), which is concerned that the funding it received from the DH is insufficient to effectively monitor all 80+ projects. The net result is that we have very little support to ensure that partners are clear on what is expected of them and little back-up when they fail to meet their partnership obligations.

Conclusion

In conclusion, the Direct Payments Development Fund has been an important message from central government that direct payments are a priority, and the Rowan Organisation is proud to have been involved in delivering a project in pursuit of this. The outcomes will, hopefully, exceed those stated in the original bid if all concerned can carry forward the (often painful) learning process. The direct consultation with all the groups that are currently under-represented in the take-up of direct payments in respect of the barriers that they encounter and their solutions to overcoming these will provide invaluable information for promoting change. The real test will be whether those solutions are effective and will lead to the full access to direct payments that we are all hoping for.

References

CSCI (Commission for Social Care Inspection) (2004) *Direct payments: What are the barriers?*, London: CSCI.

DH (Department of Health) (2003) *Direct payments guidance: Community care, services for carers and children's services (direct payments) guidance, England 2003*, London: DH.

THIRTEEN

Carers and direct payments

Margaret Fletcher

Informal carers are important: they provide most of the support received by disabled and older people today. Britain has 5.7 million informal carers, who are providing unpaid care for one in 10 of the population. One in five of these carers provide support for 50 hours a week or more (Census, 2001). This chapter will look at the contribution that direct payments can make in the crucial role played by carers in supporting people in the community. It will look at legislation and policy, the process of carers' assessments, young carers, the role of carers' centres and support services, and some of the barriers to and the benefits of direct payments, and provide conclusions and recommendations.

Background

The introduction of the 1995 Carers (Recognition and Services) Act gave carers the right to an assessment of their needs for the first time, although this placed no responsibility on local authorities to provide services to meet carers' needs. The introduction of the 2000 Carers and Disabled Children Act increased carers' rights to an assessment, even in circumstances where the person cared for refused an assessment, provided they would be eligible for community care services. This Act gives local authorities the power to offer carers' services (or direct payments) to support their caring role, or to help them maintain their own health and well-being. (Leece, 2002). Since April 2001 direct payments have been available to carers for carers' services, parents of disabled children, and young carers aged 16 and 17 years. The Carers (Equal Opportunities) Act, taking effect from 2005, amends these two previous Acts and has three main aims: to ensure that carers are informed of their rights to an assessment, to give local authorities new powers to enlist the help of housing, health and education authorities in providing support to carers, and to ensure that work, lifelong learning and leisure are considered when a carer is assessed.

In 1999 the government launched a National Strategy for Carers, which for the first time established a framework national policy to start responding to carers' issues. This Strategy gave recognition to carers as individuals in their own right and aimed to address this by "empowering carers to make more choices for themselves and to have more control over their lives" (DH, 1999, p 32).

It was not always so. In their formative paper, Bytheway and Johnson point out that "… less than forty years ago, the term 'carer' was barely in the English language", and go on to suggest that the term is "a social invention" (1998, p 241). Although family members, friends and relatives had always been present in caring and supporting capacities, they were not identified as carers by policy makers, campaigners or researchers. Bytheway and Johnson trace the history of the term to the 1980s, to the influence of feminism and the emergence of research and surveys that would underpin the shift towards community-based care, which was consolidated in the 1990 NHS and Community Care Act.

It is now generally accepted that an informal carer is someone who, without payment, provides help and support to a partner, spouse, child, relative, friend or neighbour, who could not manage without their help. This could be due to a physical or mental illness, addiction or disability. Anyone can become a carer, as carers come from all walks of life, all cultures and can be of any age. Indeed, we all, at some point in our lives, from birth onwards, will be recipients of care. What makes the carer's status different is that it is now enshrined as a recognised role within legislation.

There had been earlier attempts to identify who carers are and what they do, in, for example, the 1985 General Household Survey (Green, 1988). As Bytheway and Johnson point out, the fact that six million people were identified as carers "… came as a shock to the policy world" (1998, p 245). Since then these figures have been debated from a variety of perspectives and carers continue to be counted. Thus, for the first time, the 2001 Census asked respondents specifically whether people provided unpaid care to a family member and for details of the caring role. Responses showed that 68% (3.56 million) of carers provide care for up to 19 hours a week; 11% (0.57 million) for 20 to 49 hours; and 21% (1.09 million) for 50 or more hours a week. In addition, the Census found there were 175,000 young carers in the UK, 12,000 of whom were caring for more than 50 hours a week (Census, 2001).

When asked, more than 80% of carers say that caring has had an adverse impact on their health. With carers now playing a central part in the provision of care and support it has been estimated that carers save the government £57 billion each year in unpaid community care support (Carers UK, 2002). Statistics thus show that more and more of us can expect to be involved in a caring role during our lifetime.

Why do carers need support?

Many people feel rewarded and enjoy their caring role, but for others being a carer brings personal costs. Many people give up an income, future employment prospects and pension rights when they become a carer. An estimated three million carers also work outside the home and juggle full- or part-time employment with their responsibilities as a carer. For some people, taking on a caring role can mean facing a life of poverty, isolation, frustration, ill health and depression (Howard, 2001). Despite publicity given to carers and their central role in community care policies, the majority of carers struggle without support alone and do not know that help is available to them. Many find it hard to identify what they do, on the basis of love or obligation, as an activity which has public recognition. When they are consulted, carers say that access to information, financial support and breaks from caring are vital in helping them manage the impact of caring on their lives (Keeley and Clarke, 2002).

The Princess Royal Trust for Carers (the Trust) was founded in 1991 with the aim of developing and supporting the establishment of independently managed carers' support services across the UK. It is the largest provider of comprehensive carers' support services in the UK. Through its unique network of independently managed carers' centres, young carers' services and interactive website (www.carers.org), the Trust provides information, advice and support services. In 2005 the Trust had a network of 118 carers' centres reaching 180,000 carers, including 10,300 young carers.

Carers' centres provide carers with a range of services, including information and advice on all issues facing carers, ranging from support services and benefits to respite and physical aids. They also provide emotional support by giving carers an opportunity to discuss their situation and problems through one-to-one counselling with trained staff and volunteers, and also group sessions where carers can meet others in similar situations. Practical support is provided through advocacy, training in moving and handling, and stress management. The centres, which usually have at least a third of their board members as carers, also provide community consultation by acting as a unified voice for local carers, to influence local decision making and policy.

Carers' centres work in response to local need, forming partnerships where there are potential partners in the local authority, the primary care trusts and the voluntary sector, meeting gaps in service provision.

The Trust provides start-up funding to pump-prime new carers' centres in localities in joint partnership with local authorities and primary care trusts or health boards, and it also raises development funds to support specific carers' services and initiatives. It operates a structure of regional networks to support carers' centres, including individual consultancy advice on governance, funding and staffing issues; conferences and specialised training events; and provides funds to carers, distributing over £150,000 annually through carers' centres to carers in need of breaks, essential equipment/household items, access to vocational training, education, alternative therapies to support their mental health and well-being and also transport assistance.

Research about carers

The Trust has commissioned significant research on carers. In 2002, the 'Carers Speak Out' project was undertaken to provide feedback to the government on the implementation of the National Strategy for Carers. Using a postal questionnaire and one national and 11 regional events, 3,800 carers were consulted with the aim of finding out what their needs, priorities and issues were. This was the largest consultation event of its kind ever held. The survey questionnaire sought information on:

- caring responsibilities and characteristics of carers;
- carers' access to information, advice and support;
- carers' knowledge and experience of carers' assessments;
- the impact of caring on carers' own health;
- carers' views on taking a short break from caring, and the help and support needed to take a break.

Among carers who responded to the survey, 39% reported that they had a disability or long-term illness themselves. Again, this would seem to be relevant, as illness is different from 'health', and indicates that this group of carers had complex needs. From the carers who responded to the study more than eight out of 10 said that caring had a negative impact on their health. As these findings suggest:

> Carers even more likely to feel that caring had an impact
> on their health were those carers who were female (89 per

cent); caring for a person with a serious illness or disease (94 per cent); or a person with a mental and physical illness (90 per cent); if they had been caring for periods between 10 and 20 years or caring for 15 hours or a day (both 89 per cent). (Keeley and Clarke, 2002, p 25)

Furthermore, in terms of the negative impact on their health, almost nine out of 10 carers felt that caring had affected their mental well-being, reporting symptoms of anxiety, stress, depression and lack of sleep. And more than four out of 10 felt that caring had affected their physical well-being, mentioning back pain, strain or other injury.

Carers' assessments

Local authorities have a formal duty to carry out assessments of carers' needs, including assessing their state of health, and their wishes and ability to continue to care. To qualify for a carers' assessment, carers must be providing or intending to provide 'substantial and regular care' for another individual aged 18 or over. This assessment determines whether the carer is eligible for a 'care package' to help the person in the caring role. There is no definition in the guidance of 'substantial and regular', and Leece (2002) argues that there needs to be flexible interpretation of these terms to take into account individual carer situations and capacity to continue caring.

Following a carers' assessment a local authority may under the 2000 Carers and Disabled Children Act make a direct payment in lieu of services to carers. Carers must consent to the direct payment and be able to manage the payment with or without support (DH, 2003a). A direct payment cannot be given to a carer to buy a service for the person they care for, but it can now be given for a family member not living in the same house to be employed in the capacity of a personal assistant. A relative living in the same house can be employed as a personal assistant with the local authority's approval. (DH, 2003a).

Only a quarter of carers who responded to the 'Carers Speak Out' survey said that they had received an assessment of their needs. Most of the carers in this sample provided a great deal of support, with nearly 80% providing support for 50 hours or more a week, and so this was of some concern.

The findings correlate with the small numbers of carers' assessments recorded for local authorities in England. Carers' assessments (including combined carer/client assessments) accounted for 26% of all client, carers' and combined carer assessments in 2002-03; figures for individual local authorities ranged from 0% to 61%: "Overall performance shows a significant need for improvement in assessing carers' needs" (DH, 2003b). Unsurprisingly, therefore, there is a low take-up of direct payments for carers (for carers' services) in England with only 957 payments made in 2003. This situation is likely to improve, given that since 2003 take-up of direct payments has been made an indicator of social service performance.

As reflected in the figures for carers' assessments, there is a marked differences across the 150 local authorities in England in the numbers of carers in receipt of a direct payment in their own right, ranging from 0 in just over 50% of all local authorities to 370 in one local authority (Commission for Social Care Inspection (CSCI), 2004a), by all accounts demonstrating that access and choice to direct payments at present for carers is a postcode lottery.

The number of carers of disabled children in receipt of direct payments (for children's services) more than doubled, from 875 as at 30 September 2003 to 2,072 at 30 September 2004 (CSCI, 2004a). It is to the situation of younger people, in particular young carers, that I now turn.

Young carers and direct payments

The 2001 Census identified 175,000 young carers, but there are undoubtedly many more, as most remain hidden and unsupported. Approximately three million children (23% of all children under 18 years) live in households where there are chronic physical or mental health problems, illness or disability (Becker et al, 1998). Young carers are defined in the direct payments guidance as children and young people who provide care or support to another family member and carry out on a regular basis substantial caring tasks with the level of responsibility usually associated with an adult (DH, 2003). They are often responsible for tasks such as personal care for a family member, emotional support, household tasks such as shopping, cooking, and paying bills, and helping to look after younger siblings.

Young carers have been exposed to much media attention and there has been debate among researchers as to their status and identity. Aldridge and Becker were among the first to identify young carers as having their own needs and rights (1996). They argue for services to support children as carers and for 'giving children back their childhood'. However, some disabled people prefer to ask what leads to young people becoming carers. They argue instead that disabled parents are often forced to depend on their children because they lack support from the social and health services that would enable their independence (Olsen, 1996). For example, this could be by employing a personal assistant to provide evening support for the parent during key exam times for the child and also for assistance with school transport.

Nevertheless, the negative outcomes and disadvantages experienced by young carers continue to be identified as educational difficulties and poor health, social exclusion, stigma, limited opportunities for social and leisure activities, and an adverse effect on transition to adulthood, employment opportunities and life chances (Becker and Deardon, 2004).

With this information in view, the Princess Royal Trust for Carers Young Carers Network was established in 1991. It currently (2005) encompasses 73 projects/support services reaching 10,300 young carers. These projects offer a range of direct services to young carers and their families and also play a key role in raising awareness, offering training and in identifying gaps in services, not just for young carers but also for their parents or relatives.

In recognition of their shared concerns, in November 2004, the Princess Royal Trust for Carers launched a 'Joint Position Statement on Young Carers' in conjunction with the Disabled Parents Network and The Children's Society, with the aim of working in partnership for the rights of disabled people, and also including people with mental illness and substance misusers with parenting responsibilities, their families, and children and young people who are in caring roles. The partnership is committed to lobbying for more adequate funding for community care packages for parents who need assistance with personal care and support with respect to their parenting role, to ensure that no child or young person should take on an inappropriate level of caring responsibility. Adult services should, as a matter of course, identify if their clients are parents and what, if any, support needs they have in their parenting role. At present, a proportion of disabled parents who need assistance are unable to access support for their parenting needs until their children experience difficulties and are identified and assessed as being in 'in need' under the 1989 Children Act.

Children and young people sometimes make an informed choice to take on caring responsibilities. For example, this could occur during the final stages of a parent's terminal illness. The 2000 Carers and Disabled Children Act gives specific recognition to young carers of 16 and 17 years of age who are undertaking a substantial caring role for a disabled adult. The guidance states that they are eligible to receive an assessment and notes that a small number may choose to access direct payments in order to allow them to arrange for carer services to be delivered to minimise any disruption to their education arising from their decision to care (DH, 2003).

However, the take-up of direct payments by these young carers remains exceedingly low. The latest available statistics indicate that, across all local authorities in England, only 12 young carers are in receipt of a direct payment (CSCI, 2004a). And, strikingly, all 12 recipients are from one local authority. This may reflect the guidance for direct payments by the DH, that there will only be a "small number of circumstances" where direct payments are appropriate (DH, 2003, p 36). Indeed, only a small proportion of all young carers receive an assessment under the relevant categories of legislation, including the 1989 Children Act, the 1995 Carers Recognition and Services Act and the 2000 Carers and Disabled Children Act.

The guidance to the legislation states: "Young carers should not be expected to carry inappropriate levels of caring which have an adverse impact on their development and life chances", and further, "Services should be provided to parents to enhance their ability to fulfil their parenting responsibilities" (DH/DfEE/HO, 2000, paras 3.61-3.63, pp 49-50).

In response to this, young carer-friendly assessment tools have been developed in some local authorities, for example, in North Yorkshire. It is very clear that strategies for joint assessment and support between adult and children's services are needed to support young carers and their families. There needs to be a holistic, preventative approach to supporting young carers which also empowers disabled parents.

In the context of promoting direct payments, the Bristol and South Gloucestershire Young Carers Project (a member of the Princess Royal Trust for Carers Young Carers Network) uses a contribution by a young carer to advertise direct payments for young carers and their families. In the following extract (Box 12.1), written by a young carer of a parent with a disability, the benefits of receipt of direct payment are highlighted:

Box 12.1: Young carer, aged 15, South Gloucestershire

I'm 15 and my two sisters and I care for our mom. She has fibromyalgia, which is like ME and also has a tumour in her spine. She is not able to stay up for very long or lift things, even like pots and pans; because of this our social worker arranged that we could have a care worker come and clean our house and cook for us because my mom can't do it and my sisters and I aren't able to keep up with everything.

For about four years carers came from an agency. They came twice a day every day. Although they were helpful, the carers wouldn't always turn up and the hours weren't always convenient. Some of the carers didn't understand that we had been told what they had to do and they wouldn't listen to us because we weren't adults. Other carers were really rude to us when they thought my mom was asleep or unable to hear them.

Recently we have swapped to direct payments. This means that money is paid directly into my mom's bank account and then every month the carers are paid from that bank account. They are paid hourly and my mom and I monitor the hours so the carers know that if they don't turn up they won't get paid. We were allowed to interview the carers and because we got to choose we know that we like them and they get on with us. It is also better because we have a close relationship with the carers because it is consistently the same two people all the time..

The hours that our carers need to work are flexible so they fit in with everyone's schedules. It also means that if we want to go away for the weekend or something it is easier to cancel or with direct payments the carer can come with us. One of the carers also sleeps over once a week, which makes it easier for my sisters and I....

The benefits of direct payments

Direct payments provide carers with control over services for their support. They can choose a broader range of services that will meet the outcomes agreed at the time of the assessment to facilitate their capacity to continue in the caring role and promote their health and well-being. For example, direct payments could be used to employ a worker to undertake domestic tasks such as cooking, housework and gardening. Alternatively, one-off payments could be used to purchase a range of services, such as education, short courses, including driving lessons, holidays and short breaks, stress-reducing therapies, taxi and train fares, equipment and household adaptations.

Direct payments offer much greater potential of flexibility to meet both the needs of the carer and the person they are caring for.

Barriers to the take-up of direct payments by carers

Recent findings of the CSCI pertaining to the relatively low take-up identified a number of barriers to taking up direct payments, including:

> Lack of clear information for people who might take advantage of direct payments; low staff awareness of direct payments and what they are intended to achieve; inadequate or patchy advocacy and support services for people applying for and using direct payments; problems in recruiting, employing, retaining and developing personal assistants and assuring quality. (CSCI, 2004b, p 5)

Online consultation with carers conducted in October 2004 by the Princess Royal Trust for Carers on direct payments reflected similar barriers. The Trust has an interactive website with around 4,000 registered users. In October 2004 an online discussion about direct payments was held with a small sample group of 12 carers looking at both the benefits and some of the obstacles for users of direct payments. The carers who took part were mostly involved in looking after a partner with a long-term illness or a child with severe disabilities, or were older carers, including a carer with a disability herself. Critical to the issue of take-up of direct payments by carers in their own right for carers' services is ensuring that carers who are eligible for an assessment receive one and that the appropriate information is supplied on choices of care packages including direct payments.

Carers indicated that dealing with contractual employment and administrative issues on their own can be an additional burden and cause of stress. Unless there are in place adequate infrastructure support services, such as a payroll service, employment law advice, and so on, many potential users would be reluctant to take the option of moving from direct services to direct payments. There still remain issues for users of direct payments about accessing Criminal Records Bureau checks for personal assistants unless structures are set up to enable them to link into umbrella bodies .

Local authorities' use of discretionary powers to charge carers for services featured negatively in feedback by some carers. Many are already carrying the financial burden of caring and caught in a poverty trap, as highlighted by research. For example, one study revealed that seven out of 10 carers had found themselves financially worse off since becoming a carer (Carers National Association, 2000).

Promoting direct payments

Two carers' centres in the Princess Royal Trust for Carers Network were successful in receiving funding, from the DH Direct Payment

Development Fund, in 2003 and 2004 respectively. This case study focuses on Sefton Carers Centre.

Sefton Carers Centre is in partnership with Sefton Council and took over the management and operation of the local authority direct payments scheme in October 2003. The aim of the new service was to facilitate an increased advisory and support function and, importantly, the administration of a payroll service.

Since the inception of this new arrangement, the number of direct payment recipients has grown from 49 to 131. Of these 131 direct payment recipients, the majority are users of services or people requiring support. Of these, approximately 90% have a carer in the household. Only one carer has been recorded as being in receipt of a direct payment, or indirect payment: a one-off payment for transport purposes. However, the positive impact of the use of direct payments extends to those households where there is a family carer by reducing the number of caring hours required by family and increasing flexibility in people's lifestyles.

Many direct payments users said they were disappointed when using agency staff, and the majority choose to employ a personal assistant. As previously mentioned, family members can now be employed, and this is especially helpful where a person has dementia and needs the stability of a known person in the home.

The provision of comprehensive information, advice and a support service is key to the scheme, including assistance with recruitment and selection, a personal assistant register and advice on employment law and health and safety. The location of the direct payments scheme at Sefton Carers Centre enhances the range of benefits to recipients, as the centre already offers an extensive range of support services for carers and their families, including advocacy, training for carers in handling techniques, and an emergency respite service.

Another project, located at Northamptonshire Carers Centre, has received funding from Northamptonshire County Council to employ a direct payments advisor specifically to support parent carers: that is, carers with a parental responsibility for a disabled child. In this case there are close working links with the local social services' disabled children's services team. The scheme was initially piloted with six families in May 2004. By December 2004, referrals were up from the initial six to 45 families. In the spirit of the direct payments scheme there has been flexible application of eligibility criteria, including the provision of intense personal care, and respite care and smaller care packages. A payroll service is provided by Northamptonshire Council for Voluntary Service, which is helpful in alleviating additional pressures for parents with the heavy caring responsibilities.

A third example of promoting direct payments comes from Carers Buckinghamshire, which received a grant of £50,000 in 2004 from Buckinghamshire County Council to distribute a form of direct payments, which encompassed non-means-tested help to carers in the form of one-off grants of up to £500. Some examples of the type of services purchased include essential household equipment, transport services, a holiday for the carer, respite for the person cared for, or a holiday for both, a number of short breaks, a place at a play scheme, and a series of massage and reflexology courses.

The key issues surrounding moving successfully from social care services to direct payments related to receipt in the first instance of adequate information about direct payments and support from the care manager. In cases where a direct payment was offered to the person being supported, carers highlighted one of the key areas of help to them was provision of a payroll service or additional payments to pay for a bookkeeper. Among the comments were the following: "I think I have enough to do as a full-time carer let alone become wages clerk, manager, etc", and, "… I found the paperwork hard going, so I found a bookkeeper who does it all for me for £10 a month. Social services agreed to pay this as part of the scheme".

Often carers can find dissatisfaction with agency staff because of lack of consistency of personnel, as well as being let down badly: "I had … agency carers but had a different one each week which upset my husband, but the last straw was when they forgot to feed him and being a diabetic it was life threatening".

For the majority of carers in this small sample there were advantages of moving to direct payments: "On the whole it is a great scheme giving you lots of flexibility", and, "You can pick and choose your own carers instead of being stuck with agency staff". From another carer came the comment, "It is very good to get direct payments for you are in control [of] who you have coming in to help you and the hours [and tasks] that suit you also". Another advantage of the scheme was seen to be the recent change in policy where direct payments can be used to employ a relative: "My husband will not be looked after by anyone he doesn't know … hence I have really never had a break.… My daughter can be the carer so that is good as she knows my husband's illness so well".

The disadvantages raised were recruitment and selection of personal assistants and ensuring quality: "I am struggling to find personal assistants; that to me is the biggest disadvantage of the scheme". Finding suitably qualified staff in more rural areas can be particularly difficult, as some pointed out. Several local authorities have offered a solution in the form of a database of personal assistants.

Other disadvantages of taking on the role of employer include the possibility of having to dismiss staff and potentially having to face the stress and time of an employment tribunal.

The cost of accessing services was raised frequently, as local authorities have the discretion to charge for care packages: "The Attendance Allowance we get does not cover the cost I pay". As the Carers' Allowance is discontinued when a recipient receives the state pension, many carers can be caught in a poverty trap. The issue of charging for carers' services raises ethical questions. Carers are, after all, the unpaid community care work force.

Drawing on the experience of the three projects outlined earlier and the online consultation, it seems that if direct payments are to become a mainstream service, local authorities will need to:

- invest and train their care teams and staff to proactively promote direct payments to carers;
- invest in an infrastructure to support implementation of employment advice and support services, including payroll services;
- develop training schemes for personal assistants;
- publish clear guidelines on entitlements and operation of direct payments;
- import good practice from local authorities where direct payments have worked well;
- work in partnership with and fund the voluntary sector to develop independent advocacy and support services for carers.

Conclusions

The implementation of direct payments schemes that are operating in the spirit of the guidance definitely provides a flexible care package alternative and gives carers a greater degree of control and choice over services, including services for the person cared for when a joint assessment is undertaken. Carers need to have accessible and reliable information on their rights and entitlement to an assessment and appropriate ongoing support in moving on to direct payments if they opt for this.

The largest group of carers in receipt of direct payments are parents caring for a child with disabilities. The take-up of direct payments by carers (for carers' services) remains low and is linked to the low provision by local authorities of carers' assessments. Again, the take-up of direct payments by young carers is also low and reflects that the needs of young carers fall through the assessment net between adult and children's services.

Direct payments have the potential to improve the choice, control and quality of life for carers and the person they care for, although there is still a long way to go to put in place the appropriate infrastructure and support services to ensure some of the obstacles and barriers to delivery and take-up are removed. Direct payments should not be seen as the only solution when looking at the provision of flexible quality support for carers, but rather as a viable option from the total care services on offer.

References

Aldridge, J. and Becker, S. (1996) 'Disability, rights and the denial of young carers: the danger of zero-sum arguments', *Critical Social Policy*, vol 16, no 3, pp 55-75.

Becker, S. and Deardon, C. (2004) *Young carers in the UK, 2004 report*, London: Carers UK.

Bytheway, B. and Johnson, J. (1998) 'The social construction of "carers"', in A. Symonds and A. Kelly (eds) *The social construction of community care*, Basingstoke: Macmillan, pp 241-53.

Carers National Association (2000) *Caring on the breadline: The financial implications of caring*, London: Carers National Association.

Carers UK (2002) *Without us ...? Calculating the value of carers support* London: Carers UK.

Census (2001) (www.statistics.gov.uk/census).

CSCI (Commission for Social Care Inspection) (2004a) *Councils delivery and improvement statement*, November.

CSCI (2004b) *Direct payments: What are the barriers?* London: CSCI.

Deardon, C. and Becker, S. (2000) *Growing up caring: Vulnerability and transitions to adulthood – young carers' experiences*, Leicester: Youth Work Press for the Joseph Rowntree Foundation.

DH (Department of Health) (1999) *Caring about carers, a national strategy for carers*, London: HM Government.

DH (2003a) *Direct payments guidance: Community care, services for carers and children's services (direct payments) guidance, England 2003*, London: DH.

DH (2003b) *Social Services Performance Assessment Framework Indicators: 2002-03*, London: DH.

DH/DfEE (Department for Education and Employment)/HO (Home Office) (2000), *Framework for assessment of children in need and their families*, London: The Stationery Office Ltd.

Green, H. (1988) *General Household Survey 1985: Informal carers* (Series GH5, No 15, suppl A), London: Her Majesty's Stationery Office.

Howard, M. (2001) *Paying the price: Carers, poverty and social exclusion*, London: Child Poverty Action Group.

Keeley, B. and Clarke, M. (2002) *'Carers speak out': Project report on findings and recommendations*, London: The Princess Royal Trust for Carers.

Leece, J. (2002) 'Extending direct payment to informal carers: some issues for local authorities', *Practice: A Journal of the British Association of Social Workers*, vol 14, no 2, pp 31-44.

Olsen, R. (1996) 'Young carers: challenging the facts and politics of research into children and caring', *Disability and Society*, vol 11, no 1, pp 41-54.

Section 5
Working with direct payments

"It's not like being at work": a study to investigate stress and job satisfaction in employees of direct payments users

Janet Leece

The numbers of people using cash payments to purchase social support are likely to swell dramatically in the near future due to government commitment to increasing the take-up of direct payments. However, the relationship between direct payments users and the workers they employ to provide their support is poorly understood, as research into direct payments has largely focused on the experiences of disabled people. Employees of direct payments users have been generally ignored and the few studies to report findings from a worker's perspective have tended to predict a problematic relationship.

This chapter looks at previous research into personal assistants' experiences of working for direct payments users and reports findings from an in-depth PhD study that examines this relationship. This study is unique in that it considers job satisfaction and stress in personal assistants and compares their experiences with those of a comparable group of employees: local authority home care workers. This comparison has been missing from the literature and is of consequence, as the direct payments relationship should not be seen in isolation. For many disabled people, the alternative to direct payments is the receipt of home care, and for many personal assistants a likely alternative employment is home care work.

Background

Local authorities in England have been able to give cash payments to individuals to purchase their own support since 1997, following the implementation of the 1996 Community Care (Direct Payments) Act. Direct payments have had a low take-up nationally, although this is likely to change radically as the government has demonstrated a clear commitment to increasing numbers of people using direct payments.

On 8 April 2003 it became a mandatory responsibility rather than an option for local authorities to offer cash payments, with the direct payments guidance stating:"the government expects to see a substantial increase in the numbers of direct payment recipients and will be monitoring local councils' progress in achieving this goal" (DH, 2003, p 5). In line with this, direct payments became a performance indicator in 2004 to encourage local authorities to extend their schemes. The government has also pledged money to promote the take-up of cash payments by those groups currently under-represented by creating the Direct Payments Development Fund.

Many people using direct payments choose to spend the money by employing one or more personal assistants (Leece, 2003a). Government pressure upon local authorities to expand the number of people accessing schemes raises questions about how well this employment relationship is working. Previous research into this relationship, and direct payments generally, has been inclined to focus on the experience from the viewpoint of disabled people (for example, Morris, 1993; Lakey, 1994; Kestenbaum, 1996; Leece, 2000, 2001; McMullen, 2003; Clark et al, 2004). Only a small number of studies so far have included the personal assistant's perspective, and none of these looks specifically at job satisfaction and stress (Glendinning et al, 2000; Ungerson, 1999, 2004). These studies tend to predict a difficult relationship, and this chapter continues by considering the issues discussed in the literature.

Making direct payments for the purchase of social support results in it increasingly being treated as a commodity to be bought and sold in the market. Ungerson (2002) argues that treating support as a commodity has led to the blurring of the boundaries between paid and unpaid support, with the relationship between employers and their personal assistants often showing many of the features of informal support by family and friends. Personal assistants tend to have less clearly defined roles than local authority home care workers and provide a much wider range of support, such as gardening, decorating, pet care, companionship, help to attend business activities, social gatherings, and so forth (Ungerson, 1999; Glendinning et al, 2000; Clark et al, 2004). Warm, friendly relationships develop, with some personal assistants describing the relationship as 'like family'.

However, this blurring of the boundaries has led some academics to argue that the 'direct payments' relationship holds a number of risks for personal assistants. For example, Glendinning et al (2000) consider that feeling part of their employer's family can lead to personal assistants having the 'boundless obligations' associated with real family, while Anderson (2003) argues that 'being part of the family' benefits employers rather than personal assistants, as employers will feel able to encroach on workers' off-duty periods, but workers are unlikely to be afforded the unconditional love associated with kin relationships. A number of studies have shown instances of personal assistants doing unpaid jobs or working unpaid hours (Glendinning et al, 2000; Kestenbaum, 2001; Ungerson, 2004).

There have been suggestions that the move to cash payments will disadvantage women, who provide most of the support for older and disabled people (National Union Research, 1998; Ungerson, 2000). The shift away from public provision may result in jobs being lost in the public sector, where workers have union representation, pension provision and higher salaries, to be replaced by work with direct payments users on less beneficial terms. In some countries such as Canada, the US, Austria and Italy, the low rates of payment and the unregulated nature of direct payments schemes have led to the development of a 'grey care market', where employers are forced to recruit refugees, migrants or illegal workers (Osterle, 2003; Ehrenreich and Hochschild, 2003; Gori, 2003). In this situation, personal assistants lack employment rights and may be trapped in low paid, transient work.

While the UK has a more regulated system, where direct payments users enter into formal contracts with employees and payments are made for tax and national insurance purposes, there are few incentives for cash-strapped local authorities to upgrade hourly rates of pay for personal assistants (Ungerson, 1999). There is also anecdotal evidence that the 'recruitment crisis' within the care sector is leading to some recruitment agencies bringing foreign workers into the UK on short-term visas to provide live-in support for disabled people including direct payments users.

Ungerson (2004) draws attention to other difficulties for personal assistants, for example, where their future job prospects could be damaged as the work may not be accepted as 'valid experience', or they could feel unable to leave should they wish to take up alternative employment, and argues that personal assistants are vulnerable to emotional blackmail, because they are "frequently working alone with no colleagues and operating in a segment of the labour market which credentialism has barely touched" (2004, p 204).

The management of the relationship with personal assistants is highlighted, in a study of older direct payment users, as an important aspect in successfully handling direct payments (Clark et al, 2004). Yet

Pickard et al (2003) point to the lack of training and external support for personal assistants. Home care workers employed by social services, for example, have a supervisor or manager to consult should things go wrong, but personal assistants generally have no one other than their employer.

Overall, the commitment by government to increase the take-up of direct payments appears to pay no heed to the position of people working for direct payments users. Indeed, Cameron and Moss (2001, p 6) argue that the support worker is "a curiously under examined feature of the policy changes and debates". Much of the research into direct payments ignores the experiences of one half of the employment relationship: the employee. This chapter reports findings that examine this relationship.

Methodology

The research used a grounded theory approach with qualitative in-depth interviews that were tape recorded and transcribed in full. Three disabled people from the 'Consumers as Researchers' programme at Staffordshire University, who are trained in research methods, were involved as 'experts' in the research design for the study. This chapter has also been circulated to all the respondents who took part to ensure their experiences have been accurately reflected.

For the study, direct payments users in Staffordshire were invited to take part with their personal assistants, as were a group of home care users and workers. The direct payments users and home care users were then matched to be as similar as possible in terms of: age, gender, disability and ethnic origin, so that any differences in responses were likely to be the result of the method of support (home care or direct payments) rather than another characteristic. The characteristics of the sample can be seen in Table 14.1. The sample consists of 32 people

Table 14.1: The sample

Direct payments users	Home care users	Personal assistants	Home care workers
5 women	5 women	6 women	8 women
3 men	3 men	2 men	0 men
Age range 22-84 years	Age range 36-76 years	Age range 25-68 years	Age range 32-57 years
Average age 52 years	Average age 52.8 years	Average age 47 years 3 months	Average age 45.7 years
All 'white British' ethnic origin	All 'white British' ethnic origin	All 'white British' ethnic origin	All 'white British' ethnic origin
All with a physical disability	All with a physical disability		

(eight direct payments users, eight personal assistants, eight home care users and eight home care workers).

Measuring stress and job satisfaction is difficult, as individuals' personal situations may influence their assessment of their work, which means that a single method of evaluation is unlikely to discover the whole of a respondent's experience (Coffey et al, 2004). This study uses a multi-method approach, as suggested by Coffey: a qualitative interview where respondents are interviewed individually and prompted to talk about issues relating to stress and job satisfaction, and two questionnaires completed with respondents directly after the interview. Respondents also gave details of the terms and conditions of their employment.

To measure satisfaction at work, a questionnaire developed by Warr et al (1979) was used, which has a series of 16 questions to measure overall job satisfaction. This includes intrinsic satisfaction (features central to the job, such as control and autonomy), and extrinsic satisfaction, which refers to aspects external to the work, such as pay. To measure stress, the General Health Questionnaire (GHQ12) was used. This is a 12-item questionnaire originally developed as a self-administered instrument to detect psychiatric illness in the general population and has subsequently been used to measure stress in UK workforce studies (Buck et al, 1994).

Both questionnaires are well validated and have been used in a number of studies with social and health care workers (for example, see Willcocks et al, 1987; Balloch et al, 1999; Coffey et al, 2004). The questionnaires can be used with large samples or with small samples on an individual basis (Johansson and Moss, 2004). It is not the intention of this study to analyse the data from the questionnaires quantitatively, as given the small sample size this would be statistically flawed. This data is used to aid interpretation of the qualitative interview material and provide a greater depth of understanding of the relationship between users and workers.

Results of the job satisfaction and stress questionnaires

All of the personal assistants and home care workers in the study completed the job satisfaction questionnaire and this was scored using the system detailed in Willcocks et al (1987). Higher scores indicate greater job satisfaction than lower, with a maximum score of 105. The scores are reported in Table 14.2 and show an average score of 80.8 for personal assistants and 69 for home care workers. This shows that,

Table 14.2: Job satisfaction scores

Personal assistants	Home care workers
85	77
76	33
91	65
79	65
68	88
89	72
77	69
82	83
Total 647	*Total 552*
Average score = 80.8	Average score = 69

as a group, the personal assistants in the study reported a higher level of job satisfaction than the home care workers.

Respondents also completed the GHQ12 to measure their level of stress. This was scored as suggested in Goldberg and Williams (1988), with higher scores indicating higher levels of stress. The results are detailed in Table 14.3 and show that home care workers had a higher average score at 2.63 than personal assistants, whose average score was only 1.75. The findings show that as a group the home care workers in the study reported higher stress levels than personal assistants. Two of the home care workers appear to be particularly stressed.

The results from the job satisfaction and stress questionnaires show that the group of personal assistants in the study reported lower stress levels and higher job satisfaction than the comparison sample of home care workers. These findings are interesting given the negative predictions made about the relationship by previous studies. The chapter continues with an examination of the qualitative interview data on stress and job satisfaction to help to gain a greater understanding of these results.

Table 14.3: Stress scores from GHQ12

Personal assistants	Home care workers
0	0
0	0
1	0
0	7
4	1
3	11
4	2
2	0
Total 14	*Total 21*
Average score = 1.75	Average score = 2.63

Looking at the relationship in greater depth

A number of recent studies have indicated that individuals' satisfaction with their jobs is generally declining and employment has become more stressful due to the increased number of hours people are expected to work and the amount of work they need to undertake (Taylor, 2002). Bunting (2004) refers to this as 'work intensification' and argues that the public sector has been particularly affected by this over the last 10 years, as 50,000 jobs have been lost, while work responsibilities have become greater.

The nature of home care has also changed, following the community care reforms of the 1990s. These reforms require home care workers to move away from a predominantly cleaning role to the provision of personal support with some low-level nursing care (see Leece, 2003b). The work has become more clearly defined and task based in what Aronson and Neysmith (1996, p 62) refer to as the 'conveyer belt principle'. This aspect of the work is clearly demonstrated in my study with five of the home care workers saying they have to rush from user to user:

> "You have one of those days when everything goes wrong, I'd got this huge list of people to see but I couldn't get to grips with the times that you were going to people's houses, so they'd written them down for me and I'd got three people to see at the same time. That was really stressing me out, I was getting so worked up about it thinking oh god, oh god." (Home care worker)

One of the home care workers employed prior to the community care reforms talked about enjoying the cleaning part of the job previously and how she now feels under pressure rushing from one user to another. Her scores on the stress and job satisfaction scales indicate she is the most highly stressed and least satisfied of all the respondents in the study. This aspect of dissatisfaction with the job may link with the concept of the 'psychological contract' (Argyris, 1960). This relates to the perceptions of the obligations that both employers and employees have of the employment relationship, and Bunting (2004) argues that the psychological contract has changed for people working in the public sector with the advent of a business-orientated social care system, with many employees feeling that their jobs have changed out of all recognition. It may be that some home care workers' expectations of their job are not being met, making them feel dissatisfied and stressful.

In comparison, none of the personal assistants in the study talked about rushing from user to user, as they all work for just one disabled person. This does not mean, however, that personal assistants are unaffected by work intensification, such as working long hours or doing unpaid work. All but one of the personal assistants said that they are undertaking some work for their employer that is not paid, with three of them doing substantial amounts:

> "I mean effectively you could say I work eight to 10 hours a day for him but as he is my friend, last year I spend most of my time with him anyway, he would come round to mine for meals or for dinner, stay here overnight if we went out drinking, things like that. So I'm working eight to 10 hours a day but only paid for 16 hours a week." (Personal assistant)

> "Well, the direct payment pays for 22, but she's [the personal assistant is] here more like 40 hours ... she's here all the time really. Our kids play together. She's like my best friend, we go out together, go for meals, she's here to help me if I need anything...." (Direct payments user)

One of the personal assistants in the study is employed to live in and has problems in establishing the boundaries between paid and unpaid time. His employer highlighted this difficulty referring to the unpaid support provided as 'friendship time':

> "But he [the personal assistant] gives more friendship time in care than paid care time which is wonderful for me obviously because to be selfish I couldn't manage without but I'm not sure that it is good for him in the sense that I think there should be more time for him to be doing totally unrelated things to the house and to me, outside interests, in other words...." (Direct payments user)

While some of the home care workers in the study are also doing some unpaid jobs for home care users, such as occasionally posting letters, these are on a much smaller scale than those done by the personal assistants. The difficulty for personal assistants in establishing boundaries in their relationship with their employer and the possible problems that being 'like family' can bring has been suggested in previous research (Glendinning et al, 2000). In my study, more than half of the personal assistants describe their relationship with their employer as 'like family' or 'almost like family', two describe it as friendly, and one as 'friendly/ professional'. Interestingly, the personal assistants describing the relationship in familial terms scored higher on the job satisfaction scale than the other personal assistants and all except one of the home care workers. So, being like family appears to bring happiness to personal assistants in my study; indeed all of the personal assistants talked about how much they like the job and how well it suits them:

> "I don't class it, it as a job because I forget, I'm just here. If I didn't come round she'd miss me. That's what I always say (laughs). I do enjoy what I'm doing. It suits me it suits my kids it suits her and it suits her kids. And as I say I wouldn't want to be stuck in an office all day. No it's not like being at work." (Personal assistant)

> "It is a really comfortable job, hence the fact that I've been here just over five years and we get on really well." (Personal assistant)

A number of the personal assistants talked about things that they do in working time that they would be unable to do if working in 'traditional employment'. For example, one personal assistant takes her dog with her to work, and another brings his 14-month-old daughter with him, so that he can look after her while at work. One personal assistant does her Christmas shopping when out shopping with her employer, and another continues her hobby of making sugar flower cake decorations when her employer watches television. These types of activities could be described as 'the perks of the job' and appear to be completely lacking in the home care relationship.

Home care workers were much more likely than personal assistants to talk about the 'limits' or 'lines' in the relationship that they must not cross and the need to distance themselves from the users they support. The boundaries in the home care relationship appear much more clearly drawn:

> "It is drilled into us, do not go beyond your role of duty because if you do it they will expect other carers to do it." (Home care worker)

> "I find that sometimes I have to cut myself off 'cause I think at the end of the day it is only a job and I'm not there to be, I know it sounds callous, I am not her friend, friend. I'm her friend but only so far." (Home care worker)

None of the home care workers describe their relationship with home care users as 'like family'. Their relationships were described in more formal terms with only one home care worker describing it as friendly, almost all said it is a 'friendly/professional' or a purely professional working relationship:

> "Just purely professional, you know, I go in there, I do my job, I leave and that is it." (Home care worker)

Along with maintaining professional boundaries, all of the home care workers said that while home care users generally share their worries with them, home care workers themselves have to control their feelings and keep their worries and concerns hidden from the people they support:

> "No I wouldn't put my worries on him no. I would go in and chin about things, I've got to do this tomorrow and I've got to do that, you know, as you would. I just have a normal conversation with him." (Home care worker)

In contrast to this, five personal assistants talked about how they share their worries and concerns with their employer:

> "I mean he has helped a lot with my problems, he [the employer] helps me more than I help him to be honest 'cause I've got a little one [daughter] and a family. Stressful times, he's given me a lot of support." (Personal assistant)

The type of work that involves workers in having to control their own feelings and 'give something of themselves' has been described as 'emotional labour' (Hochschild, 1983). It entails workers using both their personality and emotional skills to do their job and can be very demanding. Indeed, Hochschild argues that emotional labour is potentially damaging to workers, because their feelings are taken out of their control and managed by their employing organisation. It may be that the less formal relationships experienced by the personal assistants, where the majority are able to share their worries with the person they support, help to protect them from the emotional labour element of the work.

The support which workers receive from managers and colleagues to do their job can be important in terms of reducing stress and increasing satisfaction (Brown et al, 2001). During the interview, home care workers and personal assistants were prompted to talk about support that they receive. Most of the home care workers said they receive good support from their manager and colleagues, although two said they feel isolated at work and would like the opportunity to mix more with their colleagues. Personal assistants do not have the support of a manager, and this has been highlighted in the literature as an area for concern. However, without exception, all of the personal assistants in the study said they do not miss having the support of a manager, and seven said they feel the lack of colleagues is a positive part of the job:

> "I can't say I do [miss having colleagues] no 'cause most jobs I worked with my colleagues have been hard to work with, I've had to leave 'cause I just don't get on. So at least this way I know, I was friends with him [the employer] before I worked for him so we got along and it is just hassle free." (Personal assistant)

So for the personal assistants in this study, the lack of management and colleagues is a positive point rather than a problem. This corresponds with research by Makin et al (1996), which suggests that having colleagues and managers can be a mixed blessing, as they can be a major source of stress. It may also be, as Ungerson (1999) suggests, that individuals who decide to work for direct payments users may choose the job precisely because it has movable boundaries between work and friendship, and a lack of organisation.

It has been suggested that the relationship between personal assistants and direct payments users may resemble that of master and servant, because of the ability of users to 'hire and fire' their assistants (Ungerson, 1997). Although Ungerson (1999) later argues that this analogy is too simplistic, as disabled employers are no longer protected by social deference in the same way that 19th-century employers of servants were, and disabled people's physical vulnerability may reduce their power. A recent study by Clark et al (2004, p 18) of older direct payments users argued that "the days of domestic service are long gone", with relationships being friendly and 'like family' instead of being dictatorial. To look at this aspect of the relationship, home care workers and personal assistants were asked during the interview whether they ever felt like a servant. One personal assistant said that there is an element of being a servant in the nature of the job, because she is being paid to 'serve' someone and another described herself as 'subservient', saying that if she was not, she could not do the job. While most personal assistants do not feel like servants, in contrast to this, the majority of the home care workers said that they do feel like servants in their relationship with some home care users.

Feeling like a servant is likely to reduce home care workers' self-esteem and could be contributing to a lower job satisfaction; indeed, one home care worker said that feeling like a servant made her feel "a bit worthless".

The chapter now moves on to look at the terms and conditions of employment described by home care workers and personal assistants.

Employment terms and conditions

The study examined the terms and conditions of employment for both home care workers and personal assistants, as these can be important elements of extrinsic job satisfaction for employees. The differences in the terms and conditions between the two groups are striking. The average hourly rate that personal assistants in the study said they receive is £5.16, which is a lot lower than the average hourly rate of £6.14 that home care workers report. This pay difference means that a personal assistant working full time (37 hours per week) would receive an average gross weekly salary of £190.92, as opposed to £227.18 for a home care worker.

All the home care workers said that they receive sickness and holiday pay, compassionate leave, unsociable hours payments, guaranteed hours and paid travelling time, and have access to a pension scheme. Over half of the home care workers are members of a trade union. In contrast, half of the personal assistants said that they do not receive sick pay, with one not receiving holiday pay or compassionate leave. Most personal assistants said that they are not paid extra if they work unsociable hours nor paid for travelling time, and none have access to a pension scheme or belong to a trade union. Two personal assistants do not know whether they are entitled to sickness pay, and one goes to work even when she is ill.

The prediction made by the literature, detailed earlier in this chapter, that personal assistants are being employed on less beneficial terms and conditions than workers employed in the public sector are borne out in this study, although it is important to make clear that the terms and conditions of employment are largely out of the control of direct payments users and are determined by individual local authorities. Despite their poorer terms and conditions, the group of personal assistants reported higher job satisfaction and less stress than home care workers and this reflects the point made by Ungerson in Chapter 15 in this book that, while working conditions may not be satisfactory, it does not mean that the experience of work itself is unsatisfactory.

Conclusion

In conclusion, the findings from the study show a mixed picture. The pay and conditions of personal assistants are markedly poorer than those of home care workers employed by the local authority, indicating that direct payments are continuing the trend in social care started by the community care reforms, of moving away from public provision with its more beneficial terms and conditions for employees. However, despite their worse terms and conditions, the group of personal assistants reported higher job satisfaction and less stress than home care workers.

The study suggests that this could be linked to the blurring of the boundaries within the direct payments relationship and the formation of friendly, family-like bonds between employer and employee. The informality of this relationship can cause difficulties, as highlighted by previous research, but it may also bring a number of beneficial effects to the worker. It could produce a more reciprocal relationship where there is 'give and take' and both parties receive benefits, so that personal assistants may do extra jobs for their employers, but they might also do things they could not do in more formal employment: the 'perks of the job'. This could account for one personal assistant saying about her job, "it's not like being at work".

A close, sharing relationship may help to protect personal assistants from the emotional stresses of providing support to their employer. It could ensure that they feel appreciated and less like servants. The informal nature of the work where there are no managers or colleagues is clearly a positive point for some personal assistants.

The direct payments relationship appears in a positive light when compared to home care work. This comparison is useful and has previously been missing from the debate. It is important that the two relationships should be compared, as the home care relationship is the likely alternative to direct payments. The new 'professional', impersonal role of the home care worker in providing task-based support may essentially be less satisfying and more stressful for some workers than the informal direct payments relationship. However, this does not justify the present system, which results in direct payments users having to offer low pay and poor terms of employment to their personal assistants. Given the government's determination to increase substantially the numbers of people using cash payments this situation should be rectified.

Acknowledgement

With grateful thanks to all the people who took part in the study, the consumer researchers at Staffordshire University, and Sue Farrier-Ray, Head of Services for Older People, Staffordshire Social Care and Health Directorate.

References

Anderson, B. (2003) 'Just another job? The commodification of domestic labor', in B. Ehrenreich and A.R. Hochschild (eds) *Global woman: Nannies, maids and sex workers in the new economy*, London: Granta Books.

Argyris, C. (1960) *Understanding organisational behaviour*, Homewood, IL: Dorsey Press,.

Aronson, J. and Neysmith, S. (1996) 'You're not just there to do the work: depersonalising policies and the exploitation of homecare workers', *Labour, Gender and Society*, vol 10, no 1, pp 59-77.

Balloch, S., McLean, J. and Fisher, M. (1999) (eds) *Social services: Working under pressure*, Bristol: The Policy Press.

Brown, D., Dickens, R., Gregg, P., Machin, S. and Manning, A. (2001) *Everything under a fiver: Recruitment and retention in lower paying labour markets*, York: Joseph Rowntree Foundation.

Buck, N., Gershuny, J., Rose, D. and Scott, J. (1994) *Changing households: The British Panel Survey 1990-1992*, Colchester: University of Essex.

Bunting, M. (2004) *Willing slaves: How the overwork culture is ruling our lives*, London: Harper Collins.

Cameron, C. and Moss, P. (2001) *Care work in Europe: Current understandings and future directions: Mapping care services and the care workforce, United Kingdom national report*, London: Thomas Coram Research Unit, Institute of Education, University of London.

Clark, H., Gough, H. and Macfarlane, A. (2004) *'It pays dividends': Direct payments and older people*, Bristol: The Policy Press.

Coffey, M., Dugdill, L. and Tattersall, A. (2004) 'Stress in social services: mental well-being, constraints and job satisfaction', *British Journal of Social Work*, vol 34, pp 735-46.

DH (Department of Health) (2003) *Direct payments guidance: Community care services for carers and children's services (direct payments) guidance, England 2003*, London: DH.

Ehrenreich, B. and Hochschild, A.R. (2003) *Global woman: Nannies, maids and sex workers in the new economy*, London: Granta Books.

Glendinning, C., Halliwell, S., Jacobs, S., Rummery, K. and Tyrer, J. (2000) *Buying independence: Using direct payments to integrate health and social services*, Bristol: The Policy Press.

Goldberg, D. and Williams, P. (1988) *A user's guide to the General Health Questionnaire*, Windsor: NFER-NELSON.

Gori, C. (2003) 'Payments for care in Italy', Paper presented at The Direct Employment of Domiciliary Care by Older People Conference, 13 May, London.

Hochschild, A. (1983) *The managed heart: Commercialisation of human feeling*, Berkeley, CA: University of California Press.

Johansson, S. and Moss, P. (2004) *Care work in Europe: Current understandings and future directions. Work with elderly people: A case study of Sweden, Spain and England with additional material from Hungary*, Work package 9, London: Thomas Coram Research Unit, Institute of Education, University of London.

Kestenbaum, A. (1996) *Independent living: A review*, York: Joseph Rowntree Foundation.

Kestenbaum, A (2001) *Older disabled people with ILF extension fund awards: Their experience and views*, Nottingham: Independent Living Fund.

Lakey, J (1994) *Caring about independence: Disabled people and the Independent Living Funds*, London: Policy Studies Institute.

Leece, J. (2000) 'It's a matter of choice: making direct payments work in Staffordshire', *Practice: Journal of the British Association of Social Workers*, vol 2, no 4, pp 37-48.

Leece, J. (2001) 'Directing support: direct payments and older people', *Generations Review; Journal of the British Society of Gerontology*, vol 11, no 3, pp 23-5.

Leece, J. (2003a) *Direct payments*, Practitioner's Guide Series, Birmingham: Venture Press.

Leece, J. (2003b) 'The development of domiciliary care: what does the future hold?', *Practice: Journal of the British Association of Social Workers*, vol 15, no 3, pp 17–30.

Makin, P., Cooper, C. and Cox, C. (1996) *Organisations and the psychological contract*, Leicester: British Psychological Society.

McMullen, K. (2003) *The direct approach: Disabled people's experience of direct payments*, London: Scope.

Morris, J. (1993) *Independent lives: Community care and disabled people*, Basingstoke: Macmillan.

National Union Research (1998) 'The hard truth about individualized funding', (www.members.shaw.ca/bsalisbury/).

Osterle, A. (2003) 'Austria's pflegegeld system', Paper presented at The Direct Employment of Domiciliary Care by Older People Conference, 13 May, London.

Pickard, S., Jacobs, S. and Kirk, S. (2003) 'Challenging professional roles: lay carers' involvement in health care in the community', *Social Policy and Administration*, vol 37, no 1, pp 82-96.

Taylor, R. (2002) *Britain's world of work – myths and realities*, ESRC Future of Work Programme Seminar Series, Swindon: ESRC.

Ungerson, C. (1997) 'Give them the money: is cash a route to empowerment?', *Social Policy and Administration*, vol 31, no 1, pp 45–53.

Ungerson, C. (1999) 'Personal assistants and disabled people: an examination of a hybrid form of work and care', *Work, Employment and Society*, vol 13, no 4, pp 583-600.

Ungerson, C. (2000) 'Thinking about the production and consumption of long-term care in Britain: does gender still matter?', *Journal of Social Policy*, vol 29, no 4, pp 623-43.

Ungerson, C. (2002) 'Care as a commodity', in B. Bytheway, V. Bacigalupo, J. Bornat, J. Johnson and S. Spurr (eds) *Understanding care, welfare and community*, London: Routledge and The Open University.

Ungerson, C. (2004) 'Whose empowerment and independence? A cross-national perspective on "cash for care" schemes', *Ageing and Society*, vol 24, no 2, pp 189-212.

Warr, P., Cook, J. and Wall, T. (1979) 'Scales for the measurement of some work attitudes and aspects of psychological well-being', *Journal of Occupational Psychology*, vol 52, pp 129-48.

Willcocks, D., Peace, S. and Kellaher, L. (1987) *Private lives in public places: A research-based critique of residential life in local authority old people's homes*, London: Tavistock Publications.

FIFTEEN

Direct payments and the employment relationship: some insights from cross-national research

Clare Ungerson

The provision of benefits and cash allowances to care users, which are designed to encourage care users to employ their own care workers directly, are not unique to the UK. Similar systems have developed in many welfare states and have been named, by the present author, as part of a process of the 'commodification' of care (Ungerson, 1997a). It is the purpose of this chapter to use some recent cross-national research to unpick some of the implications of these systems for various dimensions of the 'employment' relationship and to begin to understand how and why different funding and regulatory regimes for various schemes of 'cash for care' are likely to have differential impacts on the employment relationship between care user and care giver. The chapter also considers the way in which different systems impact on the working conditions of the care giver.

Early work on the development of direct payments in relation to disabled people tended to argue that the employment by care users of their own care workers was in itself a form of empowerment (Morris, 1993). This argument had at its core an assumption that the ability to hire and fire one's own labour would transform the relationship between care user and care giver: it would undermine professionalised definitions of 'need' and the professionalised construction of the appropriate response to that defined need. Instead, within a 'direct payments' context, disabled care users would themselves be able to articulate and act upon their self-perceptions of need, and manage their own care arrangements such that these arrangements accurately responded to their needs. This literature was therefore concerned with the rights and empowerment of the employer. There was some concern expressed about the difficulties that some care users may encounter in managing the employment relationship, particularly where it was necessary to ensure a paper trail for tax and social security purposes and to pay national insurance contributions from what amounted to rather limited amounts of money (Kestenbaum, 1996). Later critiques developed, which noted that there was a possibility that these forms of employment could result in the exploitation of low-paid and relatively unskilled casualised labour (Ungerson, 1997b), although, in the light of some empirical evidence, this view was later tempered by the understanding that care workers employed by care users in receipt of direct payments were also able to bring their employment to an end when it no longer suited them or they could find other forms of employment (Ungerson, 1999).

In this chapter, five cross-national examples will be used to illustrate the way in which different funding regimes for 'cash for care' schemes combined with different regulatory frameworks and organisational contexts appear to have considerable influence on the type and quality of employment relationship that emerges between care user and care giver/worker. The 'employment relationship' will be explored along a number of dimensions all of which constitute some of the basic building blocks of a 'relationship'. For example, it is important to consider how far the funding arrangements encourage or discourage continuity of care by particular individuals over a period of time; how far the scheme allows for the provision of care by one individual for one other individual, or by a group of individuals who only service the needs of one other individual; whether it is possible to employ someone within the scheme for very long periods of the day or night, or whether the scheme promotes task-orientated care delivery over very short bursts of time; whether or not the scheme encourages or discourages co-residence with the care user and how that co-residence impacts on the 'employment relationship'; and whether, in general, the scheme allows for the development of relatively good working conditions for the care giver/worker such that they are likely to be working within a context which underwrites good morale. This chapter is specifically not going to examine the important question of the empowerment of care users within cash for care schemes that is part of the rationale of the introduction of an 'employment relationship' in the first place. This is partially for reasons for space, but it is also an issue that has been explored in other articles that have already been published using data from this project (Ungerson, 2003, 2004).

The five country study

The examples studied arise out of a cross-national project funded as part of the Economic and Social Research Council Future of Work Programme.[1] The project was designed to explore the shifting boundaries between paid and unpaid work, particularly in relation to care of older people. Hence all the data that follows in relation to cash for care schemes is derived from that five country study (Austria, France, Italy, the Netherlands, the UK) and relates only to the use of cash to employ caring labour by older people. Each of these countries appeared, at the start of the study, to offer rather different types of funding regime, with a speculated differential impact on the labour market for care and on the employment relationship. Since 1993 Austria has placed the system of '*Pflegegeld*' at the core of its social care system for older people and disabled people. Anybody needing continuous care for more than six months and a minimum of 50 hours' care a month can apply for a long-term care allowance. In 2001, 343,782 care users were in receipt of this benefit, of whom 82% were aged over 60 (Oesterle, 2003). Care users can pay their relatives. It is an entirely unregulated system.

A rather similar system prevails in Italy where a central government-funded cash allowance – the *Indennita di accompagnamento* – has been in place for disabled people since 1980, and extended to older care users in 1988. In 2001, 5.8% of the population aged 65 and over was in receipt of this allowance. In addition, unknown numbers of care users are in receipt of similar cash payments paid by the Italian regions and municipalities (42% of Italian municipalities provide payments for care to care users, with most of those municipalities being located in the centre/north of Italy) (Gori, 2003). There is very limited regulation as to how the allowance is spent, and employers can pay their relatives. Italian commentary, previous to this research project, had suggested that the allowance is widely used to pay workers who operate in the considerable informal labour market (Gori, 1999), and that many of these informally employed workers are non-European Union nationals.

The Netherlands is another interesting example of a country where the payment of relatives is permitted. However, this is within the context of a heavily regulated system of routed wages. Since 1995 the '*Persoonsgebonden* budget' or 'personal care budget' has been in place for people needing more than three months' home care. At the end of 2002, there were 34,544 personal budget holders (Pijl, 2003). The personal budget operates within the context of long-term care insurance. The Care Insurance Office assesses need and allocates the payments, while the Social Insurance Bank pays the care workers, who are contracted by the care users, even when the care workers are relatives of the care user. The Netherlands system of routed wages has been more and more subject to regulation until it has moved into a directly opposing model of commodified care management to that which prevails in Austria.

In France, the allowance known as the *Prestation Spécifique Dependance* was made available to older care users in 1997. The allowance was means tested, but enough to employ a care worker on a part-time basis. The allowance could be used to pay relatives but not spouses, and was specifically directed towards pulling informal economic activity into the formal labour market, and workers into the social security system. At the end of 2001, approximately 150,000 older care users were in receipt of this benefit. The benefit has now been extended and renamed the *Allocation personnalisée à l'autonomie* (APA) and the expectation is that 80% of the dependent older population will be in receipt of this more generously allocated benefit, amounting to about 600,000 recipients in total (Martin, 2003).

A somewhat similar system has recently developed in the UK, where the right to choose cash rather than services has been steadily extended to disabled people of working age, culminating in the 1996 Community Care (Direct Payments) Act. This option was made available to older care users in 2000. At present, very few older care users are in receipt of direct payments, certainly in comparison with the high number of recipients of cash for care in the other countries described in this chapter. In 2003 there were just over 1,899 older care users in receipt of direct payments (Commission for Social Care Inspection, 2004) – and this low take-up is in contrast to the continuing stream of policy documents emanating from the UK government in support of direct payments (see, for example, Milburn, 2002). Careful regulation is used to oversee the system and ensure that care users do not pay co-resident carers (except a formally employed personal assistant). This means that the payment of relatives, particularly co-resident spouses, is not part of the culture of the UK scheme and currently it is generally the case that relatives cannot be paid to care, although there is some local variation, particularly in rural areas. Payment of the cash is contingent on the presentation of full documentation and evidence that the workers are locked into the social insurance system.

The data collected in this project has been largely qualitative and exploratory. We were concerned to investigate the employer/employee relationship in depth, and to develop an understanding of how and whether the presence of the cash nexus alters the care relationship, such that it emerges as a hybrid of work and care (Ungerson, 1999). In addition, the cross-national framework allowed us to look at the expected differential impact of the five funding regimes. In many respects the desire to conduct small-scale qualitative research was rendered more complicated, but also more interesting, by the attempt to make cross-national comparisons. Inevitably, the data emerges with a great deal of 'noise in the system' where we were unable to hold the variables constant. For example, in Austria, Italy and the UK, the samples of older care users were located in large urban areas: Vienna, Salzburg, Milan, Sheffield. But even here there were differences, with Vienna and Milan being cities with incoming populations, particularly internationally, while Sheffield has a very stable population with little in-migration, particularly from abroad. Both the studies in the Netherlands and in France were conducted in largely rural hinterlands of urban concentrations, and this means that it is likely that the labour markets in these areas are much less diverse, and local networks rather more solidaristic than those of the urban areas. The outlining of the differences between the areas of origin of our sample populations remains a task for the project as a whole. However, we do know that if we had attempted to hold the variables constant by, for example, using a triangulated method, the entire project would have been prohibitively expensive. So what we have emerged with is data from qualitative interviews conducted in five different countries of Europe (and five different languages), which has been selectively translated into English. In each country, interviews were conducted with 10 older care users in receipt of 'routed wages'. They were then asked to name and grant access to their care givers, and these care givers were also interviewed in depth. In each country, about 30 interviews were conducted overall.[2]

Time, continuity and 'one-to-one' care

Across the five samples contained within this study, it was perhaps surprising, given the fact that cash for care schemes are intended to underwrite 'choice', that clear differences emerged in the way that care was delivered within the different schemes. In particular, distinct patterns emerged in terms of the dimensions of time and continuity of personnel, and most of this chapter is intended to demonstrate those patterns. 'Time' can be analysed along two sub-dimensions: first, the amount of time that care givers were able to give to the person they were caring for within any 24-hour period, and, second, the period of time over which individual care givers had been providing care for their older employers. Both dimensions of time have an impact on the employment relationship. For example, if individuals are able to spend time together which is not entirely task-orientated but which also has the potential for the development of companionship, then clearly the employment relationship has the potential to develop into a hybrid which, based on companionship, begins to contain elements of affect as well as contract and service delivery. Second, a similar assumption of hybridity has to be made about those who work for employers for a very long period – but in these cases it may well be that the length of time over which an employer/employee relationship has existed is as much an *outcome* of hybridity of contract and affect as it is a driver.

As far as these two dimensions of time were concerned, it was clear that there were two different types of scheme that drove the longest periods of time, in both its senses. Paradoxically, these two types of scheme were both the most regulated and the least regulated, but their common element was that they either encouraged the 'employment' of relatives to care or, through lack of regulation, they allowed for the employment of undocumented and possibly illegal workers whose housing and employment opportunities were severely constrained. The Dutch scheme encouraged the 'employment' of relatives and the result, as far as our survey data indicates, is that commonly (but not always) it is classic 'informal' carers who are recruited to care. The majority of our small sample who were paid to care were close kin, all of whom had been caring for their 'employers' for very long periods unpaid before the introduction of the personal budget scheme. As a result of the scheme, they were now contracted to provide an appropriate number of hours of care and, depending on the type of care they were providing (whether judged to be 'domestic' or 'nursing'), they were paid the appropriate amount to do so. For example, a wife of a man who had broken his back 30 years earlier was now being paid £21,828 per annum to care for him in exactly the same way as she had cared for him before the introduction of the scheme; a friend who had visited an older woman friend for many years was now contracted and paid to do so on a regular basis twice a week. Similar cases occurred in the Austrian scheme which was run by the charity CARITAS, where care users paid a fee to CARITAS, which then contracted their kin to care for them on a paid basis.[3] In this sense, then, informal care and friendship had been wholly commodified. The amount of time, within any 24-hour period, spent by the care giver with the care user was determined not by the nature of the contract, but by the nature of the ongoing and past relationship. It was also the relationship and its history that determined how long it had lasted and how long it was likely to continue (particularly, for example, care delivered between spouses and between parents and their children, where death was the most likely event to bring these relationships to an end). Moreover, these relationships were intrinsically 'one to one', reflecting the way in which informal care and friendship are commonly configured.

While these were, as a result of the introduction of the scheme, 'employment relationships' in the sense that contracts existed and wages were paid, they were in all other senses relationships that bore closest proximity to affective relations. As one of the Dutch respondents put it, when asked if the introduction of a wage for the care she gave her husband made any difference to the relationship, "He hasn't sacked me yet!". She meant it ironically, of course. In that sense, then, these commodified informal care relationships that predated the introduction of the cash for care scheme had hardly been impacted by the scheme itself – they remained very predominantly affective rather than contractual relationships and rather different from a typical 'employment' relationship. The one thing that such schemes did alter was that they allowed for care givers to shift from more conventional paid work into commodified informal care and spend more time with the person they cared for. This clearly allowed for the amplification of affective relations – as one of the Austrian respondents put it when asked by the interviewer, "What is your experience of this type of work?":

> "Absolutely fantastic. We understand each other very well. Previously, we scarcely knew each other. The other person was always somewhere else. It's quite different now. She is sweet, grateful, and easy to look after. If I really want to go somewhere, she says: 'Of course, my dear, just go'. She doesn't cling to me either. She tries to relieve me of everything and make things as easy as possible for me."

As already suggested, in contrast to the Dutch and Austrian CARITAS schemes, which were highly regulated, there were also schemes where there was no regulation at all, and it was, paradoxically, also in these schemes that many of the care givers delivered care at any time of the day or night and over long periods of time within any single 24-hour period, and, at the same time, some of these relationships had lasted for a long period of time. These relationships also often involved one-to-one care. However, in these cases, it was much clearer that the way in which these relationships had developed was strongly determined by the funding regime of the particular scheme. For example, in Italy and Austria, where (apart from the CARITAS scheme mentioned above) there was no attempt to regulate the way in which care users spent their cash allowances, a typical care worker was a migrant, sometimes undocumented, who was also co-resident. There were both intrinsic and extrinsic reasons for this form of labour. Intrinsic to these schemes was a relatively low level of cash payment to people with high needs, which they could spend entirely as they chose. Both Austria and Italy are welfare states with comparatively limited provision of service-based care. Hence there were strong motivations built into these schemes to employ care labour that was cheap and, in the absence of service-based support, could also provide a wide array of care services including domestic work, meals provision, and personal care. Extrinsic to these schemes was the fact that, in both Austria and in the northern cities of Italy, there is a pool of labour available which is largely restricted to migrants, some of whom are illegal, who also seek to resolve their accommodation needs through co-residence with their employers. Thus, opportunistically, care users could recruit care workers who, on low levels of wage, were willing to provide them with comprehensive care based on 24/7 co-residence. Some of these employment relationships were of considerable longevity (one of the Italian sample of migrant care workers had worked for her employer for 26 years), and this reflected the development of a companionate employment relationship – this particular worker described her employer as "like a sister". However, not all the relationships had developed into hybrids of contract and affect, since many of the workers were clearly unhappy with the work that they did and considered that their occupation merely reflected their very limited alternatives. A typical comment came from a Peruvian woman working in Milan:

> "Even if I don't like it, what can I do? It is a stressful job, not easy work. Here the only work that one can do is to care for old people. What I did in my own country [nursing training] is not recognised here."

Moreover, for many, there was not so much an opportunity for companionship, as a form of compulsory companionship which was deeply irksome.

"When she watches television in the afternoon, seeing that she ... doesn't need me, I want to take the opportunity to write a letter to my family, but she does not want that. She wants me to stay always by her side, and watch television seated next to her, so if she sees me going away, she says: 'Where are you? What are you doing? I pay you to stay with me and keep me company. I don't pay you to wander about the house'. However, she has got to understand that she has not bought me with that little salary she pays me." (Italian migrant worker who is co-resident)

Thus, both these types of scheme allowed for or encouraged 24/7 care and very long-lasting care relationships, which in circumstances where both care giver and care user were in a position to choose to stay or leave, could become the basis of deeply companionate and affective employment relationships. The way in which the cash for care scheme was funded, its organisation (or lack of organisation), and the level of funding available, combined with extrinsic factors such as the nature of the local labour market, had a strong effect on the nature of the employment relationship, especially in relation to time and the ownership of time, and whether the relationship could be 'one to one'.

In striking contrast are schemes which encourage the use of agency workers, such as that prevailing in France. Here, despite the fact that French care users can pay kin – excluding spouses – to care, most of the sample in this study had used an agency to recruit their caring labour. There are incentives and a culture embedded within the French cash for care scheme to persuade care users to use visible labour recruited through the operation of the conventional labour market. Agency workers typically work for a number of care users, delivering task-orientated, non-companionate care. In the French sample, the care workers visited up to 13 older care users a day, delivering a variety of tasks including dressing, washing, shopping and cooking. These were not one-to-one relationships (although most of the care users had only one regular care worker) and they entailed the delivery of care over very restricted periods of time. Many of these relationships were, as I have described elsewhere, 'cool' in the sense that they were based on contract rather than affect, and both worker and care user felt they could exit them if they were dissatisfied with the quality of the service or with their working conditions (Ungerson, forthcoming). This is not to say that the employment relationships were unproblematic. Indeed, there was evidence of tension precisely over the question of time. For example, workers mentioned examples of clients who had a different concept of the nature of contracted care from themselves – clients phoned them at home with additional demands (one care worker said that she responded by taking the phone off the hook) and care workers found their personal time disrupted when, motivated by a combination of affect, guilt or pity, they took on additional uncontracted unpaid care tasks for particularly demanding care users.

So far, I have argued that the way in which a scheme was organised, how and whether it was regulated, and the level of payments involved had a strongly determining effect on the nature of the employment relationship that emerges. This is particularly the case in terms of time spent delivering care and the length of the relationship, and whether or not the relationship is predominantly based on contract or affect. All these aspects of the employment relationship also impacted on, and were impacted by, the possibility of establishing one-to-one care giving and care receipt. This strong determinism does not seem to be so evident in relation to the UK direct payments scheme, where, in terms of time spent in care, longevity of the relationship and along the dimensions of affect and contract, a much more mixed picture emerged from the sample in this study. There were no examples, among the British respondents, of older care users who employed their own kin, which, given the way in which paying relatives and co-resident carers in the UK scheme is regarded, is not surprising. Thus, there was no example of fully commodified informal care, with its embedded elements of longevity, affect and a one-to-one relationship. Instead we found individual older care users who had found their caring labour through a variety of networks, some relying on agency labour, while others used 'word of mouth' through informal friendship and neighbourhood networks. Yet others advertised through local post offices or used the local Jobcentre. One care user, who had owned and been the head teacher of a private school, employed a number of her one-time employees (the janitor and his wife for example) to provide her with 24/7 care (at enormous expense). It is not clear why the British direct payments scheme should necessarily lead to such a mixture of employment outcomes, and it may well be that the mixture reflects extrinsic and contextual factors rather than intrinsic elements within the scheme itself. For example, there was evidence among this sample that users of direct payments are somewhat at a loss to find a satisfactory method of recruitment given the current tight labour market in much of the UK, particularly for caring labour. Hence they improvise and innovate in their use of recruitment methods, particularly local networks. 'Word of mouth' as a mode of recruitment was not unique to the British, since it also occurred in Italy, but it may reflect common and possibly exaggerated perceptions among older people in the UK that they are very vulnerable to the activities of criminals. The use of local information networks is one way of reducing risk. The 'packaging' of care by the older care users in the UK sample such that a number of these care users had put together a group of workers who worked short hours, but only for them, may reflect the desire by some UK care workers to work to a maximum income threshold (£15.00 a week) that does not impact on their aggregate income from social security benefit. (There was some evidence from some of the care workers in this sample that this was what they were attempting to do and hence they were not interested in working long hours.)

Given these different forms of recruitment for the UK direct payments scheme, and the fact that at the time of the study it was impossible to 'employ' one's relatives, it is not surprising that continuity of care, and the incidence of 'one-to-one' relationships was variable among our small sample. Some care users who employed agency workers found themselves experiencing the same kind of employment relationship as many of the French sample – non-companionate, task-orientated delivery of care, over short bursts of time, with continuity of care workers easily interrupted by changed circumstances or either party wanting to exit the employment relationship. Others experienced one-to-one care over long periods of time, both in terms of the 24/7 time and longevity, and this was particularly satisfactory for one African Caribbean care user who had been able to find two care workers of very similar biography to herself and had been able to establish strongly companionate care. The ability to employ over extensive periods of daily time was not always so satisfactory, however: as reported in Ungerson (forthcoming) some care workers found themselves unable to provide companionate care over long periods of the day when they were employed by a care user they found 'difficult', and the consequence was a high turnover of personnel for this particular care user. On the whole, however, UK care workers said that they preferred to deliver care to one employer, comparing this to what a number of them called the 'conveyor belt' of care within residential care homes. As some of them further said, caring within the direct payments scheme meant that they felt themselves to be 'part of the family'.

Working conditions

In two of the schemes operating within this study – the Netherlands personal budget scheme and the Austrian CARITAS scheme – there was considerable bureaucratisation, through the means of elaborate contracts concerned with hours worked and rates of pay for particular types of task, of *time* spent caring. These schemes were largely orientated toward the full commodification of informal care, and it is striking that, in both of them, it was this issue of time that was carefully regulated, rather than the health and safety of the care giver/worker. It was also striking that in a situation where care givers'/workers' time was carefully allocated to caring tasks through the contract, and, for example, they received holiday entitlements, many of these fully commodified kin carers stated that they did not take their holiday entitlements, and they preferred to provide care as and when they were needed rather than according to the hours contracted. Such working beyond contract is not at all surprising, given the way in which many of these relationships predated the cash for care schemes and were more determined by affect than by contract. However, it was noticeable that there was no training available that might have helped with health and safety matters or support when health broke down. Nevertheless, these workers were protected by participation in their national social security schemes and some employment rights.

Agency workers, especially those working in France, worked to carefully regulated and scheduled hours and were trained in matters of health and safety. Indeed, a large number of the French agency workers were qualified with the French care diploma, which also meant that they worked within a strict occupational hierarchy and division of caring labour. Their working conditions were impacted by the fact that, working for multiple clients, they felt constantly rushed and unable to put into practice the holistic care that they were trained to practice. At the other end of the spectrum, co-resident care workers, such as the migrants and the fully commodified informal carers, often found that time hung heavy on their hands and/or it was not possible to establish boundaries such that they could achieve personal time for themselves (for some examples, see Ungerson and Yeandle, 2005). Again, the cash for care schemes within which many migrant workers worked were indifferent as to their health and safety and social rights.

The UK direct payments scheme contained aspects of all these elements of working conditions, depending on whether the care workers were employed through an agency, and whether or not they were co-resident. Despite the fact that all the care users in the UK sample had been in contact with and supported by a voluntary organisation whose main objective was to support direct payments users, it was noticeable that this support did not extend to the care workers employed within the local direct payments scheme: most had no knowledge of their social and employment rights and, when they experienced bad employment practice, were unable to access redress. Thus, on the whole, the working conditions of many of these care workers, in all the schemes, were not wholly satisfactory and sometimes, particularly in the case of undocumented co-resident migrant workers who felt trapped in uncongenial work with difficult employers, deeply unsatisfactory. This is not the same as saying that the work itself was unsatisfying – indeed, many of these workers reported considerable satisfaction with the work they did. It is the present author's interpretation, not theirs, that, at the same time, they were subject to risks and vulnerabilities associated with totally unprotected or underprotected paid work.

Conclusions

This chapter has argued that, on the whole, employment relationships are determined by the cash for care schemes within which they occur – except for the UK scheme, where extrinsic factors and the variety of methods of recruitment and management of caring labour entailed a variety of types of employment relationship. Given the complexity of many of these relationships it seems invidious to try to sort them into a hierarchy of relative satisfactoriness, but it is an advantage of comparative research that it can throw light on how national policy might be altered so that it attains some of the apparent advantages of other schemes. It is noticeable that in some of these schemes, particularly in the UK, both sides of the employment relationship reported difficulties – notably on the employer side, in the UK, with recruitment of reliable care workers, and on the employee side, in the UK (and in Italy), with difficult and over-controlling employers. The best employment relationships, and the longest lasting, were those where kin, often spouses, were paid to care, and as in the Dutch and Austrian CARITAS schemes, were protected by an external organisation which paid their salaries and underwrote their social and employment rights (although, as was pointed out earlier, these schemes seem to be indifferent as to the health and safety of the care workers/care givers). The high take-up, especially of the Dutch personal care budget scheme, almost certainly reflects the easier recruitment situation for those care users who have an obvious informal carer within their kin network and who can therefore simultaneously resolve the issue of labour recruitment and trust; in contrast the UK scheme, which discourages the employment of relatives and co-residents except in exceptional circumstances, means that care users have to improvise recruitment methods and recruit labour that is not necessarily well motivated, let alone proficient in care. The same is true of the unregulated Italian scheme where we encountered, in our sample, some very unhappy migrant workers who felt trapped and exploited and who may well have been delivering low-quality care. These comments do tend to drive to the conclusion that the most satisfactory working conditions and the most satisfactory employment relationships occurred in the Dutch cash for care scheme, where relatives can be employed to care. That said, it is important to note that the Dutch scheme is currently being altered so that eligibility for the personal care budget is considerably reduced and the amounts available to individual care users cut back. There is no doubt that the underwriting of good employment relationships and working conditions within a cash for care scheme is very expensive, and the politics of care users and of care givers are not yet strong enough to put these more robust and generous arrangements in place, and sustain them.

Notes

[1] The research on which this chapter is based was funded by the Economic and Social Research Council within the Future of Work Programme, grant number: L212252080.

[2] The research teams were as follows: *Austria*: August Oesterle and Elisabeth Hammer, Vienna University of Economics and Business Administration; *France*: Claude Martin and Blanche Le Bihan, Ecole Nationale de la Santé, Rennes; *Italy*: Cristiano Gori, Barbara da Roit and Michela Barbot, Istituto per la Recerca Sociale, Milan; *Netherlands*: Marja Pijl, Clarie Ramakers, Fransje Baarveld, University of Nijmegen; *UK*: Sue Yeandle and Bernadette Stiell, Sheffield Hallam University.

[3] More detail concerning many of the examples described in this chapter can be found in Ungerson (2003, 2004, and forthcoming), and Ungerson and Yeandle (2005).

References

Commission for Social Care Inspection (2004) *Direct payments: What are the barriers?*, London: Commission for Social Care Inspection.

Gori, C. (1999) *Contrasted situations at the local level: the Italian case*, Paper presented at the international seminar on 'Policies towards the frail elderly in Europe', Rennes, France: Ecole Nationale de la Santé.

Gori, C. (2003) *Payments for care in Italy*, Background briefing paper for the International Conference on the Direct Employment of Domiciliary Care by Older People, ESRC Future of Work Programme, London: Policy Studies Institute.

Kestenbaum, A. (1996) *Independent living: A review*, York: Joseph Rowntree Foundation.

Martin, C. (2003) *Brief description of the French cash for care benefit for the dependent frail elderly*, Background briefing paper for the International Conference on the Direct Employment of Domiciliary Care by Older People, ESRC Future of Work Programme, London: Policy Studies Institute.

Milburn, A. (2002), Speech to the National Social Services Conference, 16 October, Cardiff, Wales.

Morris, J. (1993) *Independent lives: Community care and disabled people*, Basingstoke: Macmillan.

Oesterle, A. (2003) *Austria's Pflegegeld system*, Background briefing paper for the International Conference on the Direct Employment of Domiciliary Care by Older People, ESRC Future of Work Programme, London: Policy Studies Institute,.

Pijl, M. (2003) *The Dutch Care Allowance*, Background briefing paper for the International Conference on the Direct Employment of Domiciliary Care by Older People, ESRC Future of Work Programme, London: Policy Studies Institute.

Ungerson, C. (1997a) 'Social politics and the commodification of care', *Social Politics*, vol 4, no 3, pp 362-81.

Ungerson, C. (1997b) 'Give them the money: is cash a route to empowerment?', *Social Policy and Administration*, vol 31, no 1, pp 45-53.

Ungerson, C. (1999) 'Personal assistants and disabled people: an examination of a hybrid form of work and care', *Work, Employment & Society*, vol 13, no 4, pp 583-600.

Ungerson, C. (2003) 'Commodified care work in European labour markets', *European Societies*, vol 5, no 4, pp 377-96.

Ungerson, C. (2004) 'Whose empowerment and independence? A cross-national perspective on "cash for care" schemes', *Ageing and Society*, vol 24, no 2, pp 189-212.

Ungerson, C. (forthcoming) 'Care, work and feeling', in M. Glucksmann, J. Parry, L. Pettingen and R. Taylor (eds) *The new sociology of work*, Oxford: Blackwell.

Ungerson, C. and Yeandle, S. (2005) 'Care workers and work–life balance: the example of domiciliary careworkers', in D. Houston (ed) *Work–life balance in the 21st century*, London: Palgrave.

SIXTEEN

Can intensive support widen access to direct payments?

Laura Luckhurst

The 1996 Community Care (Direct Payments) Act enabled local authorities to make direct payments to disabled people as an alternative to receiving services, giving them choice and control over their support. From the beginning, concerns began to be expressed that certain groups of potential users would in effect be excluded from access to direct payments (see, for example, Ryan, 1998).

Department of Health (DH) annual returns reveal that these fears have been realised. Take-up of direct payments by older people, people with learning difficulties, and mental health service users has continued to be alarmingly low. For the purposes of this study, attention was focused on these three 'marginalised' groups, because they continue to have demonstrably low take-up, despite being eligible for direct payments since 1997 (in the case of people with learning difficulties and mental health service users), or since 2000 (in the case of older people).

Research appears to indicate that one of the factors in the low take-up was that some potential direct payments users feared the responsibilities and were unclear whether and how they would receive ongoing support with these (Gramlich et al, 2002; Clark et al, 2004; Spandler and Vick, 2004). A range of proposals have aimed to address these issues. These include the promotion of direct payments in accessible formats, the training of social services staff, and so on. There have also been a number of proposals on specific schemes for supporting individuals, such as, for example, independent living trusts, circles of support, and brokering schemes. In 2003 the Direct Payments Development Fund made funding available to Direct Payments Support Services (DPSSs) for the development of projects that would address the low take-up problems, some of which focused on intensive support schemes.

In the face of low take-up by some marginalised groups, DPSSs have been requesting better guidance on good practice and, in particular, the best ways to support people. Concern specifically focused on enabling people who face barriers to communication to get their voices heard in relation to direct payments; and providing ongoing support with management of direct payments to enable independent living.

Intensive support schemes

In response to these concerns, the National Centre for Independent Living (NCIL) decided to take a close look at the support models that had been proposed, and commissioned the study discussed in this chapter, which therefore looked at the following forms of support.

Independent living trusts

These are groups governed by a trust deed. They have the power to receive monies on behalf of an individual, act for that individual and be an employer. The disabled person for whose benefit the trust and the direct payments are intended may or may not be a member of the trust. An independent living trust deed has as its objectives to enable the individual to live independently.

Third party payments

'Third party payments' (or 'indirect payments') are terms used to describe a wide variety of arrangements where someone other than the disabled person either assists with the management or receives or holds the direct payment on that person's behalf. It may be, for example, that the payment is made to an organisation on behalf of the individual. The organisation may then hold the money on behalf of the person, or pass it directly on to him or her. The organisation may assist with a range of tasks, such as recruitment, staff management, payroll, and so on. In some cases it may even employ staff on behalf of the individual. 'Third party payments' is also the term used to describe arrangements where the money is paid to the individual but managed with the assistance of (usually) a nominated person who again may help with any of the tasks of managing a direct payment. The term is also used to describe a scheme where enhanced payments are made, with the intention that the individual will use an agency's services, thereby avoiding many of the administrative responsibilities of managing a direct payment. For the purposes of this study, all these schemes are referred to as third party payments.

Brokering

A broker, who is an independent person or organisation accountable to the direct payments recipient, finds and purchases or arranges services on their behalf, according to their preferences. Being independent the broker is not tied to traditional solutions or structures in arranging services.

User-controlled personal assistance agencies

An organisation of disabled people may set up an agency employing personal assistants to work for direct payments users. Normally, personal assistants are recruited and 'ring-fenced' to work with specific individuals who choose them. The agency may, for example, assist the individual to write their job description.

For the sake of consistency, the above-mentioned schemes when referred to collectively will be termed 'intensive support schemes'. The NCIL study aimed to investigate the types of intensive support schemes currently being offered by DPSSs, and where they are operating; the factors that have influenced their provision; their impact on the take-up of direct payments by marginalised user groups; their effectiveness in supporting independent living; and the implications for policy practice.

The study reported here involved a survey of the literature; a questionnaire survey of all DPSSs in England and Wales concerning the use of the different intensive support schemes and their impact on take-up of direct payments by different impairment groups; and a more detailed investigation of intensive support schemes, by individual interviews with users, direct payments advisors and social services managers in each of three focus areas. The research was carried out between September 2003 and December 2004.

A national picture

A survey of 140 DPSSs in England and Wales was carried out between October and December 2003 and a response rate of 36% (50 responses) was achieved. The DPSSs were asked to indicate which, if any, of the intensive support models outlined above, they offered. Only those currently providing the service were counted. Fourteen DPSSs were using third party payments, five were supporting individuals with setting up independent living trusts, and three were offering other types of intensive support. None was offering brokering or personal assistance agencies.

The survey thus clearly established that intensive support schemes such as independent living trusts, third party schemes and brokering are poorly developed nationally: third party or indirect payments were found in just over a quarter of those responding (14 schemes out of 50, or 27%); independent living trusts were found in only five out of 50 (10%) of schemes, and brokering and personal assistance agencies were not found in any of the schemes responding.

Direct Payments Support Services were also asked to provide breakdowns of their users by age, user or impairment group, and minority ethnic identification. These user profiles from each DPSS were compared with the types of intensive support scheme provided. Direct Payments Support Services offering third party or indirect payments were very successful in reaching older people, who formed on average 16% of their users (compared with 12% for all services). They also did particularly well at reaching black and minority ethnic disabled people, who formed 18% of their users.

Direct Payments Support Services offering support via independent living trusts were particularly successful in reaching people with learning difficulties, who formed on average 24% of their users, considerably higher than the average for all services, which was 14.5%. More surprisingly, perhaps, this group of services was also very successful at reaching carers of disabled children, these forming 8% of their users, as opposed to 6% for all services, and was the second most successful at reaching marginalised groups as a whole, who formed 44% of their users.

Direct Payments Support Services that did not offer any type of intensive support scheme were nonetheless successful in reaching marginalised groups as a whole, who formed 45% of their users. This is likely to be partly explained by their particular success with reaching carers with disabled children. These formed 12% of their users, as compared with an average of 6% for all services.

For an indication of how well independent living trusts and third party or indirect payments work in practice, and of whether they give users choice and control, we asked DPSSs to list their impression of the advantages and disadvantages of these different schemes. As a control, they were asked to list advantages and disadvantages of 'standard' direct payments.

The perceived advantages of 'standard' direct payments placed them very firmly within the independent living agenda: independence, choice, control, flexibility and having suitable staff. The profile of third party or indirect payments differed only slightly from that of direct payments. Here, the main advantages clearly did include choice, control and flexibility, but avoidance of administrative responsibilities was also a key feature. Avoiding conflicts of interest was another advantage, while significantly some respondents actually felt that third party or indirect payments could offer greater flexibility than direct payments.

Choice and control were less evident in the responses about independent living trusts. Practical issues connected with the management of direct payments were very much to the fore. They were seen as having the advantages of sharing responsibility, coordinating support to an individual, and giving trust members a clear role where they take their responsibilities seriously. Enabling an individual to have choice and control, even though not passing the 'able and willing test' was given as one of the advantages.

Funding was reported as presenting a major obstacle to DPSSs wishing to develop intensive support schemes. Some DPSSs also said they had encountered opposition from their local authority to developing support models such as third party payments. Operational matters such as availability of suitable personal assistants, problems experienced by users in opening bank accounts, and lack of awareness by care managers and other professionals in some areas also caused difficulties. A small number of DPSSs did not want to develop any intensive support schemes, either because they did not see the need for them, or because they were actually opposed in principle to them, seeing them as a dilution of the goals of independent living, choice and control that direct payments exist to achieve.

In summary, only two intensive support schemes are being taken up in any numbers, and those are independent living trusts and third party or indirect payments. Even these are not widely available and independent living trusts were only found in five DPSS areas. The statistical data did strongly suggest that having access to these intensive support schemes widened the access to direct payments, enabling more people with learning difficulties and older people to receive them. Third party payments seem to contribute to better access by black and minority ethnic disabled people.

How intensive support schemes work in practice

In-depth investigations were carried out in three locations in England. The locations were chosen primarily to enable information to be collected about the operation of third party payments and independent living trusts, and to represent as far as possible a reasonable geographical spread around England, with some rural and some urban areas. It was decided not to pursue brokering and personal assistance agency schemes further at this stage, because the focus of the study was to gather information about schemes that were being taken up and working in practice. The survey had suggested that brokering and personal assistance agencies, at present, have not been substantially taken up, for whatever reason.

In each of the three sites, interviews were carried out with users of third party payments schemes and independent living trusts, trustees or third parties (supporters), DPSS staff, and social services managers.

The experience of users and their supporters

Both independent living trusts and third party payments schemes had been effective in enabling people who might otherwise have been excluded to access direct payments. The majority of the people using these intensive support schemes to help them access direct payments were older people or people with learning difficulties who faced considerable barriers to communication in addition to having very high support needs. It is probably no exaggeration to say that in some cases this had saved lives: several individuals had only been able to remain in the community and avoid residential care, and two people were reported as only being alive today as a result of the direct payments.

For most people using independent living trusts or third party payments, the benefits had been enormous. Individuals experienced better health, the continuity and familiarity of staff who were loyal and committed, better personal relationships with their staff and with a widening range of social contacts, and enjoyable and stimulating activities and interests, such as music, art, swimming, and holidays with or without the family. Some third party payments users additionally felt they benefited from support that was flexible and assured a quick response in emergencies, enabling them to complete their degree or other education, acquire new skills and get a job, and have a full social life.

Problems frequently experienced by users of both schemes included difficulties opening up bank accounts and not being allowed to employ relatives. (However, since 2003, the restrictions on relatives have been eased: DH, 2003.) Administration, financial monitoring and other restrictive rules about use of direct payments also caused difficulties. Independent living trust users were more likely to report difficulties recruiting staff (which may be partly explained by the fact that most of these were based in rural areas). Third party payments users, in contrast, were more likely to have experienced unsatisfactory staff at times.

Some trustees of independent living trusts complained that they had not been offered a choice as to whether to have an independent living trust or not. It was presented as the 'only way' a person could receive a direct payment, and since in some rural areas the only service available was a direct payment, they felt they had no choice but to accept.

Problems with the care management and assessment process were also reported by both groups, possibly reflecting a lower level of awareness of the wider context of independent living among these care managers, and the impact of Fair Access to Care assessments. (Fair Access to Care Services guidance was introduced in 2002 with the aim of setting a framework for local authority eligibility criteria. Levels of risk to independence were set as the main criteria for receiving a service; however, no additional resources were provided; see DH, 2002.) People reported social services professionals, for example, querying why a person needed a daily bath, or simply refusing to offer a community care assessment.

While acknowledging the undoubted benefits experienced by people using independent living trusts and third party payments, we were particularly interested in seeing whether they experienced independent living outcomes: in other words, did they have choice and control over their lives?

The key determinant of users' level of choice and control appeared to be the barriers to communication that they faced, rather than the type of intensive support scheme they were using. For those people who did not communicate verbally or had very limited verbal communication, their family and those around them relied on a range of behavioural signals and non-verbal communication to determine their choices. These people tended to be using independent living trusts, although a few used third party payments. For these people, staff selection and choice of activities were the main areas where they were able to exercise some choice, and these were obviously contributing greatly to quality of life. However, there were signs that the wider independent living agenda was not being systematically addressed: for example, one person (who had some limited verbal communication and supplemented this with an electronic communication aid) said he did not control any money of his own, and that he would like to. There was little evidence of any planning for the future where young people were using independent living trusts; indeed, one trustee expressed surprise at the notion that the trust could be used to facilitate such planning. Communication support, speech therapy, person-centred plans or advocacy might have been included in people's care plans, either to be purchased via direct payments or as additional support, to enable these young people to have more of a voice, but there were no examples of this happening in the areas we visited.

Those people who faced lesser barriers to communication tended in the main to use third party payments. These people were much more clearly in control of their support and their lives. One young man described how he had used his buying power with the agencies to find one that provided him with staff of similar age and interests to himself, and said he was "completely in control of my own money and decisions". Another told how, since getting the direct payment, he had found a job and learnt new skills, and was clearly very proud of his achievements.

Direct payments advisors' experiences

Direct payments advisors in the DPSSs studied were in the main positive about independent living trusts and third party payments, and saw it as a natural part of their role to support people with setting up and managing these schemes. There were different views as to the staff and resource implications of doing this. Some thought that, for example, supporting the set-up of an independent living trust was not overly time-consuming, although finding trustees and informing and training them did involve committing some extra time. Others perceived it as potentially more demanding than this. None of the DPSSs had staff or resources specifically allocated to this work.

In some cases, the adoption of a solution such as an independent living trust was in response to the situation of one individual. Having researched and developed procedures for implementing that solution, this then became an available option for subsequent newcomers to direct payments in that area. In another case, the option of third party payments was introduced as a general response to a perceived issue of access for older people.

The schemes were seen as hugely beneficial to users, since in many cases they would have been refused a direct payment without them:

> "It is vital, if they can't have a direct payment without it."
> (Direct payments advisor)

However, there were some concerns about the extent to which arrangements such as independent living trusts and third party payments could guarantee the person choice and control in the same way a direct payment can:

> "Families may not understand the wider issues of choice and control, independent living philosophy, etc., they just tend to look at 'better outcomes' for their son or daughter."
> (Direct payments advisor)

It was felt that having a larger number of trustees (at least three) was helpful in terms of bringing in fresh views, and holding regular meetings where all trust members could be involved in decisions helped to safeguard the independence of the user. A strong view was expressed that, for some people with very high support needs and facing communication barriers, the issue of getting their voice heard was there anyway, and it was not the independent living trust, third party or, indeed, direct payment that was causing this to be an issue.

Nevertheless, the setting up of a direct payment is an opportunity to consider a person's wider independent living needs and, indeed, is intended to provide independent living, choice and control. It is important that such opportunities are not lost, and that independent living outcomes are not overlooked in the struggle to achieve what is, in effect, good quality community care.

All direct payments advisors had experienced difficulty accessing information about independent living trusts and third party payments. The information produced by Values Into Action (Holman with Bewley, 1999; Holman and Bewley, 2001), was appreciated, but was not widely publicised. Their main sources of information apart from this were NCIL and networking with other support services.

Some advisors had found social services to be over-cautious, and wanted to see more training for social workers and care managers. Government policy initiatives affecting people with learning difficulties and older people, such as Fair Access to Care (DH, 2002), and Supporting People (ODPM, 2004), had not been found particularly helpful in supporting people's moves towards independence. There were calls for simple guidance on how independent living trusts work and how to set them up, more training and ongoing support to independent living trustees, and more access to advocacy for users. One team had been making links with local banks and wanted to use this to educate bank staff about their responsibilities towards disabled people wanting to open bank accounts.

Social services managers' views

The social services managers interviewed had a general overview of independent living trusts and third party payments, but were not always familiar with the details of how these operated. They all felt that information was hard to obtain. Interpretations of when it was appropriate to use an independent living trust varied from "when a person is unable to manage but able to consent", to "a way of determining whether or not they consent, when their ability to consent is not clear", to "it being a way of supporting a person to manage a direct payment where a parent didn't feel able to manage it on their own [on behalf of the direct payment user]".

There was also questioning of the motivations behind the use of third party payments, which some felt were more because people lacked confidence than because they were actually unable to manage. Generally, however, independent living trusts and third party payments were seen as very important, and definitely the way forward for some people. One manager suggested that what was most helpful was having a range of different support options, to enable people to choose what suited them best.

It was acknowledged by some that social services staff could be an obstacle due to their lack of expertise and confidence. Legal departments were also understood to find these schemes challenging. There were calls to make the guidance on direct payments simpler, although the 2003 guidance, which permits direct payments users to have help from any other person with managing their direct payments and frees up the restrictions on who may be employed, was found to be very helpful (DH, 2003). The fact that local authorities now had a duty to provide direct payments had also been found useful.

A number of other initiatives were also helping to extend direct payments to groups such as older people and people with learning difficulties: in one area, the Valuing People Implementation Team had supported the building up of a direct payments network within learning difficulties teams. A champions group was being set up in another area, and a training department was being asked to include direct payments in the foundation training for social services staff.

Conclusions from in-depth interviews

Users had undoubtedly benefited greatly from both third party payments and independent living trusts. High-quality community care outcomes were being achieved, and in most cases some independent living outcomes were also happening. However, there were some situations where the opportunities for independent living had not been fully exploited.

Conclusions

The study set out to investigate a range of intensive support schemes: independent living trusts, third party schemes, independent brokering agencies, and user-controlled personal assistance agencies. None of these is widely used nationally, but independent living trusts and third party/indirect payments are now available in a few areas. Circles of support, brokering and personal assistance agencies appear not to have been developed to any great extent.

Fourteen DPSSs offered third party payments schemes, while independent living trusts were found in five DPSSs. The reasons for the adoption of particular forms of 'intensive support' were not always clear, reflecting the uncertainty of DPSSs and social services departments over both the guidance around 'willing and able' and the relative value and effectiveness of different options. This also reflected the general lack of information and guidance on different schemes and what is involved in setting them up. The reasons for having independent living trusts are not clearly established, and different social services managers appear to work from different assumptions about them.

In some cases, the adoption of a scheme such as independent living trusts was in response to the situation of one individual. Having researched and developed procedures for implementing that solution, this then became an available option for subsequent newcomers to direct payments in that area. There were a significant minority of DPSSs for whom local authority policy was a barrier to them developing third party schemes. The reasons for brokering and user-controlled personal assistance agencies not being adopted are unclear. In general, DPSSs referred to lack of funding and other resources, local authority policy, and uncertainty over guidance, as barriers to developing all types of intensive support.

Rural DPSSs were more likely to adopt independent living trusts. We should be cautious in reading too much into this, due to the small numbers of DPSSs involved; however, individuals suggested that this is associated with the lack of any alternative services in these areas. Third party payments were more evenly distributed around the country, although again they are very small in number. Resourcing of direct payments support schemes is an issue that needs careful attention: it would appear that the larger, better-resourced schemes have been better able to develop 'intensive support' schemes. There was a continuing need for better and more accessible information about intensive support schemes, and for care managers to receive better training. Information needs include clarification of the guidance around people's ability and willingness to manage direct payments.

Offering intensive support schemes did enable authorities to reach more people in marginalised groups. Where independent living trusts were offered, a significantly higher percentage of users were people with learning difficulties. Where third party schemes were offered, a higher percentage of users were older people.

Where independent living trusts had been used, it was almost exclusively with people with learning difficulties who faced very significant communication barriers. It remains less clear whether the provision of independent living trusts influences the availability of direct payments to the whole range of people with learning difficulties or, for example, older people. It would be very useful to see some action research looking at the relevance of independent living trusts with a wider range of users. Third party payments, on the other hand, seemed to be used and actively welcomed by a range of users including older people, people with learning difficulties and younger people under 25 years old with physical impairments.

The benefits for some of those using independent living trusts cannot be overestimated: they were literally life-saving. Users additionally benefited from good personal relationships with their staff, improvement in their social contacts, and continuity and flexibility of care. They experienced a very good quality of life compared with anything else that was available. At the same time, independent living trusts were sometimes perceived as a 'way around' the legal restrictions on direct payments, rather than in terms of an opportunity to involve the direct payments user in decisions about their life. There was a feeling expressed by some people that independent living trusts were an imposition by the local authority, and possibly an intrusion into the family's affairs. Their potential in terms of enabling the user to have a voice in his or her day-to-day support was not always being exploited to the full, and ambitions and social contacts could remain quite limited for the trust beneficiary.

Third party payments came in a wide variety of forms, but a common theme was the perceived advantage of shared responsibility. They were sometimes seen as flexible, and giving consistency and reliability. Younger disabled people could find them empowering, enabling them, for example, to complete their studies without all the responsibility for administration that direct payments might otherwise entail. Third party payments were seen as enabling the advantages of direct payments without the administrative disadvantages, although sometimes they could also be inflexible and give users less choice and control.

Government policy and local authorities were perceived by some respondents to this study as unsupportive of the development of third party schemes. Direct Payments Support Services expressed much interest and enthusiasm for developing appropriate intensive support schemes. The resource implications were not thought to be prohibitive, but there was clearly an issue of staff time at an early developmental stage in order for staff to bring themselves 'up to speed' so as to be able to support and advise on setting up independent living trusts. The resource implications of third party payments depend to a large degree on the type envisaged. Some, for example where the arrangement is simply for a friend, relative or neighbour to assist the person with managing direct payments, probably take up very little more time to set up than 'standard' direct payments. However, these schemes could be open to the accusation that they provide very few safeguards to the direct payments recipient. On the other hand, setting up a scheme where, for example, the DPSS administers the direct payments on behalf of the user, would require a considerable input of staff time both to develop and set up, and in order to run the scheme. It seems likely that a very small DPSS would not have the resources to develop this type of support scheme.

Schemes such as independent living trusts also require DPSS schemes to develop skills in working with parents, spouses and other relatives to ensure that all those involved in supporting an individual with direct payments understand the aims of independent living and their role.

Direct payments are a means to an end: that end is independent living, and independent living means choice and control over one's life. Independent living trusts and third party payments have achieved some important independent living outcomes for individuals whose choices would be very limited indeed without them: having a choice over staff and being able to form positive personal relationships with them, choosing their own daily activities and pursuing their own interests, being able to eat the food they like, and experiencing a widening of social contacts are extremely valuable outcomes. For some, these schemes have achieved even more: learning new skills, completing training and education, getting a job, achieving personal goals. However, for some people, barriers to communication may mean there needs to be significant investment in enabling them to make and express choices in their daily lives. For some people, support with communication and decision making and ensuring that they have access to independent advocacy may therefore be vital elements in ensuring the success of direct payments. It is critical that these elements are considered at the stage of setting up direct payments.

This study suggests that the provision of intensive support schemes is a vital component of direct payments support, enabling many to access direct payments who would not otherwise do so. By giving people access to direct payments, these intensive support schemes do open the door to significant independent living gains for some people. However, attention to such issues as communication support, advocacy and supported decision making could greatly enhance the outcomes for some intensive support scheme direct payments users.

While resources are not always the main issue, there will undoubtedly be some local authorities in which resourcing of direct payments support could be reviewed in the light of these findings. Government could also help by clarifying that there are no restrictions on the development and/or continuation of third party and indirect payments schemes by DPSSs. Clear and accessible guidance on intensive support schemes has not been readily available, and would help DPSSs, social services, users and their families to understand the types of intensive support which could be used and when they might be appropriate.

References

Clark, H., Gough, H. and Macfarlane, A. (2004) *'It pays dividends': Direct payments and older people*, Bristol: The Policy Press.

DH (2002) *Fair access to care services: Guidance on eligibility criteria for adult social care*, London: DH.

DH (2003) *Direct payments guidance: Community care, services for carers and children's services (direct payments) guidance, England 2003*, London: DH.

Gramlich, S., McBride, G., Snelham, N. and Myers, B. with Williams, V. and Simons, K. (2002) *Journey to independence: What self-advocates tell us about direct payments*, Kidderminster: British Institute of Learning Disabilities.

Holman, A. with Bewley, C. (1999) *Funding freedom 2000: People with learning difficulties using direct payments*, London: Values into Action.

Holman, A. and Bewley, C. (2001) *Trusting independence − a practical guide to independent living trusts*, London: Values into Action and Community Living.

ODPM (Office of the Deputy Prime Minister) (2004) *Supporting people guidance*, (www.spkweb.org.uk).

Ryan, T. (1998) 'Questions of control and consent', *Care Plan*, vol 5, no 2, pp 10-14.

Spandler, H. and Vick, N. (2004) *Direct payments, independent living and mental health – an evaluation*, London: Health and Social Care Advisory Service.

SEVENTEEN

Care managers and direct payments

Annette Lomas

"Direct payments can offer people a new beginning and a chance of a better quality of life." (Care manager)

Direct payments offer the opportunity for older people to have far greater power, choice and control over the way their support is delivered (Leece, 2001; Clark et al, 2004). Yet despite the growing merits of using direct payments with older people, the indications are that their take-up of direct payments remains low. With high expectations by the government that local authorities will significantly increase the number of older people using direct payments, the possible barriers affecting take-up need to be explored.

This chapter briefly explains the background to direct payments and details findings from a study of two areas in one local authority, undertaken early in 2003 for a post-qualifying award in social work. Previous research has identified that care managers are key to enabling older people to access direct payments (see Glasby and Littlechild, 2002; Clark et al, 2004), and this study explores care managers' knowledge, confidence and views about direct payments, to consider whether these factors have influenced the take-up by older people. The study posed three research questions: what is the level of care managers' knowledge of direct payments (the term 'care manager in this study refers to a social worker or an unqualified social care assessor)? Do care managers feel confident about advising and implementing direct payments with service users? Do care managers feel that direct payments are a good way of meeting service users' needs?

Background

The 1996 Community Care (Direct Payments) Act, implemented in April 1997, originally limited eligibility to people under 65 years of age but was extended to include older people from 1 February 2000. While the power to provide direct payments was initially optional, it became a mandatory duty upon local authorities to offer direct payments to service users in April 2003 (after this research was undertaken), under the 2001 Health and Social Care Act (see DH, 2001). There are no studies as yet that examine whether making direct payments a duty has made a difference to care managers' practice with regard to direct payments, although early data from a survey of all local authorities in England, gathered almost a year after direct payments were made mandatory, found that on average 58% of service users with physical or sensory disabilities said their care manager had not told them about direct payments (DH, 2004). Making direct payments a mandatory responsibility may not change practitioners' views about whether direct payments are a good way to meet service users' needs. While care managers may (or may not) now be offering direct payments, if they are offered without enthusiasm then it is unlikely that people will take them up (Hasler and Campbell, 2000). Whether care managers feel confident about offering direct payments and see them as a viable option is crucial.

There is little published work on direct payments which focuses specifically on the needs and views of older people, and the research that exists suggests that older people benefit from direct payments in the same way as younger disabled people (Clark and Spafford, 2001; Leece, 2001; Glasby, 2002; Clark et al, 2004). In particular, older people value the continuity of support that direct payments can provide; as one Staffordshire direct payment user said: "Before I had direct payments I had about 40 Homecare Workers in 2 years" (Leece, 2001, p 24).

In the study by Clark et al (2004), undertaken in three different local authorities in England, older direct payments users reported feeling increased happiness and motivation, with direct payments seen as crucial in enabling some older people to remain living at home. However, despite service users reporting higher satisfaction levels with direct payments than with directly provided services, take-up of direct payments remains slow among older people. Indeed, provisional figures from the councils' delivery and improvement statements (September 2003) report that, although there were around 12,600 people receiving direct payments in England, fewer than 2,000 were older people (CSCI, 2004).

There are a number of barriers to the progress of direct payments (Witcher et al, 2000), key among which may be the lack of knowledge and confidence of care managers (Hasler and Zarb, 2000; Glasby and Littlechild, 2001). The Social Services Inspectorate (SSI) carried out a national programme of inspections during 1999 and found that some staff were 'ambivalent' about the introduction of direct payments and lacked knowledge about direct payment legislation (Fruin, 2000). As one social worker from a multi-disciplinary team put it:

> "I am very worried about direct payments – vulnerable people managing their own services." (Fruin, 2000, p 17)

Consequently, service users could be disadvantaged in terms of opportunities for accessing direct payments (DH/SSI, 1999).

Similar findings also emerged from research into direct payment pilot schemes in Norfolk (Dawson, 2000) and Staffordshire (Leece, 2000), where the need to promote awareness of direct payments not only among service users but also among care managers was highlighted. Data from Dawson's (2000) work suggest that the most crucial factor in determining whether or not a person takes up direct payments is the approach of their care manager. Other research studies such as Rainey (1999), Maglajlic et al (2000) and CSCI (2004) have mirrored these findings, in that social workers continued to have a poor knowledge of direct payments and limited training opportunities generally.

Early research conducted by Age Concern (1998) indicates similar findings in the area of older people, in that few staff within social services *at that time* knew anything about direct payments. A much more recent report highlighted how direct payments are still not part of the culture of care management. Care managers were found to lack confidence and sufficient knowledge when offering direct payments to older people. As one care manager said:

> "I just don't understand it. It's not user friendly. Because I don't understand it, I don't think I can explain it." (Clark et al, 2004, p 41)

This research raises serious questions as to how service users are to be kept informed, especially as Clark et al (2004) found that care managers are the single most common source of information for older people to find out about direct payments. With pressure from the government to "make direct payments a reality" for older people (Milburn, 2002), my study aimed to discover whether care managers are acting as a barrier to take-up in one local authority in England. More specifically, the study aimed to examine care managers' knowledge, confidence and views on direct payments, to consider if these factors have influenced the take-up of direct payments by older people.

At the time of this study in early 2003, the local authority had been operating a direct payments scheme for five years; having extended direct payments to older people in the year 2000. For adults and older people, the scheme focused on offering support with personal care. Direct payments for respite and day care had not been implemented, neither had the restriction been lifted on using direct payments to secure support from a relative. A service level agreement had been established with a local charity to offer support and act as advisors to service users interested in direct payments. Figures collated in March 2003 for the local authority showed that out of 176 people on direct payments, only 21 were older people.

Methodology

The research method used in this study was a semi-structured questionnaire designed to collect both quantitative and qualitative data. As a research tool, questionnaires are time-efficient for the respondent to complete and provide an understandable and respected means of gathering data (Bryman, 2001). Although it would have been more reliable to use a questionnaire previously developed (Gibbs, 1991), this was not possible due to the lack of past research undertaken in this particular area.

The questionnaire requested brief personal details from the respondents, including how many service users they had helped on the direct payments scheme. By collecting this data, knowledge would be gained as to how many respondents had actually implemented direct payments. Under each of the three research questions, a tick box was included to provide a baseline of factual information, and the respondent was then invited to comment on their experiences in greater depth. The questionnaire was designed to be completed anonymously with details kept confidential, to encourage the respondents to express their views honestly and openly.

The local authority in which the study took place is in the north of England. Two areas of the local authority were chosen based on use of direct payments to enable comparisons to be made. One chosen area had the lowest take-up rate for older people in the local authority and the other area the highest take-up rate, with three and 13 older people using direct payments, respectively. These areas will be referred to as the low take-up area and the high take-up area. Twenty questionnaires were sent to each area for distribution to care managers. In response,

11 questionnaires were completed and returned from each area (22 in total). Of those returned, five care managers from the high take-up area had implemented direct payments compared to none in the low take-up area.

Care managers' knowledge of direct payments

In response to the questionnaire, the majority of care managers (17) answered that their knowledge base of direct payments was satisfactory. Interestingly, none of the care managers in either area felt that they had a good knowledge of direct payments, with three care managers in the low take-up area and two care managers in the high take-up area saying that their knowledge of direct payments was poor.

The respondents' comments on the questionnaire revealed a key theme of limited training opportunities available in both areas. Seven care managers across both areas commented on the need for more training, with two care managers in the low take-up area and one care manager in the high take-up area describing training as 'infrequent'. Ten care managers who stated they had undergone training had participated in only one training course since direct payments were implemented. However, care managers in the high take-up area did note that they had gained knowledge from other sources such as team meetings, colleagues and through practical experience. Worryingly, eight care managers across both areas commented that they were not aware of any recent changes to policy or legislation, with one care manager saying:

> "I've been on one training day on direct payments approximately three years ago, with no update on policy.... As a result, the knowledge begins to fade and direct payments become a less immediate consideration when carrying out assessments."

These findings suggest that care managers do lack knowledge in the area of direct payments and that there were few training opportunities. This corresponds with other research undertaken (Rainey, 1999; Maglajlic et al, 2000; CSCI, 2004) which found that workers had limited knowledge of direct payments, with insufficient training given. Similarly, the SSI found that some staff members lacked knowledge about direct payments legislation and local procedures (Fruin, 2000).

This indicates that care managers should have access to frequent, local training to increase and maintain their knowledge base. Training should not only focus on the aims and philosophy of direct payments, but also on advantages and practical implementation issues, with clear, relevant and up-to-date information to enable care managers to explain to older people what direct payments involve.

Care managers' confidence about direct payments

The results show that a significant number of care managers (15) were only confident in some aspects of direct payments and nearly a quarter (five) were not confident at all. Surprisingly, two care managers in the low take-up area felt completely confident compared to none in the high take-up area, whereas three more care managers in the high take-up area were confident in some aspects of direct payments than those in the low take-up area.

Key themes of levels of practical experience and the frequency with which service users are told about direct payments emerged from the comments gathered. Interestingly, of the two care managers in the low take-up area who responded they were completely confident, only one of them had practical experience and noted, "I would not use direct payments again". Two other care managers in the low take-up area said that they had some practical experience, compared with five care managers in the high take-up area. Surprisingly, eight care managers across both areas said that they do not always tell service users about direct payments, and this may reflect that direct payments were not a mandatory duty at this time. However, recent statistics show that 48% of service users with a physical or sensory disability in the local authority in this study said their care manager had not told them about direct payments, and this was almost a year after direct payments were made mandatory (DH, 2004).

These results suggest that the majority of care managers in both areas were only confident in some aspects of advising and implementing direct payments, and several care managers were not confident at all. From the comments gathered, it appeared that confidence levels were linked to levels of practical experience, as two care managers summarised:

> "It is my lack of practical experience in direct payments that affects my confidence in this area."

and

"As I've only helped one person and that ended in an unsatisfactory arrangement and the direct payment had to be withdrawn, I do not feel confident in advising people."

These results mirror previous studies such as Carmichael et al's research in 2001, which highlighted a lack of confidence and a high level of anxiety among care managers regarding the complexity of direct payments. Similarly, Clark et al (2004) reported that care managers do not always feel confident about offering direct payments to older people. Interestingly, they too found links between confidence levels and practical experience, as care managers who were confident in this study had arranged direct payments and attended training.

Clearly, these findings highlight that care managers need more support and training in the area of direct payments to build their confidence levels and reduce the anxiety and tensions that have been created. Research has indicated that direct payments 'champions' can offer positive support and be inspirational to front-line workers (Hasler and Stewart, 2004). Given the outcome of this research, it would certainly be beneficial to ensure that each care management team has a worker with a lead role in direct payments, to offer support and encouragement to his or her colleagues. Allowing time for joint visits with the local support service could also be an important contributing factor in building care managers' confidence and experience with direct payments.

Care managers' views about direct payments

The results indicated that almost all of the care managers (20) felt that direct payments are only appropriate sometimes as a service option. However, care managers in the high take-up area were shown to be more positive about direct payments with two care managers answering that direct payments are a good way to meet service users' needs, compared with none in the other area.

Key themes as to the benefits and drawbacks of direct payments emerged from the respondents' comments. In terms of benefits, two care managers from each area responded that direct payments enabled greater control, with one care manager from each area saying that direct payments can be tailor-made for each individual. One care manager from the low take-up area and three care managers from the high take-up area felt that direct payments enabled more choice. Two successful direct payments cases were highlighted in the high take-up area involving older people with dementia, living at home with a large care package.

Many drawbacks were mentioned by respondents in both areas. A number of the disadvantages interlinked with each other, such as direct payments being too complex and, therefore, causing the process to be lengthy and not suitable for crisis situations. Two of the main drawbacks stated were that care managers felt that service users did not want the responsibility of direct payments and that direct payments were unsuitable for individuals with mental health needs. Two care managers also said that family should be able to claim direct payments to support their relatives.

This study shows care managers having doubts that direct payments are a good option for service users. Although benefits of direct payments were acknowledged, which echoed previous findings (Glendinning et al, 2000; Clark et al, 2004), more drawbacks were noted and most care managers said that direct payments were only appropriate sometimes as an option. As one care manager concluded, "Direct payments appears to be a complex and messy process, which could take a long time to set up. I'm not convinced that there are great advantages to service users".

Interestingly the drawbacks raised reflect previous findings such as Witcher et al's study in 2000 that found barriers such as demands on care managers' time, restriction on relatives as personal assistants and restrictive eligibility criteria.

With regard to the restriction on employment of family members, this could be a significant barrier for older people. In a study by Barnes (1997) the preferred option for older people was to employ relatives as personal assistants. However, since my study was completed, the restriction on employing close relatives has been lifted, as long as the local authority "is satisfied that it is necessary to meet satisfactorily a person's needs" (DH, 2003, p 26). This is a breakthrough for older people, especially those diagnosed with dementia, who are likely to respond better to a known and trusted face.

In terms of whether care managers' knowledge, views and confidence levels influence take-up of direct payments by older people, the results shown here indicate that these factors do have an influence. In the high take-up area, the care managers were generally more knowledgeable, confident and positive about direct payments than the care managers in the low take-up area. This appeared to be because care managers in the high take-up area had practical experience of actually implementing direct payment cases, thereby having opportunities to increase their knowledge. These results therefore suggest that care managers' lack of knowledge and attitude towards direct payments can act as a barrier to the take-up of direct payments. This is consistent with previous findings such as Clark et al's study (2004), which found that the less care managers understand about direct payments, the more unlikely they are to suggest them to older people. Dawson's study (2000) also highlighted that:

> As the direct payments pilot project progressed, it became increasingly apparent that the single most significant factor in determining who became an employer through direct payments was the potential employer's social worker. (p 22)

Linked to this, my study also indicated that, in both areas, care managers acted as powerful gatekeepers with regards to giving information about direct payments, and this is again consistent with previous literature (Dawson, 2000; Glasby and Littlechild, 2001). For example, care managers appeared to have a tendency to forget to tell service users about direct payments. Comments included:

> "I tend to forget."

> "Should advise all clients but do not always remember to do so."

These comments mirror Clark et al's findings (2004), where direct payments were found to be not in the forefront of care managers' minds, with one care manager saying: "I don't always think about it straight off" (p 46).

Without information about direct payments, it is impossible for service users to make informed choices about the support they want. As Zarb and Oliver (1993, p 9) have emphasised, "Information poverty as a major constraint on providing appropriate and adequate solutions to disabled people's needs".

The results discussed here also highlight the influence of care managers' judgement as to the ability of service users to manage direct payments. This too is in line with more recent research (Clark et al, 2004; CSCI, 2004). For example, many care managers commented that direct payments were unsuitable for people with mental health problems:

> "Many of my clients have mental health difficulties, therefore, I cannot offer the service."

Of course it can be problematic for care managers to assess whether a person is able to consent and manage a direct payment; however, it appears from the questionnaires that blanket assumptions were being made about clients' ability to manage direct payments. Therefore as Clark et al (2001) found, there could be service users who would have benefited from direct payments but were not offered the chance.

While it is important to recognise the pressures practitioners face, this does raise wider issues of equity of service provision for people. It is therefore crucial to assess each individual's ability to manage direct payments separately. Indeed, as Leece (2001) explains, direct payments for people with cognitive impairment have great potential for more effective support because they allow more scope for meeting needs at home than traditional services. Interestingly, the two cases in my study that were highlighted as being successful with direct payments were where users had significant cognitive impairment and were enabled to continue living at home.

However, the findings also show that care managers felt that some older people did not want the responsibility of direct payments. Care managers' comments included:

> "Older people feel too jaded to take on this extra responsibility."

> "Most individuals are frail and vulnerable and are seeking assistance from external sources – they do not feel able to take on a new administrative system which needs understanding and managing."

While it is recognised that older people can be concerned about managing the bureaucracy involved with direct payments (Barnes, 1997), they do not value their independence any less than younger adults (Macfarlane, 1991). The misconceptions that older people cannot manage direct payments can be partly explained by ageist attitudes in society generally. Many older people are likely to have internalised stereotypes of ageism and feel that they are 'past their best' (Thompson, 2001). Workers, too, may hold preconceived ideas that older people cannot manage the process of direct payments. Indeed, the CSCI (2004), which hosted two events on direct payments, found patronising attitudes among local authority staff. Risks were overemphasised, which in turn exacerbated service users' fears surrounding direct payments, rather than support and encouragement being offered to them. This response highlights the need for a significant cultural change before direct payments can become a reality for many older people. In order for this change to evolve, care managers need to embrace the strengths and skills older people possess and shake off the notion that ageing means a reduced lifestyle.

Conclusion

Direct payments offer enormous potential for many older people to lead the lives they want yet, despite this, take-up of direct payments has been slow. This study, which confirms other research findings, highlights that care managers' knowledge, confidence and views are a key to the promotion and, therefore, take-up of direct payments by older people. Since this study was undertaken, direct payments have become a mandatory responsibility for local authorities, but early data show that care managers are still not telling many service users about the option of direct payments (DH, 2004).

In order to make direct payments a reality for older people, care managers need to inspire older people about direct payments by offering this option positively. To achieve this, care managers themselves need to be inspired. The sharing of good practice among colleagues, having access to frequent support and training, and being proactive in listening to the views of older people who use direct payments will help to reinforce the benefits of this initiative. As Hasler and Campbell (2000, p 22) argue: "Unless the people carrying out the assessments are informed and enthused about direct payments, most users will never get to hear or be put off by them". Only then, may the door to direct payments be open to older people.

References

Age Concern (1998) 'Extend direct payments to over 65s', *Care Plan*, vol 5, no 2, pp 14-16.

Barnes, C. (1997) *Older people's perceptions of direct payments and self-operated support schemes*, Leeds: BCODP Research Unit, University of Leeds.

Bryman, A. (2001) *Social research methods*, Oxford: Oxford University Press.

Carmichael, A., Evans, C. and Brown, L. (2001) *A user-led best value review of direct payments*, Report for Wiltshire County Council (unpublished).

Clark, H. and Spafford, J. (2001) *Piloting choice and control for older people: An evaluation*, Bristol/York: The Policy Press/Joseph Rowntree Foundation.

Clark, H., Gough, H. and Macfarlane, A. (2004) *'It pays dividends': Direct payments and older people*, Bristol/York: The Policy Press/Joseph Rowntree Foundation.

CSCI (Commission for Social Care Inspection) (2004) *Direct payments: What are the barriers?*, London: CSCI.

Dawson, C. (2000) *Independent successes: Implementing direct payments*, York: York Publishing Services/Joseph Rowntree Foundation.

DH (Department of Health)(1997) *Community Care (Direct Payments) Act 1996: Policy and practice guidance*, London: DH.

DH (2001) *Explanatory notes to the Health and Social Care Act 2001*, London: DH.

DH (2003) *Direct payments guidance: Community care, services for carers and children's services (direct payments) guidance, England 2003*, London: DH.

DH (2004) *Statistical bulletin: Personal social services survey of physically disabled and sensory impaired users in England aged 18–64: 2003–04*, London: DH.

DH/SSI (Social Services Inspectorate) (1999) *Inspection of independent living arrangements for younger disabled people: Poole Borough Council*, Bristol: South and West Inspection Group, SSI.

Fruin, D. (2000) *New directions for independent living*, London: DH.

Gibbs, L.E. (1991) *Scientific reasoning for social workers: Bridging the gap between research and practice*, New York, NY: Macmillan.

Glasby, J. (2002) 'Independence at a price', *Community Care*, 29 August–4 September, pp 30-1.

Glasby, J. and Littlechild, R. (2001) 'Independence pays?: Barriers to the progress of direct payments', *Practice*, vol 14, no 1, pp 55-66.

Glasby, J. and Littlechild, R. (2002) *Social work and direct payments*, Bristol: The Policy Press.

Glendinning, C., Halliwell, S., Jacobs, S., Rummery, K. and Tyrer, J. (2000) *Buying independence: Using direct payments to integrate health and social services*, Bristol/York: The Policy Press/Joseph Rowntree Foundation.

Hasler, F. and Campbell, J. (2000) 'What users want', *Community Care*, 7-13 September, p 22.

Hasler, F. and Stewart, A. (2004) *Making direct payments work: Identifying and overcoming barriers to implementation*, Brighton: Pavilion Publishing.

Hasler, F. and Zarb, J. (2000) 'Direct payments and older people: the principles of independent living', *Research, Policy and Planning*, vol 18, no 2, pp 7-12.

Leece, J. (2000) 'It's a matter of choice: making direct payments work in Staffordshire', *Practice*, vol 12, no 4, pp 37-48.

Leece, J. (2001) 'Directing support: direct payments and older people', *Generations Review – The Journal of the British Society of Gerontology*, vol 11, no 3, pp 23–5.

Macfarlane, A. (1991) 'Ageing and disability', in L. Laurie (ed) *Building our lives: Housing, independent living and disabled people*, London: Shelter.

Maglajlic, R., Brandon, D. and Given, D. (2000) 'Making direct payments a choice: A report on the research findings', *Disability and Society*, vol 15, no 1, pp 99-113.

Milburn, A. (2002) 'Reforming social services', Speech to the 2002 Annual Social Services Conference, Cardiff, 16 October.

Rainey, C. (1999) *Evaluation of direct payments pilot, West Sussex County Council*, Derby: National Centre for Independent Living.

Thompson, N. (2001) *Antidiscriminatory Practice*, 3rd edn, London: Macmillan.

Witcher, S., Stalker, K., Roadburg, M. and Jones, C. (2000) *Direct payments: The impact on choice and control for disabled people*, Edinburgh: Scottish Executive Central Research Unit.

Zarb, G. and Oliver, M. (1993) *Ageing with a disability: What do they expect after all these years?* London: University of Greenwich.

Section 6
Developments in direct payments

EIGHTEEN

Direct payments and health

Caroline Glendinning

There are multiple intersections between direct payments and health. For example, direct payments can enable users to experience improvements in their mental health and well-being as a result of being able to exercise greater choice and control over who supports them, how and when. High levels of continuity and good-quality relationships with personal assistants can make significant contributions to improving mental health and reducing anxiety and depression. Direct payments can also facilitate the establishment of support arrangements that cross the blurred – and highly contested – boundaries between the 'health' and 'social' elements of personal care, creating integrated support arrangements that include elements of both.

This chapter focuses on the latter of these links – the use of direct payments to bridge the 'Berlin Wall' between health and social care. This is a highly problematic area of direct payments policy and practice, and one of concern and uncertainty for users of direct payments, professionals and managers alike. The chapter will first of all set out the wider policy contexts within which these uncertainties arise, particularly the shifting boundaries between 'health' and 'social' care; the recent introduction of measures to break down the 'Berlin Wall' between these sectors; and the growing pressures to deliver integrated or seamless services to older and younger disabled people and people with mental health problems.

The chapter will then report on research carried out during 1999 into the use of direct payments to purchase health-related support and services. Drawing on direct payments schemes in three different localities, the research investigated how far direct payments users constructed packages of support that included health-related as well as social care needs; and their views on the advantages and challenges of using direct payments in this way. These views were complemented by the perspectives of personal assistants (see Glendinning et al, 2000a, 2000b and 2000c for the full study findings).

The research was conducted two years after the implementation of the 1996 Community Care (Direct Payments) Act. At that time, direct payments were restricted to adults aged between 18 and 65; their extension to older people, young adults and parents of disabled children had yet to take place. At that time too, the government had signalled its intentions to encourage partnerships between the National Health Service (NHS) and local authority services on which integrated services could be developed. However, the 1999 Health Act, which contains significant measures to facilitate such partnerships, had yet to be implemented. In reflecting on the research findings, these subsequent developments will be taken into account. The chapter will conclude by discussing some of the issues in the policy and practice relating to direct payments, health care needs and health care provision that remain to be clarified.

Direct payments and health: current policies and practice

The 1946 NHS Act that forms the legislative underpinning to the British post-war health service contains no mention of the possibility that health care might be provided in the form of cash payments rather than services in kind. However, definitions of what constitutes health care have changed considerably over the subsequent half century; they remain subject to legal challenges; and they are characterised by local and regional variations in practice. These changing boundaries between 'health' and 'social' care help to explain the current difficulties around direct payments and health.

Since 1946 there has been a marked contraction in the scope of NHS responsibilities, particularly in relation to the long-term nursing and social care of frail older people and other adults with long-term health problems or disabilities. Long-stay hospitals and other NHS accommodation have closed and responsibilities have shifted to local authority social services departments. These changes were partly the result of explicit community care policies in the 1980s; thus section 28a of the 1977 NHS Act allowed NHS resources to be transferred to local authorities in order to fund community-based accommodation and support services for former patients (their health care needs remained the responsibility of the NHS). Changes in NHS responsibilities were also covertly facilitated by the availability of social security funding during the 1980s that stimulated the growth of a substantial private residential and nursing home sector. Long-term NHS provision for older people predominated in this latter shift, although shifts in responsibilities for people with learning disabilities and other groups were also involved to some extent. Financial responsibilities for these services were eventually transferred to local authority social services departments with the 1993 community care reforms. Significantly, local authority social services departments were rarely consulted about changes in NHS responsibilities, and service users even less so (Means and Smith, 1998; Means et al, 2002).

However, the withdrawal of NHS responsibilities for funding and providing long-term care has been subject to challenges from lawyers acting on behalf of disabled and older people. In response, the government has made repeated attempts to define the responsibilities of the NHS for providing 'continuing' health care and has encouraged local NHS bodies (health authorities, now primary care trusts and strategic health authorities) to review their policies and to reinvest in long-term provision, particularly for people with substantial, ongoing nursing needs. The courts have also concluded that the NHS has a continuing responsibility to fund accommodation and services for people whose "primary need is for health care services" (*R v North and East Devon Health Authority ex parte Coughlan* 1999 2 CCCL Rep 285). However, the precise definition and application of eligibility criteria for continuing NHS funding have remained the responsibility of local NHS organisations. These criteria and their implementation can vary from one area to another; may, in practice, be drawn up with little reference to the services provided by the respective local authority; and may exclude specialised health care needs such as stoma or catheter care or anyone not living in a hospital or nursing home (Kestenbaum, 1999; RCN, 1999; Dow, 2003). These local variations may be reduced in future, as the government announced in December 2004 the intention of developing a single national framework of criteria governing eligibility for NHS-funded continuing health care.

In view of the resistance by many disabled people to the medicalisation of their impairments (Oliver, 1991; Wood, 1991; Morris, 1993), the withdrawal by the NHS from many of its former areas of responsibility for long-term care funding and service provision would arguably be welcomed. However, this shift has been largely decided and implemented unilaterally, without corresponding transfers of resources to local authority social services departments. This has created something of a 'no-man's-land', with considerable scope for dispute over who is responsible for funding and providing support for people with high levels of long-term health and social care needs, but who are nevertheless able, with appropriate support, to live independently in the community (Lewis, 2001; Glendinning and Means, 2004). A study of disabled people with high support needs in six different localities found considerable variation in the extent to which the NHS was contributing to the funding of their support (Kestenbaum, 1999). Overall, there were very few instances where NHS continuing health care funding formed part of an integrated package of community care support. Moreover, even where NHS resources were being contributed for continuing health care needs, these were usually negotiated on an individual, case-by-case basis and were as likely to be met through the provision of qualified nursing services as through user-controlled mechanisms.

Since 1997 the government has made substantial progress in improving collaboration between health and social services: "exhortations to be decent about joint working have been replaced by [a] panoply of sanctions, incentives and threats" (Hudson, 1999: p 199). Joint planning and commissioning of services for specific groups of service users has been encouraged; substantial financial resources have been 'ring-fenced' to support collaboration between the NHS and local authority social services; and new 'flexibilities' have relaxed some of the structural barriers to closer collaboration. These flexibilities, contained in section 31 of the 1999 Health Act, allow budgets for specific services to be pooled; joint or overlapping commissioning responsibilities to be delegated to a single 'lead' organisation that commissions services on behalf of both sectors; and health and social care staff to be employed by a single integrated provider organisation (DH, 1998; Glendinning et al, 2002). In many localities, the section 31 'flexibilities' have been used to create integrated health and social care services for adults with learning disabilities and people with acute and long-term mental health problems – two of the groups of service users who are now being encouraged to increase their take-up of direct payments. The flexibilities also form the legislative underpinnings of wholly integrated care trusts (Glasby and Peck, 2004).

These two policy trends form the backdrop for understanding the difficulties that now surround direct payments and health. On the one hand, NHS funding and service responsibilities have become increasingly restricted to clinical treatment and (perhaps) specialised nursing care. This raises the question of who is responsible for the funding of specialised personal and nursing care – particularly where this is intensive, continuous or highly specialised – for people living in the community. At the same time, current pressures, incentives and 'flexibilities' encourage collaboration and cooperation between NHS and local authority social services in order to deliver integrated services to people with complex needs.

Cutting across these trends, however, is the active promotion of direct payments as the means of delivering flexible, user-controlled and integrated support. Does the direct payments option apply only to the 'social' care elements of a complex package of support; and, if so, how can this be compatible with policies that promote integrated services? The 1996 legislation introducing direct payments was linked to the statutory duties of local authorities as set out under the 1990 NHS and Community Care Act. In March 2005, the Department of Health (DH) reaffirmed its view that the direct payments legislation relates only to certain local authority social services. Consequently, any identified health need which is the responsibility of the NHS cannot be met through a direct payment; this includes the health elements of integrated health and social care support services being provided under the 1999 Health Act section 31 partnership arrangements. Local authorities can certainly make direct payments for services that have an *effect* on health, so long as those services fall within social services responsibilities and are also covered by direct payments legislation. However, the DH maintains that assessed health care needs cannot be met through direct payments.

This restriction creates problems for local health and social services authorities working together to provide integrated packages of support to disabled people, whether through a pooled budget established under section 31 of the 1999 Health Act or not. Normally the resources contributed to a pooled budget would lose their 'identity', so that they do not need to be spent on health and social care services in the same proportions as they are contributed. Indeed, early guidance on the Health Act flexibilities (DH, 1999, para 119) reminded health authorities that they could contribute resources for joint 'packages' of services that could be provided in the form of direct payments rather than conventional services in kind; health authorities were also reminded of their responsibilities to provide support that was compatible with the increased independence offered by direct payments. However, this apparently applies only to expenditure on services in kind, and official guidance on direct payments (DH, 2003) makes no mention of these opportunities.

An early study of direct payments implementation (NCIL, 1998) found that a few health authorities were contributing NHS resources towards integrated direct payment 'packages', but concluded that concerns about financial probity and audit were likely to inhibit the wider use of such arrangements. Moreover, whether or not pooled budgets are being used to fund integrated health and social care services, these are still subject to separate charging arrangements. The social care elements of the funding package are subject to user co-payments that depend on assessments of users' income and/or assets (Thompson and Mathew, 2004), while the health elements of an integrated direct payment funding package remain free of charge.

The experiences of direct payments users

In 1999, research was carried out on whether people with complex, high-level support needs were using direct payments to create personalised, integrated packages of care; and to ascertain their views on the relationships between direct payments and health care. Interviews were conducted with 44 direct payments users from three direct payments schemes in different parts of England. In only one of the three schemes had any jointly funded direct payment 'packages' covering both health and social care needs been formally negotiated between the local health and social services authorities (see Glendinning et al, 2000a, 2000b, 2000c).

Direct payments users were asked about their definitions of 'health' and 'social' care and how these mapped onto their use of direct payments. Over three quarters of those interviewed were receiving help, treatments or support through their direct payments that fell within their definitions of 'health' care. All of this help formed part of a cluster of activities that direct payments users termed 'personal' care, which, they argued, could not be divided into health and social care components:

> "In my mind, you can't split personal care into separate components – personal care, health care, social care. It's a holistic approach ... it all contributes to the well-being and health of the whole person."

Most of the help was provided by personal assistants, as part of users' daily care routines. The range of health-related tasks that personal assistants performed included helping with medication – applying ointments or lotions, reminding to take tablets and, in a few instances, giving injections. Half the direct payments users received regular physiotherapy exercises from their personal assistants, including massage to receive discomfort, exercises to maintain joint mobility and chest physiotherapy to keep airways clear. Half also received help with toileting, including emptying catheter bags, stoma and catheter care and help with suppositories and manual bowel evacuations. Many personal assistants changed dressings and provided foot care. Personal assistants working for some very severely disabled users were also involved in tissue care to prevent pressure sores. Many direct payments users reported receiving nursing care from their personal assistants during periods of illness at home, and a small number of personal assistants helped with the maintenance and use of oxygen equipment in the home.

There were three main reasons why direct payments users received health-related care like this from their personal assistants. First, mainstream health services were simply not available, either because of strict limits on the range of tasks that community health staff were allowed to perform or because of restrictions on their long-term availability. For example, prior to receiving direct payments, one severely disabled man had received a twice weekly visit from a district nurse to give a suppository as part of his bowel management regime. However, the district nursing service did not regard help with toileting as its responsibility, so he had to wait until the social services home care worker arrived to help him to the toilet. With direct payments, both these tasks could be carried out by his personal assistant. Direct payments users frequently reported that physiotherapy was not available for adults on a long-term basis, because NHS priorities lay with acute rehabilitation:

> "You get a matter of six treatments ... and then you're left out. I had a period when I was going for about two months and it helped my mobility tremendously, but then it just stopped dead because they can't afford to do it."

Second, some disabled people reported that once a personal assistant was available to provide hands-on care, they were assigned a lower priority by community health services and pressured to allow tasks to be transferred to the personal assistant so that NHS professionals could withdraw:

> "To be honest, the district nurses were putting verbal pressures on me that they are health carers not social carers and they did want to move away from doing [manual bowel evacuations]...."

Third, and most important from the perspective of the direct payments users, many of them asked their personal assistants to carry out health care tasks because they could do this flexibly and reliably as seamless elements of their daily routines. They recounted numerous experiences of inflexible community health services that could accommodate neither their own ordinary daily routines nor the constraints imposed by other health treatments they were receiving:

> "I was coming home from dialysis at 9pm and trying to have a meal and they [district nurses] were wanting to put me to bed at 8pm, so there was no way it would work out."

> "If I ring up and ask them [district nurses] to come in and give me a bladder wash-out, they assume that disabled people don't go out, they're willing to sit around all day long and wait for them to come in at their convenience."

Involving personal assistants in the health-related aspects of their personal care extended the choice and control that direct payments users could exercise over their daily routines:

> "It gives you a sense of independence, have some control over your illness, ... [it] has really enhanced my life a lot."

Direct payments also allowed choice and control over who provided intimate health-related care, and how that was provided:

> "I can do what I want, as I want, when I want. I can use certain people for certain tasks that I feel comfortable with. I don't use all my carers [to help me with] a bath, for instance."

The increase in choice and control had benefits for direct payments users' mental health; this was particularly important for people at risk of depression or other mental health problems:

> "Previously, waiting for that knock on the door, if it didn't go well it could actually mess up your mind for two or three days. You'd got so worked up about it, het up about it, about the attitude of the carers. All that has vanished. The general sense of well-being is a lot better."

Almost all the direct payments users in the study wanted the scope of direct payments formally extended so as to acknowledge and legitimate the help their personal assistants already gave with health-related care or to enable them to receive more in this way. Direct payments-funded help with physiotherapy was a particular priority:

> "There would be advantages to having physio through the intermediary of a personal assistant, because I need physical exercise every day. I wish the physio could give it to me every day, but that's not possible."

Users also argued for direct payments to be extended to cover chiropody, which they wanted to purchase from private professional sources; a wider range of general and specialist nursing tasks provided by their personal assistants; and for cash payments with which they could purchase their own equipment such as wheelchairs, special cushions and protective clothing.

Nevertheless, these wishes were not unqualified; several constraints on the use of direct payments to purchase health-related care were acknowledged. One was the need for confidence in the training and professional supervision of personal assistants who might carry out complex or skilled health care activities:

> "It's one thing to be replacing dressings and ointments and it would be another thing to do injections...."

One user had already asked community health professionals to provide training for her personal assistant, for which she had been willing to pay, but had been refused.

However, set against the perceived need for training and qualifications was a widespread anxiety that this risked undermining the principles of user control that characterised direct payments:

> "They'd be insisting on bloody doctor's notes and bloody more bureaucracy!"

> "What I don't want is my personal assistant making professional judgements over my life.... We'd start creating a professional culture again and, you know, we'd lose control.... You'd get the 'Well, I know best' environment."

Some direct payments users thought this tension could be resolved by using direct payments to purchase additional specialist professional services – for example, from physiotherapists in private practice with skills in neurology or cystic fibrosis – rather than paying their personal assistants to provide health care.

A second set of constraints related to users' support for the principles of equity that they felt underpinned a universal NHS. Some direct payments users had already seen the NHS withdraw from aspects of health care provision – the shifting boundaries described in the previous section of this chapter – and they argued that the NHS should contribute financially to the health-related support they received from personal assistants:

> "Why should it come out of social services' budget when it's a health thing? Often they try to dump their costs onto social services anyway."

However, users were also concerned about the implications for equity, should they become able to purchase treatments and health care that were not available to non-direct payments users. Whether direct payments were used to purchase physiotherapy or chiropody from private professional sources or from personal assistants, some users were concerned they would be 'jumping the queue', or at least obtaining access to services that were not available to their peers. Rather, they argued that access to such treatments should not depend on 'your purse strings' or on 'the sharp elbows of the middle class'.

The experiences of personal assistants

The study also examined the experiences of 14 personal assistants through a series of focus group discussions. Several personal assistants had previously worked in home or residential care services and confirmed that they now undertook tasks such as bowel management that, in other settings, would be performed by qualified nurses. In addition, they drew attention to the important role they played in monitoring their employer's health, including occasionally suggesting that a visit from a qualified doctor or nurse might be appropriate. This was particularly common when the direct payments user had a learning disability, limited communication, or mental health problem. In such situations, personal assistants' close familiarity with their employer's usual health status and behaviour patterns inevitably drew them into considering whether additional interventions might be needed. However, this monitoring role was highly problematic, as it could encroach on their employer's autonomy over such decisions:

> "I've got instances where he [employer] won't particularly say, and I have actually to tell one of the nurses – this is the nurse at the surgery – that I'm a bit worried. Because he won't do it himself. So that's probably over-stepping the mark – over-stepping on one hand and on the other hand looking after health care."

In situations like this, personal assistants had to rely on a more generalised duty to act with care and in the best interests of their employer, although finding the balance between this duty and the employer's expressed preference was not always straightforward.

In the course of transferring responsibility for specific aspects of a direct payments user's health care, a number of personal assistants had been shown by health professionals how to perform tasks such as changing dressings or bowel evacuations. This had often simply involved watching the professional perform a procedure, sometimes on only one occasion and with no subsequent check on the quality of ongoing care. Consequently, some personal assistants were asked by the direct payments user to perform health care tasks that they did not feel confident or competent to undertake. However, the status of the direct payments user as their employer, combined with the explicit principles of user control and autonomy that underpin direct payments, made it difficult to refuse such requests. Personal assistants were also uncertain who they were accountable to for health-related tasks and about their liability if, for example, an infection resulted from an incorrectly performed procedure. Even where training had been given by a health professional, this did not include assessing risks and how to avoid them:

> "If you administer an injection wrongly but actually end up killing your client – I know it's extreme – but who is accountable, the person who trained you because you didn't have quite enough training or you because you didn't listen properly?"

Conclusions

Given demographic and technological developments, there is likely to be increasing pressure on the NHS to contribute to intensive packages of support for people with complex and high levels of needs, so that they can live independently in the community. However, in policy terms the use of direct payments to finance health-related care is highly problematic. This problem is intensified by long-term changes in the boundaries between 'health' and 'social' care and a consequent divergence between the respective responsibilities of the NHS and local authority social services for funding community-based support for people with extensive and complex health and social care needs.

Consequently, practices relating to direct payments and health care are likely to vary considerably across England. Although direct payments users in the research reported here argued that the 'social' and 'health' aspects of personal care are indivisible, the introduction of statutory definitions of 'social' and 'nursing' care might help to end the current local variations in responsibility for funding the more specialised personal care procedures such as bowel management, stoma management and treatment of pressure sores. Without such definitions, severely disabled people, whether direct payments users or not, remain at the mercy of local NHS purchasers and service providers as to the boundaries of their responsibilities for health care.

Furthermore, recent legislation has facilitated resource transfers between the NHS and local authorities and the creation of pooled budgets that can be spent in any proportions on 'health' or 'social' care services. In contrast, direct payments legislation only applies to the social care services that local authorities may provide following a community care assessment. Thus even where a pooled budget is established to fund integrated health and social care services, it is apparently not legal to use the 'health' component of the pool for direct payments. Moreover, even if an integrated direct payment covering both 'health' and 'social' care needs were to be made from a pooled budget, the 'social' care elements would be liable to means-tested charges while the 'health' elements remain free.

Given the significant but intangible health-related benefits that many users derive from the enhanced choice and control they experience in using direct payments, this distinction is increasingly untenable. Until these contradictions are resolved, practice across the country is likely to remain inconsistent and confused. The London Borough of Richmond has proposed a solution to these difficulties that involves redefining any needs for continuing health care as 'heavy duty' social care, thus bringing them within the statutory responsibilities of local authority social services departments (London Borough of Richmond, personal communication). Resources to meet these needs could be transferred from the NHS to the local authority, which also has the powers to waive its charging policy for the services (or direct payments) it provides. It may be that the DH has accepted the underlying logic of this argument, as its most recent guidance (DH, 2005) bears the disclaimer that it is not intended to constitute a comprehensive legal statement and advises local councils to seek their own legal advice.

From the perspective of direct payments users, their personal care needs – and therefore their personal assistants' daily tasks – are indivisible; they cannot be separated into 'health' and 'social' elements. Consequently, significant aspects of the personal care provided by personal assistants are likely to include tasks that in other settings might be carried out by qualified nurses and therapists or their respective ancillary assistants. These tasks do not simply include physical, 'hands-on' care, but the direct and indirect provision of social and psychological support. Research (Glendinning et al, 2000c) has shown that such support, derived from the nature and quality of the relationship with an employed personal assistant, can be just as important for people whose disabilities are primarily physical as for those with mental health problems or learning disabilities.

Providing a range of individualised personal support and assistance, at times and in ways that are controlled by the user, remains at the heart of direct payments. Yet, so long as the boundaries between 'health' and 'social' care funding and professional responsibilities continue to run like a fault line through the broad spectrum of 'personal' care, then it is inevitable that direct payments will fund some elements of support that are widely regarded as 'health' care. This is a legacy of the broader changes in the scope of NHS responsibilities that have taken place over the past half century. The situation is not unique to direct payments users. Studies of technology-dependent children (Kirk and Glendinning, 2002) and frail older people (Pickard and Glendinning, 2002) have shown similar broad overlaps between the responsibilities and tasks carried out by professional nursing and therapy staff and close relatives who provide day-to-day care in the home. As with the personal assistants whose views were reported in this chapter, these overlaps are accompanied by tensions and uncertainties about appropriate levels of training and responsibilities for risk management.

There are yet further dimensions to this confusion. The legislative links between direct payments and local authority responsibilities for community care mean that the resources allocated to individual direct payments users are generally based on the costs of community care services in kind. Official guidance (DH, 2003, p 22) states that a direct payment must be equivalent to the local authority's estimate of the 'reasonable cost' of securing the support needed. However, this is an area where local authorities can exercise discretion over how that 'reasonable cost' is calculated and the extent to which they take into account very high, intensive or complex support needs. Consequently, in the research reported in this chapter, some direct payments users reported difficulties in recruiting personal assistants with specialist skills or qualifications within their direct payments budget. Only a small minority of direct payments users are likely to have additional private resources (for example from an accident compensation award) that they can contribute towards the costs of employing personal assistants.

Finally, personal assistants occupy a complex and potentially conflicting position between their disabled employers and health professionals with formal qualifications. On the one hand, the philosophy of independent living and principles of user control assume that the primary accountability and commitment of personal assistants is to their disabled employer. On the other hand, because of the continuity of the relationship with their employer, personal assistants are likely to find themselves monitoring their employer's health; they may also be required to perform a range of 'health'-related personal care tasks, either because of their employer's preferences or because such activities have been delegated by NHS professionals. Although the latter may show personal assistants how to perform a task, this informal training can still leave personal assistants unclear about where responsibilities for maintaining their employer's health and managing risk lie.

The pooled NHS and local authority budgets that can be created under the section 31 'flexibilities' in the 1999 Health Act offer an opportunity to break down the unhelpful distinction between the 'health' and 'social' aspects of personal care and provide integrated direct payment packages to disabled people needing complex or high levels of support. However, legal confusion about the use of NHS-related resources for such purposes remain. Moreover, even if these legal and policy issues are clarified, some difficult tensions may remain about how skilled or expert health-related support can be provided within integrated direct payments 'packages' without compromising the choice and control that is at the heart of the direct payments scheme.

Acknowledgements

The research reported in this chapter was carried out at the National Primary Care Research and Development Centre, University of Manchester, as part of its programme of research funded by the DH. The author is grateful for advice from the DH and the London Borough of Richmond on the legal limits and opportunities relating to direct payments and health. However, any opinions expressed in the chapter are those of the author alone.

References

DH (Department of Health) (1998) *Partnership in action: New opportunities for joint working between health and social services*, London: DH.

DH (1999) *Draft guidance and regulations on the s31A partnership arrangements*, (www.dh.gov.uk), London: Health and Social Care Joint Unit, DH.

DH (2003) *Direct payment guidance: Community care, services for carers and children's services (direct payments) guidance, England 2003*, London: DH.

DH (2005) *Direct payments and health*, (www.dh.gov.uk/PolicyAndGuidance/OrganisationPolicy/FinanceAndPlanning/DirectPayments), accessed 1 March 2005.

Dow, J. (2003) 'Continuing health care – where now in the continuum of care?', *Journal of Integrated Care*, vol 11, no 6, pp 43–5.

Glasby, J. and Peck, E. (eds) (2004) *Care trusts: Partnership working in action*, Oxford: Radcliffe Medical Press.

Glendinning, C. and Means, R. (2004) 'Rearranging the deckchairs on the Titanic of long-term care: is organisational integration the answer?', *Critical Social Policy*, vol 24, no 4, pp 435-57.

Glendinning, C., Hudson, B., Hardy, B. and Young, R. (2002) *National evaluation of notifications for use of the section 31 partnership flexibilities in the Health Act 1999*, Final project report, Manchester/Leeds: National Primary Care Research and Development Centre/Nuffield Institute for Health.

Glendinning, C., Halliwell, S., Jacobs, S., Rummery, K. and Tyrer, J. (2000a) *Buying independence: Using direct payments to integrate health and social services*, Bristol: The Policy Press.

Glendinning, C., Halliwell, S., Jacobs, S., Rummery, K. and Tyrer, J. (2000b) 'Bridging the gap; using direct payments to purchase integrated care', *Health and Social Care in the Community*, vol 8, no 3, pp 192–200.

Glendinning, C., Halliwell, S., Jacobs, S., Rummery, K. and Tyrer, J. (2000c) 'New kinds of care, new kinds of relationships; how purchasing services affects relationships in giving and receiving care', *Health and Social Care in the Community*, vol 8, no 3, pp 201-11.

Hudson, B. (1999) 'Dismantling the Berlin Wall: developments in the health–social care interface', in H. Dean and R. Woods (eds) *Social Policy Review 11*, Luton: University of Luton, Social Policy Association.

Kestenbaum, A. (1999) *What price independence? Independent living and people with high support needs*, Bristol: The Policy Press.

Kirk, S. and Glendinning, C. (2002) 'Supporting "expert" parents – professional support and families caring for a child with complex health needs in the community', *International Journal of Nursing Studies*, vol 39, pp 625-35.

Lewis, J. (2001) 'Older people and the health–social care boundary in the UK: half a century of hidden policy conflict', *Social Policy and Administration*, vol 35, no 4, pp 343-60.

Means, R. and Smith, R. (1998) *Community care: Policy and practice*, Bristol: The Policy Press.

Means, R., Morbey, H. and Smith, R. (2002) *From community care to market care?*, Bristol: The Policy Press.

Morris, J. (1993) *Independent lives? Community care and disabled people*, Basingstoke: Macmillan.

NCIL (National Centre for Independent Living) (1998) *National Centre for Independent Living newsletter*, London: NCIL.

Oliver, M. (1991) *The politics of disablement*, Basingstoke: Macmillan.

Pickard, S. and Glendinning, C. (2002) 'Comparing and contrasting the role of family carers and nurses in the domestic health care of older people', *Health and Social Care in the Community*, vol 10, no 3, pp 144-50.

RCN (Royal College of Nursing) (1999) *Rationing by stealth: A review of health authorities' continuing care policies in England and Wales*, London: RCN.

Thompson, P. and Mathew, D. (2004) *Fair enough?*, London: Age Concern.

Wood, R. (1991) 'Caring for disabled people', in G. Dalley (ed) *Disability and social policy*, London: Policy Studies Institute, pp 197-204.

NINETEEN

The future of direct payments

Jon Glasby, Caroline Glendinning and Rosemary Littlechild

When direct payments were formally introduced in the UK under the 1996 Community Care (Direct Payments) Act, there was considerable resistance in the field, and a range of practical barriers to be overcome. As the chapters in this volume have demonstrated, those keen to promote the take-up of direct payments have had to challenge professional concerns about loss of status; fears about the potential threat to in-house social services; and common assumptions about the inability of certain user groups to manage a direct payments package. As a result, progress to date has been slow and uneven, with some areas of the country lagging behind others and with some user groups massively under-represented among those who currently benefit from the increased choice and control offered by direct payments.

At the same time, achievements to date should not be underestimated. Direct payments were pioneered by disabled people and were only implemented following longstanding, organised pressure from the independent living movement (for a summary of the debate, see Glasby and Littlechild, 2002). However, direct payments have gradually become more and more mainstream, aided by dedicated disabled activists and by user-led centres for independent living. Direct payments were initially introduced only on a restricted and discretionary basis, following research suggesting that they might be more cost-effective than directly provided services (Zarb and Nadash, 1994). They have since been extended to more and more user groups; the number of recipients is constantly growing; and the option has become mandatory, backed by a new performance indicator. By late 2003, the Community Care Minister, Stephen Ladyman, was arguing that:

> "The assumption should be not only will care be delivered by a direct payment; the assumption should be that the person can manage a direct payment and the only times when care should be delivered, in my view, other than by a direct payment, is when the individual themselves has

made a personal and positive choice to receive the care directly and not via a direct payment." (NCIL, 2003).

By late 2004, Ladyman was calling for direct payments to be a central feature of social care, with care managers and social services staff 'immersed' in direct payments (Community Care, 2004a). In March 2005 the government published a Green Paper on the future of social care services for adults in England (DH, 2005a) that proposed further encouragement for direct payments; new forms of support to help currently excluded groups in using direct payments; and 'individual budgets', in which users can chose how their allotted resources for social care are used without necessarily having to handle cash payments. In many ways, therefore, the introduction of direct payments can be seen as heralding the most fundamental reform of social care for many years and there has been substantial progress from a seemingly unpromising start.

Nevertheless, despite this positive encouragement from central government, the persistence of marked variations in the take-up of direct payments – between localities and between groups of disabled and older people within these localities – suggests that some intractable barriers may still exist. Some of these barriers are discussed in the contributions to this volume. Other challenges are suggested in this chapter. In particular, we advocate a degree of caution in assuming that direct payments will or should become the preferred option for *all* people – adults, older people, carers, young adults – otherwise eligible for social care services, particularly before some of these outstanding barriers are addressed.

The remainder of this chapter locates the development of direct payments within a wider policy context and, in particular, shows how the experience of direct payments may constitute the first steps in a wider transformation of social welfare arrangements in England. However, there also remain a number of difficult unresolved or under-researched aspects of the direct payments experience. The chapter will argue that, in the same way as these difficulties have affected the implementation of direct payments, they are also likely to affect the wider policy ambitions that have been outlined for the coming decade.

The legacy of the struggles for direct payments

From direct payments to individualised funding

By early 2005, two potential landmark policy proposals seemed likely to shape the consolidation, extension and further evolution of direct payments. In February 2005, *Improving the life chances of disabled people* called for disabled people to be fully included as equal members of society (Prime Minister's Strategy Unit, 2005). Among a wide range of proposals, this comprehensive strategy document called for individualised budgets, formed from a number of different funding sources (for example, from local authority social services, housing, adaptations and equipment, independent living funds and other sources) and placed under the control of disabled service users. The intention was to enable existing resources to be used in more flexible and individualised ways. The proposal built on a national pilot scheme – *In control* – that is working with seven local authorities to develop an individualised approach to funding for people with learning disabilities (for further information, see www.selfdirectedservices.org). Currently, typical social services practice is to assess people, and identify (often quite limited) services to meet these needs. In contrast to this professional gate-keeping, *In control* assesses the severity of a person's needs according to a limited number of criteria, determines which level of severity they fall into and on this basis gives them entitlements to a specified sum of money to spend on their support needs (much more like the social security system). With appropriate support, people can then choose how this money is spent: via direct services; via voluntary or private provision; via direct payments; or via some combination of all three. Crucially, people know in advance how much money they are entitled to, how much relevant services might cost and how they can best use the resources available to meet their needs.

Improving the life chances of disabled people focused on a broad range of different sources of support, but applied only to disabled people of working age, disabled children and young people and their families. Complementing this, a Green Paper entitled *Independence, well-being and choice*, published in March 2005, spelt out the health and social care dimension of this vision, including the implications for older people (DH, 2005a). The Green Paper called for greater opportunities for older and disabled people to exercise greater choice and control over how their needs are met. Further action to encourage the take-up of direct payments, particularly among older people, people with mental health problems and young people moving to adult services was proposed, although the only concrete proposal for this was the suggested introduction of 'agents' to help people whose level of disability is so severe that they are currently unable to consent and use direct payments themselves (DH, 2005a, appendix C). The Green Paper also took up the theme of individual budgets and the experience of *In control* that enables users to exercise choice and control without the legal and employer responsibilities of direct payments. Following assessment, resources would be allocated to each individual that could be used to buy the services they want to receive:

> This is ... about providing people with choice, empowerment and freedom.... The budget would be held by the local authority. People could have individual support to identify the services they wish to use, which might be outside the range of services traditionally offered by social care.... For those who choose not to take a direct payment as cash, the budgets would give many of the benefits of choice to the person using services, without them having the worry of actually managing the money for themselves. (Department of Health, 2005a, p 34)

As with *Improving the life chances of disabled people, Independence, well-being and choice* suggested that a wider range of resources (including resources currently allocated to the supply of minor equipment and adaptations, independent living funds and Access to Work and Family Funds) should be pooled and included in individual budgets. Individual budgets would also enable their holders to 'buy' services from their local authority, an option that is not available to direct payments users. Ultimately, it was hoped that giving purchasing power (if not the actual cash payments) to service users would stimulate the social care market to provide more flexible, high-quality and person-centred service options, as well as providing an incentive for councils to match standards in the private sector (and vice versa).

These two major policy documents are highly significant for both the legacy and the future of direct payments. They show just how far the ideas initially promoted by a small group of determined disability activists have moved from the margins to the mainstream of public policy in England, in a space of little more than 10 years. However, the history and experiences of direct payments also hint at some of the challenges which still need to be tackled if these current visions are to become reality in the future.

From disability to citizenship

If these changes are successfully piloted and rolled out, the implications are potentially revolutionary. People do not live their lives according to the categories created by welfare services and agencies (for example, Glasby and Littlechild, 2004; see also Chapter Eighteen by Glendinning in this volume), and individualised budgets offer a real chance to design more holistic support packages that can meet a much wider range of needs. With clear entitlements to specified levels of funding, service users would no longer be passive recipients of professionally defined and controlled services, but active citizens with rights to specified levels of support. Moreover, if needs are identified via self-assessment and person-centred planning, then people with support needs would be able to be involved in articulating their own chosen lifestyles and deciding how the resources of the state can best be mobilised to help them achieve desired outcomes. In theory, this should be both better for people 'using' services and more liberating for social care and other practitioners, who become 'care navigators' and service 'brokers' rather than 'care managers'.

Individualised funding does not automatically lead to individualised solutions; it does not prescribe a necessary movement away from local authorities' direct provision of services (one of the concerns alleged to have inhibited the wider use of direct payments) or from collective service provision. On the contrary, there is considerable scope for exploring which activities and support needs service users wish to meet together with their peers and friends, and which they prefer to meet by themselves. As an example, a group of people with learning difficulties who have got to know each other over a number of years at a social services day centre may decide that they no longer wish to receive conventional 'day care', but nevertheless acknowledge that they still need support to engage in meaningful social activities. Some may wish to use direct payments to employ personal assistants to help them go to college or to enter employment. However, because they liked meeting their 'mates' at the day centre, they may also decide to carry on meeting as a group on a regular basis, perhaps going bowling or to the cinema. Here, they may not each need a personal assistant, but could get together as a group to employ one or two people to support them in this activity.

A similar example comes from one local authority where a residential home for people with learning difficulties was closed down by the local authority after the residents expressed their desire to live more independently (personal communication). In response, the families of the people concerned formed an independent living trust to rent a property, in which three of the former residents lived together as house mates. Pooling their direct payments enabled these people to hire their own staff to support them; some were workers they knew and liked from the former care home, while others were new people they had recruited directly.

In both these examples, people received personalised support via direct payments, but could choose to use some of their resources in collective ways to do things with friends and to secure economies of scale. This raises all kinds of possibilities about the scope for more imaginative use of direct payments and about links to collective and cooperative activities that current policy has barely begun to consider. *Independence, well-being and choice* includes encouragement for voluntary and community sector organisations and services, and refers to the potential of time banks for enhancing community solidarity and social inclusion (DH, 2005a, chapter 12) but these are merely starting points.

The success of direct payments has also helped to transform popular and policy thinking and debate in another, more fundamental way. It has drawn attention to the distinction – central to a social model of disability – between impairment and disability. While debate has tended to focus on the apparent predominance of people with physical impairments among the users of direct payments, a social model focuses not on the individual impairment of the person concerned, but on the societal and environmental barriers to independent living (see, for example, Oliver and Sapey, 1999; Swain et al, 2004). This has the advantage of moving the debate beyond a preoccupation with individual diagnoses and 'user groups' to consider the ways in which different groups of people with impairments are discriminated against and excluded by society, and the changes that need to take place to enable them to exercise greater choice and control over their services and therefore over their own lives. Viewed from this angle, the availability of direct payments and personal assistance is a citizenship right, and the emphasis correspondingly shifts to consideration of the full range of support required to help people with different needs benefit from direct payments, individualised budgets and other mechanisms for achieving independent living. Thus, both *Improving the life chances of disabled people* and *Independence, well-being and choice* draw attention to the physical and other barriers that can prevent disabled and older people taking advantage of universal services such as education, transport and leisure, and the need to make these accessible to everyone in the community.

In addition, a social model also enables us to take a step back from debates about the barriers faced by disabled people, to consider the way in which discrimination operates more generally. Once again, the focus shifts from looking solely at disability to a more inclusive approach which considers gender, race, sexuality, age and a range of other social divisions. It is this perspective that is so dominant in the Prime Minister's Strategy Unit proposals for improving the life chances of disabled people. It is arguable that such proposals might not have seen the light of day without the extensive discussion and debates that have surrounded the struggle for direct payments.

Outstanding challenges and problems

However, these are still early days, and individualised funding remains an aspiration for the future rather than a practical reality. Moreover, the experience of implementing direct payments suggests that some major challenges still remain. In some instances, evidence about the nature and extent of these challenges is also lacking. Tackling both the difficulties and the gaps in knowledge are absolutely essential if the visions set out above are to be effectively implemented.

Macro- and micro-level resource issues

First there are a number of macro- and micro-level resource issues. Despite the rhetoric of choice and personalisation, political pressures to keep local Council Tax rises low, combined with wider uncertainties about the future of local government funding, could deny social care the resources that are needed to deliver significant change. Moreover, with the Gershon (2004) review of public sector spending recommending efficiency savings, it is difficult to see how choice and personalisation (DH 2005a; Prime Minister's Strategy Unit, 2005) and investment in low-level preventative services (ODPM, 2005) can co-exist alongside rationing and financial restrictions. In housing, financial constraints are reducing the number of people using 'Supporting People' services (Community Care, 2005a).

Moreover, there is no evidence on the extent to which the amount of support required by current users of direct payments is typical or not. It may be that these users reflect a process of 'cream-skimming' – the use of direct payments by those who are best able to manage the employment and other responsibilities involved. Despite the best intentions of those involved, such processes can result from high-profile performance targets. If this is the case, then it may be difficult to achieve a further substantial take-up in the numbers of direct payment users without also offering very intensive help and support, not just in the form of recruitment and payroll services but also brokerage and the use of agents for those without capacity to consent, as proposed in the Green Paper (DH, 2005a, chapter 4). However, more intensive support for direct payments users risks undermining arguments that direct payments constitute a more efficient form of support than directly provided services (Zarb and Nadash, 1994). On the other hand, if additional resources are *not* invested in advocacy, brokerage and other support services, whether for direct payments users or in relation to personalised or individualised budgets, it may be difficult for the promise of choice to become a reality.

Moreover, despite Standard One of the National Service Framework for Older People (DH, 2001), there continue to be substantial differences in the range of needs that are recognised in the community care assessments of older people, compared to their younger disabled counterparts. These needs are then translated into the levels of financial support that are made available through direct payments. Nowhere was this restricted range of needs more starkly demonstrated than in Clark et al's (2004) study of older direct payments users. Some respondents who had used direct payments before reaching retirement age described how, on reaching 65, support for their wider social and community participation was no longer included in their assessed needs and, therefore, in the amount allocated for their direct payments. As a result, some older users were supplementing their direct payments from their own resources in order to sustain their social contacts and activities outside the home.

Moreover, the Social Exclusion Unit acknowledges that the take-up of direct payments is increasing only slowly for older people, particularly among those groups which already have difficulties accessing mainstream social care and health services (ODPM, 2005). One issue that therefore needs wider discussion and debate, whether in the context of direct payments or individualised budgets, is the range of support needs that these options are intended to cover and the levels of resources that are consequently made available to individual disabled and older people. It would be disappointing if the opportunities for wider social participation and engagement that direct payments currently offer working-age disabled people were not also extended to older people as part of the new proposals outlined above.

Staffing direct payments

A second area of difficulty concerns the implications for human resources. This has two dimensions. First, the future of direct payments needs to be considered within the wider context of the social care labour market. This is typically beset by difficulties of recruitment, retention and low pay (Henwood, 2001; Williams et al, 2001). In some areas of the country, particularly London and south-east England, these problems are acute and affect both local authority services and independent providers (Robinson, 2004). In rural areas, out-of-town shopping developments may offer alternative part-time, flexible and better-paid employment. Yet these are exactly the same labour markets from which direct payments users will be seeking to recruit personal assistants. Some social care workers may value the opportunity to leave the pressures of working for a home care service or in a residential home, and to move to more flexible and varied employment, involving a closer, more rewarding relationship with only one disabled or older employer. On the other hand, as Jan Leece and Clare Ungerson point out in this volume (Chapters Fourteen and Fifteen, respectively), this means that they will have less clearly defined roles than care workers employed in formal organisations, with the more family-like relationship also holding a number of risks. In promoting the take-up of direct payments, little attention is apparently being given to stimulating the supply and retention of personal assistants and other people employed by direct payments users, or to considering the mechanisms by which such employees can be encouraged and enabled to provide high-quality services.

The factors likely to help the recruitment and retention of personal assistants are the same as those affecting the wider social care workforce – pay, status, training, support and career opportunities. However, Leece in Chapter Fourteen of this volume found that the personal assistants in her study actually received lower hourly rates of pay than conventional home care workers. Moreover, personal assistants are further disadvantaged by their isolation; this means that they are likely also to find it difficult to access training opportunities and take advantage of collectively negotiated terms and conditions of employment. It is not clear, for example, how many local direct payments schemes or support services have established arrangements that allow personal assistants to take paid sick leave or paid holidays. Certainly these were not common among the personal assistants in Leece's study, who were also unlikely to be paid extra for working unsociable hours or for their travelling time. Moreover, while in general new care standards are requiring more care staff to be trained and qualified, it is far from clear how far these opportunities are available to personal assistants, nor what career opportunities are open to those who do gain qualifications. To the extent that such opportunities involve moving to new employment situations, this is likely to undermine the continuity in relationships that is so highly valued by direct payments users.

Moreover, little is known about the capacity of private home care and home nursing agencies to meet the needs of direct payments users. Many agencies are relatively new and are financially heavily dependent on large block contracts from local authority social services department purchasers. Indeed, one small-scale study (Patmore, 2002) found that independent agencies could be reluctant to respond to small-scale individual purchasers, given the time taken to negotiate and provide individualised services; instead, a large block contract from the local authority took priority. It is far from clear that home care agencies will be able to meet increased demands for personal assistants, especially given the comparatively high 'transaction costs' involved in negotiating individualised support arrangements for direct payments users.

There is another dimension to the human resource challenges of increasing take-up of direct payments – the paradigmic shift that will be required in the roles and identities of those front-line social services staff who are currently responsible for conducting assessments and drawing up care plans. Some researchers and commentators (for example, Bewley, 2000; Dawson, 2000; Fruin, 2000; Clark et al, 2004) have attributed the low take-up of direct payments in part to front-line staff who either do not know enough about the option or fail to discuss it appropriately with potential users when carrying out community care assessments. This situation may change in future, as current cohorts of social work students who have learned about direct payments as part of their professional training graduate and start to practise. However, with the roll-out of a single assessment process from older people to other groups of service users, it will be imperative for direct payments also to become an integral part of the training of other front-line professional staff such as community nurses and occupational therapists. Even though *Independence, well-being and choice* notes the importance of cultural change and leadership in meeting the challenges set by a more personalised approach to social care service delivery (DH, 2005a, chapter 11) it contains few specific proposals on how the necessary changes in the knowledge, behaviours and activities of front-line staff might be brought about in order to deliver the new adult social care 'vision'.

Increasing choice and maintaining equity

A third area of concern is around the actual level of demand for direct payments. Quite simply, it is far from clear whether the majority of those who want (with support) to use direct payments are now doing so or whether there remains potential to increase their take-up yet further – and if so, whether there are particular forms of support that they require to do so. Assessing potential demand is difficult. One factor that may impact on demand is the approach of front-line staff, as described above. Another factor is potential users' perceptions of the available supply of appropriate support that can be purchased with a direct payment. Evidence from other countries such as the Netherlands (Kremer, 2004) and Germany (Schunk, 1998) suggests that many older people receiving cash payments for care opt to give the money to a close relative (including a spouse). In contrast, direct payments regulations in England proscribe the employment of many categories of close relatives.

Moreover, it should be remembered that some people simply may not want – perhaps because of illness or because they simply value other priorities more than choice – to exercise choice through direct payments. Again, little is known about the priorities and preferences of different groups of older and disabled people, particularly those who, for whatever reason and whatever the level of support available, do not want to exercise the option of accessing direct payments and would prefer directly provided services. In extending direct payments to a wider group of people than those who currently access them, there may be a risk of 'creaming off' people for whom direct payments can be relatively easily arranged, thereby leaving residual resources (as well as very limited choices) for those who simply do not want to use direct payments. It will be important to ensure that they too can be assured of receiving good-quality, appropriate services. The future development of direct payments and of individual budgets needs to take place with full attention to the implications for equity.

The role of regulation

A further unresolved debate concerns the role of the state – in the form of local authority social services departments and national regulatory bodies – in regulating the quality of support provided to disabled and older people. The issue of local authorities' liability for any errors or injuries experienced by users or personal assistants in the course of using direct payments has proved contentious and may have inhibited some local authorities from promoting the take-up of direct payments more widely. In announcing the Green Paper on Adult Social Care, the Minister Stephen Ladyman ruled out any role for local authorities in ensuring that services purchased through direct payments are closely regulated and checked. On the other hand, some organisations representing groups of direct payments users, such as people with learning disabilities, have deplored this decision as "very very risky and wholly irresponsible", on the grounds that it exposes vulnerable people to the risk of employing potential abusers (Community Care, 2005b, p 16). Future discussions about the role of direct payments therefore need to be accompanied by open debate about acceptable levels of risk and protection, and about the respective responsibilities of direct payments users and local authorities in this regard.

Direct payments and wider policy developments

Finally, there may be some conflicts between the promotion of direct payments (and, in future, individualised and personalised budgets) and other concurrent policy developments. In social care, the Gershon (2004) review is prompting debate about whether the purchasing of services would be more efficient if done at a regional rather than the current local authority level. It is difficult to see how this level of commissioning is compatible with the simultaneous devolution of purchasing power down to individual service users. In the NHS, the advent of practice-based commissioning and case management seems to be placing a similar emphasis on more responsive and proactive services, but control is being firmly retained within the hands of local services and of the medical profession. Rather than giving individual patients access to their own budgets, the talk here is of 'liberating the talents' of nurses (not of service users) and of 'promoting clinical engagement' (not of choice and control for citizens) (see DH, 2004a, 2004b, 2005b).

The discrepancies between the promotion of direct payments and current NHS policies also become apparent in proposals to reduce the number of regulatory bodies, particularly the plans announced in the 2005 Budget to transfer responsibility for the inspection of social care services to the Healthcare Commission.

For specific user groups, there are also mixed messages. In mental health, debates surrounding the proposed reform of the 1983 Mental Health Act seem to be placing more emphasis on public safety and risk management than on citizenship and inclusion (Beresford and Croft, 2001; Grounds, 2001; Laurance, 2003). For people with learning difficulties, there are fears about the re-creation of an institutional approach to care in new private sector, out-of-area placements; and concerns about the extent to which future legislation on capacity will promote self-determination and supported decision making (see, for example, Community Care, 2004b; DH, 2004c). While there is much to be optimistic about in the current policy context, therefore, there is also much to ponder.

Conclusions

Contributors to this volume have repeatedly noted the tendency of direct payments projects to date to focus primarily on people with physical impairments. From the beginning, it was people with physical impairments who were at the forefront of the campaign for independent living; who lobbied for the successful introduction of direct payments; who established centres for independent living; and who now form the majority of direct payments recipients. In contrast, there are a range of other user groups – people with mental health problems, older people, people with learning difficulties and others – who have fared less well and who are still significantly under-represented.

Overall, social care has come a long way in a relatively short time, and direct payments are now reaching a stage where they are posing some much more fundamental questions about the future of social work and the future life chances of disabled people and other groups. However, it may not be appropriate to assume that direct payments are the solution for all people who are eligible for community care services. Throughout this volume we have seen examples of many people, particularly people with physical impairments, whose quality of life has been significantly improved by accessing direct payments. We have also seen evidence of seemingly intractable barriers which have prevented access to direct payments by other people. As yet we have insufficient evidence of how and whether these barriers can be overcome so that direct payments become more widespread, or whether there may be other, more appropriate, means by which some groups of disabled or older people can exercise greater choice and control over their support services.

Ultimately, direct payments are a major and exciting step forward for social care and have already helped many people achieve greater choice and control in their lives. Nevertheless, a number of important questions remain to be answered if direct payments are to reach their full potential in the 21st century.

References

Beresford, P. and Croft, S. (2001) 'Mental health policy: a suitable case for treatment', in C. Newnes, G. Holmes and C. Dunn (eds) *This is madness too: Critical perspectives on mental illness*, Ross-on-Wye: PCCS Books.

Bewley, C. (2000) 'Care managers can be champions for direct payments', *Care Plan*, vol 6, no 4, pp 13-16.

Clark, H., Gough, H. and Macfarlane, A. (2004) *It pays dividends: Direct payments and older people*, Bristol: The Policy Press.

Community Care (2004a) 'Ladyman to act on councils that are slow to promote independent living', *Community Care*, 16 September, (www.communitycare.co.uk), accessed 10 March 2005.

Community Care (2004b) 'Does the Bill add up?', *Community Care*, 15 July, (www.communitycare.co.uk), accessed 10 March 2005.

Community Care (2005a) 'Fall in clients is cue for cutback fears', *Community Care*, 9 March, pp 10-16.

Community Care (2005b) 'Abuse fear grows as Ladyman rejects further controls over direct payments', *Community Care*, 17-23 March, pp 16-17.

Dawson, C. (2000) *Independent successes: Implementing direct payments*, York: Joseph Rowntree Foundation.

DH (Department of Health) (2001) *National service frameworks: Older people*, London: DH.

DH (2004a) *The NHS improvement plan: Putting people at the heart of public services*, London: The Stationery Office.

DH (2004b) *Practice based commissioning: Promoting clinical engagement*, London: DH.

DH (2004c) *Commissioning service close to home: Note of clarification for commissioners and regulation and inspection authorities*, London: DH.

DH (2005a) *Independence, well-being and choice: Our vision for the future of social care for adults in England,* Cm 6499, London: DH.

DH (2005b) *Supporting people with long term conditions: Liberating the talents of nurses who care for people with long term conditions*, London: DH.

Fruin, D. (2000) *New directions for independent living*, London: DH.

Gershon, P. (2004) *Releasing resources for the frontline: Independent review of public sector efficiency*, London: HM Treasury.

Glasby, J. and Littlechild, R. (2002) *Social work and direct payments*, Bristol: The Policy Press.

Glasby, J. and Littlechild, R. (2004) *The health and social care divide: The experiences of older people* (2nd edn), Bristol: The Policy Press.

Grounds, A. (2001) 'Reforming the Mental Health Act', *British Journal of Psychiatry*, vol 179, no 5, pp 387-9.

Henwood, M. (2001) *Future imperfect: Report of the King's Fund care and support inquiry*, London: King's Fund.

Kremer, M. (2004) 'Where are we going to when consumers are in the driver's seat? The Dutch Personal Budget (PGB) and its impact on the market, professionals and the family', Paper presented at 'Professionals between people and policy' seminar, 'Transformations in care and welfare in Europe, Amsterdam, 7-8 October.

Laurance, J. (2003) *Pure madness: How fear drives the mental health system*, London: Routledge.

NCIL (National Centre for Independent Living) (2003) Transcript of speech by Stephen Ladyman, Parliamentary Under Secretary of State, Department of Health, at National Centre for Independent Living launch event, 30 October 2003, London, (www.ncil.org.uk/Stephen_LadymanNCILLaunch.asp), accessed 20 November 2003.

ODPM (Office of the Deputy Prime Minister) (2005) *Excluded older people: Social Exclusion Unit interim report*, London: ODPM.

Oliver, M. and Sapey, B. (1999) *Social work with disabled people* (2nd edn), Basingstoke: Macmillan.

Patmore, C. (2002) *Flexible, person-centred home care for older people: Results from the telephone survey of home care providers*, SPRU Working Paper DH1918, York: Social Policy Research Unit, University of York.

Prime Minister's Strategy Unit (2005) *Improving the life chances of disabled people*, London: Prime Minister's Strategy Unit.

Robinson, J. (2004) *Care services inquiry interim report: Concerns about care for older Londoners*, London: King's Fund.

Schunk, M. (1998) 'The social insurance model of care for older people in Germany', in C. Glendinning (ed) *Rights and realities: Comparing new developments in long-term care for older people*, Bristol: The Policy Press.

Swain, J., French, S., Barnes, C. and Thomas, C. (eds) (2004) *Disabling barriers – enabling environments* (2nd edn), London: Sage Publications.

Williams, L., Parry-Jones, B., Hill, J. and Apsitis, Y. (2001) *The retention and recruitment of home care workers in Wales*, Bangor: Centre for Social Policy Research and Development, University of Wales, Bangor.

Zarb, G. and Nadash, P. (1994) *Cashing in on independence: Comparing the costs and benefits of cash and services*, London: BCODP.

TWENTY

Holding the dream: direct payments and independent living

Frances Hasler

This is a personal view, not the view of any organisation I have worked for. It is based on more than two decades of work in the independent living movement, and draws on the work and friendship of many disabled people. However, it does not pretend to represent anyone's views but my own.

> Direct payments are a means to an end: that end is independent living.

This quote appears in many books and training packs about direct payments, and I have used it regularly in presentations. I first heard it from one of the pioneers of direct payments in the UK, John Evans. But, as direct payments become more widely used, does it still hold true? Another of the pioneers, Philip Mason, gave me the title for this chapter. Speaking to a group of European activists, he said that the early days of campaigning for direct payments had been inspired by a dream, "… that disabled people would be enabled to fulfil their roles in terms of taking the opportunities society offers and meeting the responsibilities society requires". At the end of his speech he exhorted his audience to "hold the dream" (Mason, 1999, p 22) to keep the link between direct payments and independent living a strong one. What made him feel the dream was under threat?

There are two forces pushing direct payments and the ideals of independent living away from each other. One is the brutal reality of budgets: trying to achieve independent living on a survival budget will never be easy. The other is the continuing dominance of the custodial model of care. Despite plenty of rhetoric to the contrary, the instinct of many community care professionals is to limit the risks taken by (and thus the autonomy of) disabled people.

Defining independent living

The Disability Rights Commission defines independent living thus:

> The term independent living refers to all disabled people having the same choice, control and freedom as any other citizen – at home, at work, and as members of the community. This does not necessarily mean disabled people 'doing everything for themselves', but it does mean that any practical assistance people need should be based on their own choices and aspirations. (Disability Rights Commission, 2004)

For people who need regular practical assistance in their lives, direct payments offer both choice and control in the way that assistance is delivered. But direct payments will only help people to achieve independent living if they are administered within a system that supports independent living values.

Independent living is more than an individual aim. It encompasses a change in social relations. It is both a philosophy and a practical approach. It brings disabled people together to work for civil and human rights. Achieving the social aims of independent living requires collective action. Independent living is developed through the self-organisation of disabled people. The movement is based on collectively developed solutions to individually experienced barriers. The movement recognises that many disabled people will not manage to achieve independence on their own, that the support provided through organisations such as centres for independent living (CILs) is vital.

Centres for independent living

In the early days of direct payments it was accepted that their development would be linked to the development of a network of CILs, to help disabled people get the most from their payments.

A CIL is an organisation controlled by disabled people, providing support for independent living. This can take many forms, but usually includes support to employ personal assistance. CILs were the leading bodies in the campaign to legalise direct payments.

This basic link was lost as direct payments were mainstreamed, for a number of reasons. Local authorities were reluctant to invest in CILs. Traditional disability charities were hostile to CILs. One explanation given for this reluctance or antipathy was the assertion that CILs were not wholly inclusive of all disabled people. The administrative response to impairment in the UK is to divide disabled people into separate impairment and age groups for purposes of service delivery. Initially, CILs reflected this divide, being predominantly managed by people of working age with physical impairments. This does not mean that they cannot provide direct payments support across impairment and age groups.

Developing to encompass all potential users takes time, contacts, and money. But most CILs are constantly struggling for funds. In several places, a local independent living organisation has developed direct payments in the area only to see the contract for direct payments support go to an outside organisation. Local authorities could – and should – be much more supportive of the independent living movement. This would help to embed direct payments in the local culture.

Reality and dreams

Centres for Independent Living struggle with inadequate and insecure funding (Morgan et al, 2000). Disabled people struggle with reductive assessments of their need, and rates of direct payments that do not allow them to offer either the wages or the conditions of service they feel their assistants deserve. Promoting the 'dream' of independent living in this context is very difficult.

The move to make direct payments mandatory and to introduce a key performance indicator on their use has led many local councils to concentrate on getting the numbers up as best they can. Direct payments support workers fear this is at the expense of independent living ideals. Some users are not referred to a support scheme at all. In some places, the support scheme does not become involved until after direct payments have started. For users who have had no opportunity to experience independent living in the past, this deprives them of the opportunity to explore options for using direct payments in creative and empowering ways. In these circumstances it is possible for direct payments to become a burdensome rather than a liberating option. Recipients are still using the support they get to do the same tasks as always, yet now they have all the responsibility of arranging and accounting for the support.

Holistic support

This is not how the pioneers of direct payments ever envisaged their use. Independent living means having choice, control and autonomy. It does not mean being left unsupported to get on with things by yourself. Direct payments support organised by an independent living organisation will be based on the idea of peer support – other disabled people helping to spread knowledge, to develop solutions to problems, to encourage people to try new things, to share experience. This does not mean that expertise is not required: knowing the rules governing being an employer is important. But being conversant with the law is only one element of being a successful manager of staff: techniques for selection, training and ongoing supervision of staff are all equally vital. Too often, commissioning of direct payments support focuses just on the narrow legal requirements, not on the wider aspects of what people need to know.

Assessment

Even where the support scheme is able to operate to an independent living model, the ideals of independent living are often stymied by a narrow approach to community care assessment. Although guidance on 'Fair Access to Care Services' is supposed to ensure that assessments give equal weight to participation in family and community life as to personal care issues, in practice this does not always happen. In particular, assessments for older people often miss these elements.

Amounts

Where either the number of hours or the hourly rate offered (or both) are inadequate, the disabled person will struggle to achieve independent living outcomes. It can be easy for people who are struggling to recruit successfully, because they can only offer short hours and small wages, to blame direct payments rather than the system within which direct payments are delivered. Some of the decisions made by local authorities are perplexing to users. If the direct payments hourly rate is only two thirds of that paid for agency care, how are users expected to compete with agencies for staff? In these circumstances, direct payments packages can offer only limited choice. Independent living can still seem like a dream.

Attitudes

A poor assessment will lead to a poor direct payments package. But even where the amount of money offered is adequate to meet the need, the monitoring of spending can be unnecessarily heavy-handed and can defeat the objectives of independent living. I have heard of places where users have been told that they must use the same amount of money every week, and I have heard it suggested that if a user can do with a lesser amount one week (because they are budgeting their hours to spend more another week), this proves that their original assessment was too generous! This sort of attitude from care managers is incompatible with independent living. It is also frustrating for their more enlightened colleagues who are supportive of independent living.

Direct payments allow people to choose their own staff. This is a fairly basic expression of choice and control. Some care managers are very sceptical of this; I have frequently been challenged about the risk of people employing 'unsuitable' workers. Particularly where children are involved, some authorities have attempted to set policies giving them veto over who may or may not be employed. This undermines the basic idea of handing control to the user. Like attitudes to resource allocation, attitudes to risk vary within and across authorities. Changing these organisational cultures is a necessary part of ensuring that direct payments remain a part of independent living.

If people are taking risks, these need to be conscious rather than unconsidered ones. Having the information and the confidence to judge risk is part of independent living. To ensure that people have the information and the skills to make these judgements, it is vital that they have access to a proper support service before they start using direct payments. This means that support schemes need to be inclusive of all disabled people who are eligible to use direct payments. The present situation is that some are better at this than others.

Inclusion

The independent living movement is grounded in values of civil and human rights, committed to equality. But it is easy to get caught up in day-to-day administration of direct payments support and to lose sight of the necessity to keep making and renewing links with excluded or less included groups. Even well-meaning voluntary organisations can be institutionally racist. For small organisations it can be hard to make the time or find the resources to train staff, to do the outreach. But being small can also be an advantage. Changing the culture in a small, well-motivated group is easier than doing so in a large bureaucratic setting. If direct payments are to remain a tool for independent living, support organisations need to rediscover and reinvent the links between the independent living movement and race equality organisations, gay rights groups, older people's organisations, and so on. And, of course, independent living organisations need to be inclusive across impairment groups.

The supported living debate

To be inclusive of all disabled people, independent living needs to keep developing. The disabled people's independent living movement says that independent living means being able to live in the way you choose, with people you choose. It means having choices about who helps you and the ways they help. It is not necessarily about doing things for yourself, it is about having control over your day-to-day life. Is this the same dream that champions of supported living put forward on behalf of people with learning difficulties?

> Supported living starts off with a fundamental belief that every person has the right to lead their own life – determine how they live, with whom they live, who provides them with help and support and how they live their lives. (Kinsella, 2001, p 4)

Supported living is based on a number of principles that directly echo the principles of independent living – all people, no matter what their impairment, can live in the community; disabled people should be enabled to have choice and control over their lives. It has one significant element missing from the literature on independent living:

> Where people can not make some of these choices, those who know, care about, and love the person should be instrumental in making informed guesses. (Kinsella, 2001, p 1)

The stumbling-block in direct payments for this group of people is the requirement that users consent to have payments and are able to manage the payments, with assistance if needed. The 'willing and able' clause was initially supported by campaigners for direct payments, including representatives of People First (a self-advocacy organisation run by and for people with learning disabilities), as it offered some measure of certainty that the disabled person would be in control of the arrangements made. But it was opposed by those working with people with severe learning difficulties, as it effectively ruled them out of this potentially life-enhancing option.

I have witnessed fruitless debate between those who promote independent living and those who promote supported living. One group believed the other to be avoiding the issue of giving real control to disabled people and perpetuating 'carer-managed' services. The second group believed the first to be ignorant or uncaring about the reality of life for people with severe learning difficulties.

Should direct payments be adapted to include people who are deemed unable to make some choices, on the basis of informed guesses of those who have their best interests at heart? Or is this a step backwards, towards the days when disabled people were expected to be passive, with other people deciding what was good for them?

To take direct payments forward, to make CILs inclusive, and to keep the link between direct payments and independent living, it is necessary that people on both sides of this perceived divide recognise how similar, perhaps even identical, their dreams are. This recognition has started to occur recently, and the debates in some places are now far more fruitful. One example is the cooperation of a CIL and a self-advocacy group of people with learning difficulties on research about direct payments. This research explores how people with learning difficulties can be supported to manage their direct payments in ways that are truly empowering.

A gift to the community

A direct payments support worker said to me: "Direct payments are the independent living movement's gift to the community". Part of what he meant was that once you have given a gift you cannot dictate how the recipient uses it. Direct payments may develop in ways that we did not envisage.

Holding the dream, of direct payments being a means to the end of independent living, requires a vigorous and forward-thinking independent living movement, supported both financially and philosophically by local authorities.

Holding the dream requires better use of money. This includes redirecting funds from assessment and monitoring and putting them into direct payments packages. It requires adequate funding for social care, especially for older people, and the ending of charging for non-residential care services.

Holding the dream means being proud of what disabled people have achieved so far, in pioneering direct payments and in getting them on the statute books. It means reiterating again and again that everyone has both the right and the capacity to make choices.

My dream is that more people will take time to learn the history of the independent living movement and in doing so will come to respect its philosophy and understand how direct payments and independent living are related.

References

Disability Rights Commission (2004) *Policy statement on social care and independent living*, (www.drc-gb.org/publicationsandreports), London: Disability Rights Commission.

Kinsella, P. (2001) *The changing paradigm – from control to freedom*, (www.paradigm-uk.org/pdf/Articles/changingparadigms.pdf), accessed 15 March 2005, pp 1-10.

Mason, P. (1999) *Shaping our futures*, London: National Centre for Independent Living, in association with Hampshire Centre for Independent Living.

Morgan, H., Barnes, C. and Mercer, G. (2000) *Creating independent futures – an evaluation of services led by disabled people*, London: National Centre for Independent Living/Centre for Disability Studies.

Glossary

BCODP	British Council of Disabled People
CDC	Council for Disabled Children
CIL	centre for independent/integrated living
CILT	Centre for Independent Living Toronto
CLBC	Community Living British Columbia
CRB	Criminal Records Bureau
CSCI	Commission for Social Care Inspection
DH	Department of Health
DPS	Direct Payments Scotland
DPSS	Direct Payments Support Service
ESRC	Economic and Social Research Council
GCIL	Glasgow Centre for Inclusive Living
HSS	health and social service trusts
ILF	Independent Living Fund
LIG	local implementation group
LTID	long-term illness or disability
NCIL	National Centre for Independent Living
PASS	personal assistant support services
PSSRU	Personal Social Services Research Unit
SCIE	Social Care Institute for Excellence
SDRC	San Diego Regional Center
SPAEN	Scottish Personal Assistance Employers Network
SSI	Social Services Inspectorate
VIA	Values Into Action

Index